# Water in the West

## A HIGH COUNTRY NEWS Reader

# Water in the West

A HIGH COUNTRY NEWS Reader

*Edited by Char Miller*

**Oregon State University Press**
**Corvallis, Oregon**

For My Sisters

The paper in this book meets the guidelines for permanence and durability of the Committee on Production Guidelines for Book Longevity of the Council on Library Resources and the minimum requirements of the American National Standard for Permanence of Paper for Printed Library Materials Z39.48-1984.

**Library of Congress Cataloging-in-Publication Data**
Water in the West : a High Country News reader / edited by Char Miller.
   p.  cm.
Includes bibliographical references and index.
ISBN 0-87071-480-5 (perm paper)
1. Water-supply—West (U.S.) I. Miller, Char, 1951-
TD223.6 .W38 2000
     00-008140

**OREGON STATE
UNIVERSITY**

**Oregon State University Press**
101 Waldo Hall
Corvallis OR 97331-6407
541-737-3166 • fax 541-737-3170
http://osu.orst.edu/dept/press

# Preface

**W**hether it is bottled up behind dams, sold via markets to distant consumers, diverted from Native American lands, or just plain absent, water is on every westerner's lips. Their conversations about it are as intense (if differently constructed) in Portland or Phoenix as they are in the Inland Empire or the Intermountain Basin, and as important if emanating from the Colorado's Front Range or any golf course Back 9. With its keen ear trained on these many regional discussions, *High Country News* has offered a steady stream of analysis on the history of and current struggles over the West's most precious resource. Culled from *HCN*'s back pages—with the earliest entries dating from the mid-1980s, and the latest from 1999—the articles that are republished in *Water in the West* testify to the newspaper's enduring commitment to being the "Paper for People who Care about the West."

The depth of its concern is manifest in the fact that this is the second collection of *High Country News*' writings on water. Like the first, the archly titled *Western Water Made Simple* (Island Press, 1987), this book depends heavily on the insights of an array of journalists and scholars, and I am grateful to them for their permission to republish their words. I am grateful as well for the enthusiasm, efficiency, and good humor of *HCN* publisher Ed Marston, Marketing Director Steve Mandell, and Production Manager Cindy Wehling (and others behind the scenes), who dug out articles, answered my many queries, and made this such a fun project to work on. As always, Eunice Herrington, Senior Secretary of the History Department at Trinity University, has been a huge support, as has Junior Secretary Elizabeth Reed. So have been my sisters who, although living many miles away, and in more humid climes, are never far from my thoughts: I take great delight in dedicating this volume to Heili, Bibi, Kathy, and Niki.

# Contents

# Water Pressure:
# An Introduction

## Char Miller

**H**ere's an urban legend out of the New West, a region we might now better call *West.com*. In the middle-1990s, a mid-sized desert city, dependent on an aquifer for its water supply, fell all over itself to lure a massive computer chip manufacturer to town. To secure the promised thousands of high-paying jobs, the community and its state cobbled together what Bruce Selcraig reported in *High Country News* was at the time "the most lucrative come-hither campaign [this] state had ever seen": $57 million in property tax abatements, $36 million in waived new-equipment sales taxes, and $20 million in manufacturing tax credits, among assorted (and irresistible) incentives. Intel could not resist this package of giveaways, and although other cities and states had heavily courted it, the corporation established a new plant just northwest of Albuquerque in 1994.[1]

The dominant chip manufacturer in the world, Intel has made good on its promise of jobs and economic growth—the plant employs thousands of workers, with salaries providing an impressive boost in income for The Land of Enchantment, which then ranked as the fifth poorest state in the Union. Less enchanting has been the plant's impact on the region's water supply. Essential to the courtship between New Mexico and Intel, as Selcraig pointed out, was that "the Albuquerque area could provide all the water Intel would ever want." It would want a lot: to manufacture a single 8-inch silicon wafer can require upwards of 5,000 gallons of water; given Intel's production targets of thirty thousand of these wafers a month, the company projected pumping six million gallons a day. No wonder, as Selcraig noted, "Intel and all semiconductor companies freely admit they are, by the nature of their technology, world-class water hogs."

It is one thing for those hogs to drink deep in a well-watered land, but in the arid Southwest their massive thirst has had a profound impact on regional water supplies. Albuquerque's woes already were evident a year before Intel's Rio Rancho plant opened; in 1993, the U.S. Geological Survey reported that the city "was pumping out its groundwater three times faster than it could be replenished." That disturbing trend intensified when the well-rinsed silicon wafers started rolling off the Intel assembly line. By March 1996, levels in area wells were dropping faster than predicted, as first Intel and then other semiconductor plants—Honeywell, Motorola, Philips, and Sumitomo were also lured to the Albuquerque Basin in the middle 1990s—began to expand production. These five companies extracted close to two billion gallons of water from the local aquifer in 1995, and although they have since instituted conservation measures and Intel, for one, has not yet matched its earlier stated need of six million gallons a day, the rate of pumpage has continued to increase; in 1998 Intel withdrew four million gallons, up from 2.75 million gallons four years earlier.[2]

A falling water table is not the only indicator of stress on the system: tied to the rapid increase in hydromining are important changes in the patterns of water consumption. As New Mexico has become more urbanized and industrialized, expanding communities and utility districts have bought up preexisting water rights, a move that has had a profound impact on the state's long-standing agricultural and ranching interests. The politics of the state have become correspondingly more complicated, as forces in favor of environmental justice, Indian rights, and rural peoples and economies have protested against the new New Mexico. As an Intel spokesman acknowledged to Bruce Selcraig in 1994: "I think New Mexico is more complex than [we] thought. This isn't California or Arizona."

But in other respects New Mexico is like its neighbors in the West. Albuquerque is not the only city in the wider region to have gambled that rapid resource extraction would yield high employment and considerable wealth; it is not the first to discover that its actions have jeopardized its future. Its late twentieth-century dilemmas are time honored, a matter of old water in new bottles.[3]

Westerners, after all, have long worried about white gold, a concern that has bordered on an obsession—understandable in this oft-arid region—sparking an unending series of brawls over its control and distribution. Central to this historic, regional struggle is a curious legal finding, the Doctrine of Prior Appropriation. Initiated during the California Gold Rush in 1848, and sustained until the early 1990s, the doctrine determined a simple code: those who first laid claim to water could do with it what they wanted. Johnnys-come-lately might protest, but they could expect little legal support if they challenged the diversion or reduction of a river's flow. In the West, these six words ruled: "First in time, first in right."

No one knew better than John Wesley Powell just how wrong-headed this legal principle was. A Civil War hero, an explorer, and founder of the U.S. Geological Survey, he had been the first Euro-American to raft down the Colorado River through the Grand Canyon, the first to map portions of the arid landscape beyond the 98th Meridian, the first to think seriously about the significance of the Doctrine of Prior Appropriation in a region of little rain. Those Americans who pushed out into this forbidding terrain, he predicted, would be confronted with a choice between what he desired (the establishment of cooperative, small-scale communities dependent on the "new industry of agriculture by irrigation") and what he feared (the creation of an economic environment monopolized by "a few great capitalists, employing labor on a grand scale, as is done in the great mines and manufactories of the United States"). That agribusiness early on dominated the size, scope, and character of western farming and ranching perfectly illustrates how completely Prior Appropriation directed the flow of water away from Powell's Jeffersonian fantasy.

His were not the only dashed hopes, as the essays in *Water in the West* make clear. Native Americans had even less chance of successfully combating western water grabs than had enfranchised, if undercapitalized, white settlers. The Utes' experience is representative. In 1861, in the midst of the bloody Civil War, Abraham Lincoln wrote Brigham Young to ask if the Uinta Valley in northeastern Utah was a suitable site for a new reservation for the Ute peoples. Young replied, according to political scientist Dan McCool, that "the land was so utterly useless that its only purpose was to hold the other parts of the world together." In that sense, it was "perfect for an Indian reservation." So perfect that by the early 1880s Congress even had increased its size to four million acres, a good-sized sanctuary far from the pressures of white settlement.

But as demands for water escalated in arid Utah, the state and federal governments conspired with the local power structure to carve up the reservation. Land along the Duchesne River was appropriated for white farmers; Strawberry Reservoir was created in western portions of the reservation, with its impounded waters dedicated to off-reservation agricultural and urban users; the USDA Forest Service peeled off a large chunk of mountainous terrain to establish a national forest designed to protect another watershed. By the mid-twentieth century, the Ute reservation was three-quarters smaller than it had been one hundred years earlier. Its resource base would shrink even farther when in 1965 the Central Utah Project (CUP)—one of a series of vast, federally funded surface water systems throughout the intermountain west—was announced. To secure CUP's success, which required tapping into the Uinta Mountains drainage area, the federal government urged the Utes to sign a treaty that would transfer the requisite water rights in exchange for a reservation water project. Now here's a shock: the promised irrigation system never materialized, a story of fraud that was consistent with the experience of Arizona's Pima-Maricopa Indians and the Shoshones of Wyoming. Theirs has been an unending Trail of Tears.

Bound up with this long train of abuses has been the wholesale assault upon western flora and fauna. No species has been more devastated by western water policy than the salmon of the Pacific Northwest. Its once-complex habitat extended up along the Columbia, Snake, and other regional river systems but, beginning in the 1930s, the salmon have have been bottled up behind an ever-increasing number of federally funded dams. These engineering marvels created a new environment that historian Richard White has described as an "organic machine." It is responsible for the production of vast quantities of cheap hydroelectric power, an ever-widening range of irrigated desert lands, a series of locks and canals that turned Lewiston, Idaho—a bit more than four hundred miles from the Pacific—into an ocean port, and accelerated logging on public and private lands. The material goods that resulted from these physical alterations were of considerable benefit to the human economy, but savaged the reproductive cycle of the salmon; later, half-hearted attempts to provide "fish ladders" so the salmon could leap around the dams proved ineffective. The species declined rapidly, and as it did so it severed the link between the salmon's migratory patterns and the Elwah, Skokomish, and Skagit tribes, for whom the fish has had great economic value and cultural significance. This disheartening set of consequences will only be reversed if the dam infrastructure is removed.

Those walls might come tumbling down, too, as tribes and environmental groups use nineteenth-century treaties, the Endangered Species Act, and appeals to the Federal Energy Regulatory Commission, which licenses dams, to press for the "re-reclamation" of the Columbia River watershed. If it were reclaimed, the indigenous peoples would be able to restore their "traditional cultures and livelihoods," a prospect for which they have fought since losing tribal sovereignty and territorial integrity more than a century ago.

That dams might be "decommissioned," and thus removed, terrifies many westerners. Why? Because if we are compelled, finally, to acknowledge their deleterious impact on indigenous societies and riparian ecosystems, we will also be forced to acknowledge their vital role in nurturing the extraordinary postwar boom in western urban population and development. Consider the massive complex of dams and reservoirs that capture water from the Rockies and Wasatch, the Sierra Nevada, Cascade, and other mountain ranges, and from which it is then pumped to Denver, Las Vegas, or Los Angeles, Phoenix, Portland, or Seattle. Without the seemingly limitless flow of federally subsidized (and therefore cheap) water, these cities would not have leapt into national prominence; (the same could be said of their urban counterparts located along the Missouri and Arkansas river basins, and throughout Texas' waterways). It was the "Dam-icans" and the "Water-crats" who made it possible for industry and population to flow south and west over the last three decades, giving the region immense political clout. Were we to pull the plug on any of the cisterns that pockmark the West, we would quickly discover just how unsteady were its economic foundations, how ephemeral its social stability.

The region may not dry up soon, but the certainties that once dominated its water politics no longer hold sway, complicating its future. The Doctrine of Prior Appropriation, for example, has been effectively challenged in the federal courts, the same judicial system that has at long last started to confirm the claims of Native American peoples to a share of western waters. Once-impotent rural areas, whose water regularly has been diverted to slake the thirst of distant metropolitan centers, have risen up in opposition to such grandiose schemes as the Central Arizona Project, Denver's Two Forks Dam, and the Central Utah Project. Add to this the interstate and interurban battles over stream flow, and it appears that the demand for water has never been more contested.

These contests have forced water suppliers to become more creative, and belatedly they have launched a series of conservation initiatives. Most promising is the recycling of water, a strategy particularly suited to the corralling of those "world-class water hogs." Many computer chip corporations, like Intel, migrated to the West because of low labor costs and good, clean, and very inexpensive water. Until recently, these companies would suck down millions of gallons to turn out thousands of chips, and simply flush the waste (and the toxins) down the drain. But some municipal water systems have initiated plans to pass that waste water through urban sewage systems and relevant filtration processes, the end result of which is the creation of "gray water"; it will be sold for non-potable purposes only, and be of a high enough quality to be utilized once more in the construction of computer chips. Other proposed consumers are municipal and corporate landscapes and, not inconsequently, the Southwest's ubiquitous (and strikingly green) fairways. This is a nice reuse loop, and western cities are at various stages in their development of this resource. But the costs are high and the water is pricey—the San Antonio Water System is marketing "gray water" at a higher rate than that pumped directly from the local Edwards Aquifer—a situation that surely will hinder the expansion of this important conservation measure.

Less constrained, but not less troubled, is the fast-emerging free market system of water allocation. Its supporters argue that no longer should we conceive of water as something captured in a particular place for consumption in a particular place; instead, they claim it is more rational and efficient to conceive of water as a commodity that can be sold to the highest bidder without geographical or political constraints. An acre-foot of water stored in Lake Mead could be sold to suppliers in Denver or Las Vegas, Salt Lake City or Portland, creating a more fluid and profitable marketplace; one side benefit of this money-making venture would be the collapse of the current federally regulated method of distribution that has produced so much litigation. It sounds too good to be true, and it is. Nothing has sparked more lawsuits than marketers' attempts to purchase "unclaimed" water rights. *High Country News* tracked one instance of this—American Water Development Inc.'s 1986 claim to 200,000 acre-feet of water stored in an aquifer beneath Colorado's San Luis Valley. The local citizenry went up-in-arms, the state became embroiled, and the U.S.

Department of Justice jumped in, representing the National Park Service, Bureau of Reclamation, and other regulatory agencies whose missions this claim may have compromised. The case was litigated until 1994, when the Colorado Supreme Court ultimately ruled against AWDI, a bitter conclusion for its investors, and not a happy resolution for anyone concerned about regional water needs.

But then what else is new? Great hopes, deep doubts, even despair, have been integral to the history of western water policy; predictions about the prospects for change in the twenty-first century are an exercise in futility. Or so warned *HCN* publisher Ed Marston in 1989: "The best one can say is that there is a race between ecological and economic collapse and thorough-going reform, with no oddsmakers in sight."

## Notes

1. Bruce Selcraig, "Albuquerque learns it really is a desert town," *High Country News,* December 26, 1994; see also p. 318-26, this volume.
2. Albuquerque's experience is mirrored in Austin, Phoenix, and San Jose. See "Case Study #3: Albuquerque, New Mexico: Silicon Mesa," in *Sacred Waters: Life Blood of Mother Earth,* (Southwest Network for Environmental and Economic Justice, and Campaign for Responsible Technology, 1997), p.66-90; Andrew Padilla, "Intel Reports Water Conservation Success," *Albuquerque Journal,* June 27, 1998.
3. Olivier Uyttebrouck, "Rio Rancho Plan To Pump More Water in Limbo," *AJ,* June 30, 1999; Juliet V. Casey, "Parks Laps Up Too Much Water," *AJ,* November 20, 1999; Casey, "City Has Own Ideas for Growth," *AJ,* December 2, 1999.

# 1

## History

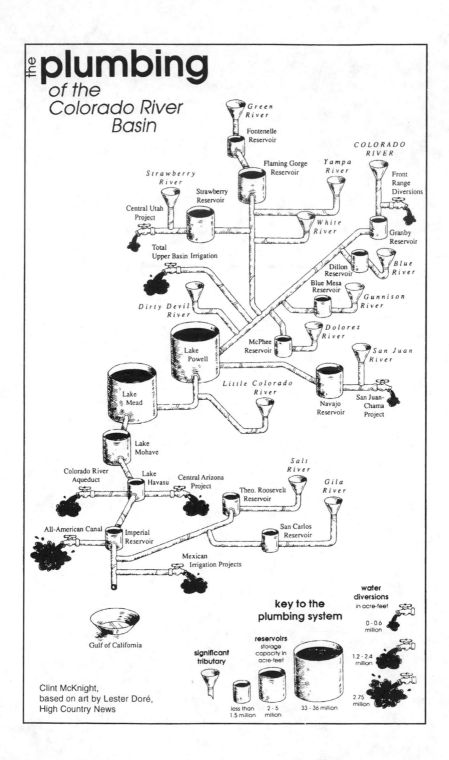

# River Basins and Closed Basins of the West

The West is composed of four major bathtubs. Three are river basin bathtubs: the sprawling Missouri, the compact Columbia, and the elongated Colorado. The major river in each basin collects water that falls within the natural boundaries of that basin and dumps it, eventually, into the Atlantic, in the case of the Missouri, and into the Pacific, in the cases of the Columbia and Colorado. The fourth of the West's major bathtubs, the Great Basin Utah and Nevada, has no outlet. Its water drains into the Great Salt Lake and other closed sinks, and stays there.

Humans have not been willing to live the natural division of the West into these basins. So, when it suits us—and it often suits us— we build canals, tunnels, and pumping stations to move water from one basin to another. The San Juan-Chama diversion moves Colorado River water into the Rio Grande basin, and thence on to the Gulf of Mexico. Denver's Front Range captures water out of the Colorado River basin and sends it under the Continental Divide into the Missouri. On the other side of the Colorado River basin, the Central Utah Project transfers water from the Colorado to the Great Basin. Southern California, the greatest diverter of all time, pulls water out of many places, including the Colorado River and the Owens River (of *Chinatown* fame) in the Great Basin. The desert irrigators on the California-Mexico border transfer Colorado River water into the closed Salton Sea basin. The megalopolis around Los Angeles dumps its water into the Pacific Ocean.

*September 29, 1986*

# The Politics of Western Water Have Changed Forever

## Dan Luecke

In 1977, when President Jimmy Carter unveiled his water projects "hit list" of federal dams he had targeted for deauthorization, the political fallout left him stunned and despised in the West. Virtually every elected official west of the 100th Meridian, including members of his own party, attacked him savagely for his failure to understand western water and the political realities of a semi-arid region. In retrospect, we see that Carter understood western water better than his critics. His problem was timing. Today, a water projects hit list would still raise eyebrows but there would be no firestorm of criticism. The politics and economics of western water have changed.

The "good old days" of western water development lasted from the turn of the century through the 1960s. During that time, the Bureau of Reclamation managed massive transfer payments from the federal treasury to dam sites in western river valleys. With the money, local sponsors of water projects, federal engineers, and congressional representatives concocted grand schemes for turning rivers into quiet and cooperative pools that stair-stepped up the river beds.

The passage of the National Environmental Policy Act in 1970 changed this situation. Dam builders now had to give some consideration to nature. And the public was involved in the review process the law created. Under the old rules, beneficiaries had been limited to those with a direct or indirect interest in water. Now, new players were elbowing their way to the table.

To accommodate nature, the public, and the federal government, "mitigation"—measures to avoid, reduce, or compensate losses due to water projects—was invented. Mitigation quickly became a process of negotiation between the dam builders and all those who purported to speak for river protection and natural systems.

Theoretically, there was hierarchy to the mitigation measures—avoiding insults to nature was preferable to replacing, in a new location, what was lost. In practice, however, compensation or replacement were the only options given serious consideration; negotiations usually boiled down to counting picnic tables, parking spaces, and outdoor toilets. Everybody grumbled—the developers about the costs and the nature lovers about what was lost.

Despite the grousing, the new process worked, particularly for those who saw progress in dams, through most of the 1970s. Then certain economic realities set in. These included a slowdown in the nation's industrial productivity, an erosion of its share of world markets, an increase in the rate of inflation, and an expansion of the share of the federal budget going to those programs known as "entitlements." The economy was seen as weak, and the federal government was stretched thin. These circumstances, along with the ideological stance of the Reagan years, took some of the money out of the hands of western dam builders. The Bureau of Reclamation's exit from the dam-building arena was accelerated by unprecedented deficit spending and the resulting enormous federal debt. By 1984, the Bureau no longer had a mission.

Local dam builders were now on their own. Their loss of a sponsor and funding was further aggravated by federal efforts to turn back to state and local governments programs that until then had been Washington's responsibility. At the same time, the states were beginning to realize that the upkeep of large capital systems built with federal money, such as wastewater treatment plants, was their responsibility. As a result, local tax dollars were squeezed and the public was increasingly wary of expensive new projects.

Just as financial resources were shrinking or vanishing, dam builders were faced with more and more expensive projects. The inexpensive, cost-effective dams had been built first. The remaining sites were losers—projects that were costly, environmentally damaging, and, often, only marginally useful.

Not that all the earlier projects had been absolutely necessary. Long-standing policies had often encouraged profligate use, or waste, of water in order to create demand for dams. Using water projects and their water efficiently had very low priority in the water development community. Efficiency, to water developers, meant less dam building.

Environmentalists saw a way to use the dam builders' past construction successes against them in this new, penny-pinching era. With the flow of both local and federal tax subsidies to dam builders shut off, environmentalists could now get to the heart of the issue: what projects were really needed, which, if any, were cost-effective, and what were the alternatives? This approach, a switch from defense to offense, has been very successful.

Dam builders who ignore the new reality do so at their peril. The Denver Water Board has learned an expensive and bitter lesson in Two Forks Dam on the South Platte River. The Sandstone Dam in Wyoming will eventually fall of its own weight, as will the Clear Creek Dam, the Union Park project and the Collegiate Range project in Colorado. The unfinished portions of the Central Utah Project are in serious trouble and, in California, the Auburn Dam has been shelved and Pam Dam is on the skids.

Large dam construction, the twentieth-century equivalent of pyramid building, is too expensive to command much public support today. Over time it has resulted in lost opportunities by diverting capital. The real economic benefits of dams have been limited, especially if we count the energy and political capital that have gone into coaxing the funds out of Washington. Now, capital-intensive water projects have to compete with a host of other community needs for resources. Given their dubious benefits, few dams are likely to stand up well in contests played on level fields. Both the environment and the economy will be better for the struggle.

But questions remain about whether the water management institutions in the West, which dominated the region's economy for so long, can themselves adapt to the new realities. In *Rivers of Empire: Water, Aridity and the Growth of the American West*, historian Donald Worster suggests that the West, a hydraulic society and a colony within a nation, has fought a long, fierce battle to "get out from under" by expanding its resource base through dam construction. But instead of rising above colonial dependency, the West has been ensnared in its own "hydraulic trap," Worster writes, creating a rigid political, economic, and social system that could lead to stagnation. This inflexibility is to a large extent institutional, a characteristic that environmentalists have long recognized and one that some elected officials are beginning to recognize, too.

As Colorado Governor Roy Romer observed in remarking on the lessons of Two Forks, the state has changed profoundly since its system for planning and developing water was designed. As a result, he said, its institutions are "out of step ... with the values of its citizens and in need of 'reform or overhaul.' "

But recognizing the hydraulic trap is one thing, escaping is another. In his review of the historical record of societies that have relied heavily on water development to sustain themselves, Worster sees plenty of reasons for pessimism. But he also points out that the environmental movement and its willingness to question established authority offers evidence "that the old obedience" has begun to crack.

*February 26, 1990*

# West's Grand Old Water Doctrine Dies

## Charles F. Wilkinson

As has been so widely reported, Prior Appropriation passed away in January of 1991 at age 143. Prior was a grand man and led a grand life. By any standard he was one of the most influential people in the history of the American West. It is a tall order, but with these few thoughts I will try to recount his life, and assess some of his accomplishments and shortcomings.

The story of Prior's birth has been told so often it is part of the bedrock of western history—how, on January 26, 1848, James Marshall, literally shaking with exhilaration moments after his epic discovery of gold, came upon a babe on his mad rush back to Sutters Mill to spread the news. The child was so young he must have been left by the side of the American River that very day. And although botanists deny the species ever existed in the Sierra Nevada foothills, legend persists that Marshall found the infant Prior wrapped in a blanket nestled in bulrushes.

The young boy was raised by the miners in as remarkable a time as ever existed, passed from miner to miner in the diggings in California and Nevada. Smart, exuberant, and savvy, Prior was a favorite of this nearly all-male society from the beginning. There was that moment of moments in September 1851 at Rich Bar, on the Feather River. Dame Shirley, author of the acclaimed Shirley Letters was in Rich Bar that autumn and wrote:

> A precocious, curly-haired three-year-old boy was playing
> jubilantly by the creek one afternoon. He had laboriously built
> a sand and gravel castle with a moat. An elderly miner came
> down with a bucket to fetch his (must I say it?) weekly bath.
> He never saw the boy, his castle, or the moat, the flow to
> which the old man had disturbed by plunking his bucket in the
> stream. My heavens! All at once the September air was filled
> with the din of commotion. The boy shrieked with a purple
> rage and threw his favorite toys—his 2 1/2-pound Colt 45

*revolver, his Green River knife with the six-inch blade, his*
*molded iron mining pan—in every direction.*
*    And then, as the chastened old miner departed with an*
*empty bucket, the boy thrust his index finger in the air and*
*bawled out that word that bespoke to perfection the spirit of*
*these mines: "First! First!! First!!!" From that day on, the*
*adopted boy had a name and his idea about water became the*
*byword in those rough camps.*

Prior rose again to glory in 1855. Matthew Irwin, one of Prior's
foster parents, had diverted the water—all of the water—from the
South Fork of Poor Man's Creek near the Sierra Nevada mining town
of Eureka. But Robert Phillips, a would-be water user, had come to
Poor Man's Creek after Irwin, and so Irwin brought suit in California
Supreme Court to make sure that his claim to the creek was
paramount over Phillips'.

The case was argued in the small courtroom in Sacramento amid a
judicial scene rare even in those boisterous days. In the back of the
courtroom sat Matthew Irwin and the many miners and storekeepers
who had bought water from him. When the five judges entered the
chambers, the crowd stood, initially respectful and silent; but then
Prior climbed one of the benches, turned to the Irwin contingent
and, like a conductor, caused them to begin to chant: "We're
number one! We're number one! We're number one!" Chief Justice
Murray first looked startled, then grinned, then gently raised his
hand for silence, then just stopped and drank in the simplicity and
justice of the chant.

The court ruled for Matthew Irwin and those he supplied—and
for Prior. Even today, nearly a century and a half later, is there one of
us who could say we would have done differently back then?

Prior spent much of his youth in the Gold Country, but he also
took many trips with miners or merchants who wanted his
company. Those early journeys presaged a life spent exploring every
nook and cranny of the West. Prior's very first trip was to the
Mormon settlements in Utah. He went in 1852, when he was just
four. How the Mormons doted on him: tossing him in the air,
teasing him with tickles and jests, taking him out to the irrigation
fields where the languid summer evenings were heavy with the
breath of the new green crops.

He even met Brigham Young, who, when he saw Prior, did a
double-take, grabbed the boy, hoisted him into the air, looked up at

him and, beaming beatifically, exulted: "When I came to this valley
five years ago, I had a vision of a boy and an idea, and you are the
boy whom I saw at that gilded moment." From that day on, there
was a religious dimension to Prior's ideas.

He loved the generous and hardworking Mormons so. Years later,
when Prior, who had no formal schooling, began a life of self-taught
reading, he learned of the agrarian ideal and said of the Mormons,
"That's what Jefferson had in mind."

But most of Prior's growing-up days were spent in the Gold
Country. His best and tightest pal would later earn fame as a military
man—General Mining Law. I personally think it wrong for some
late-twentieth-century commentators to term the General, who
came from a large and distinguished family, as "the Law with no
brain," but the description has stuck.

Prior and the General grew up fast and grew up about the best any
boys could. They went to all the gold camps—in California, Oregon,
Idaho, Colorado, Arizona, even Mexico and Alaska in later years.
They saw shootings and hangings. Once they even saw the ultimate
Gold Country act—one burly miner carved another's heart out
"Maltese style," with a single motion from a curved-blade knife
imported from the Mediterranean. Prior and the General clinked
their shot glasses and the General hooted: "He probably deserved it;
if he didn't steal water, he must have jumped a claim." To which
Prior replied, "First in time, first in right."

Prior and the General knew every bar from Columbia to the
Klondike and from Virginia City to Cripple Creek, and they caroused
and cursed and drank and whored and fought in them all. They were
men's men—broad-shouldered, barrel-chested, and square-jawed.
Prior, who knew Mark Twain, was fond of quoting Twain's comment
upon his first visit to Nevada in the 1860s: "This is no place for a
god-fearing Methodist and I did not long remain one."

But Prior did marry, and while he married late—at thirty-three—
he married well. Ramona was a black-eyed beauty, half Indian and
half Mexican. They settled down near the heart of the West, in the
farm-ranch country out near Vale, Oregon.

Prior went everywhere in the West and he took Ramona with him
whenever he could. He gave most of his adult life to public service—
to furthering the cause he believed in. In the beginning, it was easy.
Colorado bought in in 1882. So did his beloved Utah. With some
town-square oratory, Fourth-of-July backslapping, and Sunday-

meeting preaching, nearly all of the others came into line. Prior was messianic and he developed a cult following that spread the word. Everywhere, his message was the same, logical and true. "The water is our heritage. Take it—take it all, if you can. This is the American century. Progress will result." And, he would usually add, "Take it now. I'm traveling upriver to other towns and states; if you don't take it they will. Be first. Achieve progress first."

To be sure, not everyone listened at first. Washington, Oregon, and California bought part way into Riparian Law. Riparian was the General's outcast cousin who eventually moved back east to Newark. But no real matter. Everyone knew that by the 1890s Prior had won out basically everywhere west of the 100th Meridian. He had done it by knowing the land and the people, and by giving the people what they wanted and needed.

Ramona would say, "Prior, oh Prior. We've gone everywhere and seen so much and I admire you so. You're the man of the miners, yes, but you're also the man of the farmers. You're always so right."

It was about then, about 1890, when the frontier closed, that things began to change and Prior's work began to take on a much harder edge. His first confrontation came in Wyoming. Prior had learned of the expert engineer, Elwood Mead, who had brought innovations to Colorado water policy (a century later, Coloradans wait for another innovation) and who then moved to Wyoming as statehood drew near. Mead was a major figure at the Wyoming constitutional convention in 1890, and Prior was concerned; he had heard that Mead wanted the new constitution to make water the property of the state, with appropriations allowed only if in the public interest.

Their meeting was inevitable. When it came it was a study in contrasts—the big, ebullient, charismatic Prior sitting opposite the quiet, scholarly Mead, with his round, wire-rimmed glasses. "Well, what is this, Elwood? I thought water was for the people, not for big government."

"It is, Mr. Appropriation, but who would you say owns it before our farmers put it to use? The federal government, which will own most of the land and all of the watersheds in Wyoming after statehood? The Arapahoe and Shoshone are the second biggest landowners in Wyoming. Do you want them to claim ownership before diversion?"

"I see your point, Elwood. But the state is only a front, right? The people can just take the water, right? State ownership is just a fiction, right? A way of explaining how the settlers can just take the water. Right?"

"That's generally correct, Mr. Appropriation."

Prior pressed on. "State law is really no law. Each individual settler decides. Is that right?"

"I'd say so, yes."

"Now, what about this 'public interest,' Elwood? Everybody knows you're going to be the first Wyoming state engineer. You're not going to go running around deciding what's right and what's wrong, are you?"

"No, that's for the settlers to decide."

"Well, all right. It sounds like you're just prettying up the people's rule, 'first in time, first in right.' I'll need your assurance, Elwood, because you know damn well if I go to those farmers and tell them that this here new state is going to deny or regulate their water, then you know damn well there isn't going to be any constitution, and there isn't going to be any new state engineer. You understand me?"

"I've given you my interpretation, Mr. Appropriation."

In the years to come, Mead kept to his interpretation. He distributed water to people according to their priorities, and he hardly ever used the "public interest" provision. Prior had been right. Whatever the constitution said, the water users owned the water. They had vested rights.

No sooner was Prior done with Elwood Mead than he was locked into a confrontation that changed the course of history more than anything he ever did. If there was another great man of the West in the late nineteenth century, it was John Wesley Powell. He was the visionary who in 1869 was the first to float the Colorado River, and who wrote his famous Arid Lands Report in 1878. In it, Powell urged steps to induce more ordered settlement and a better fit between settlement and the limits imposed by the scarcity of water. Prior hated the widely read and admired report. Those who liked it, he said, were "a bunch of goddamned blind, thick-headed Easterners." And he hated the idea of limits. "Human beings can accomplish anything. There's no point in being negative."

Without Prior's knowledge, Powell was appointed head of both the U.S. Geological Survey and the Bureau of Ethnology. In 1888, Powell convinced Congress to commission him to conduct a comprehensive survey of potentially irrigable lands and possible reservoir sites in the West. It seemed innocuous. But then Powell persuaded the Interior Department to close all lands west of the 101st Meridian to settlement pending completion of his study. It was the most sweeping public lands withdrawal in history. To boot, the 1889 withdrawal was made retroactive to 1888, the date of the original congressional resolution requesting Powell's survey.

Prior became as furious as he had been that day four decades earlier at Rich Bar on the Feather River. He was everywhere. He even traveled to Washington, which he detested more than any place in the East, which in turn he detested more than any place on earth. He first met with Senator William Stewart of Nevada—Big Bill— Prior's old bar-hopping friend from Gold Country days, but he also found time to meet everyone he knew. And on the way home, he stopped in Omaha to see William Smythe, the untiring booster of big irrigation, big dams, and more development. He was always direct, but with Stewart and Smythe he was most direct. "This Powell sumbitch [Prior was always careful to use the preferred pronounciation] is a madman," he exhorted, the veins standing out on his neck. "Get him. Get the sumbitch."

And they did. In August 1890, Congress, at Stewart's relentless urging, overturned the 1889 withdrawal. Then Smythe took over. He organized the Irrigation Congress in 1891, followed two years later by the most notorious Irrigation Congress ever, in Los Angeles. There, Smythe, Prior, and nearly the whole crowd—a gang, really— shouted Powell down. He was a pariah, he was against progress. They finally drove him from office in 1894, when he was forced to resign.

Wallace Stegner, who saw it differently from Prior, described Powell's downfall this way in his book, *Beyond the Hundredth Meridian: John Wesley Powell and the Second Opening of the West*:

> *But they hadn't given him time. They had beaten him when he was within a year of introducing an utterly revolutionary—or evolutionary—set of institutions into the arid West, and when he was within a few months of saving that West from another half century of exploitation and waste. It was the West itself that beat him, the Big Bill Stewarts and the Gideon Moodys, the land and cattle and water barons, the plain homesteaders, the locally patriotic, the ambitious, the acquisitive, the myth-bound West which insisted on running into the future like a streetcar on a dirt road.*

Ramona, who knew of the Powell confrontation, remained silent.

Prior stayed busy. He lobbied through the great Reclamation Act of 1902. He knew it would never pay its way, although he kept that to himself during the debate over the act. He knew reclamation was good because it meant more farms and more farming towns. Besides, water users should be subsidized. That's how you made progress in the West.

Prior had grown to respect southern California, although not as much as Utah, for sure. But he saw there the beginnings of a great city. He wanted to help. So in 1903 he traveled to Los Angeles by rail, riding in the plush coach car specially designed for Leland Stanford. Prior had arranged for a meeting with William Mulholland, the tall, dapper, mustachioed head of the Los Angeles Department of Water and Power. It was a match made in heaven.

"Owens Valley," Mulholland mused after hearing Prior's careful, detailed, two-hour presentation in the wood-panelled, high-ceilinged room. "That's a long way from here, nearly 250 miles."

"That's exactly the point, Mr. Mulholland. If this city is going to be what you want it to be, you're going to have to think big. Imagine all the jobs you'll create building the canal and the facilities. Besides, and I've got to be direct with you, I can either head back home or go on to Las Vegas and Reno. They want to grow, too, you know."

"Prior, may I call you Prior?"

"You sure can ... Bill."

"Prior, you've got a deal. But let's keep this to ourselves."

"We sure will, Bill."

Then Mulholland got up from his mahogany desk and walked to the window. "Do you think there's any problem with those folks up in the Owens who are planning their own reclamation project? We'll have to take the water out of their watershed, and my impression is that water law pretty much favors irrigation."

"Bill, don't worry about a thing. This Riparian Law you sometimes use here in California is no problem. Just quietly, through a third party, buy up all the landowners along the stream. The only water law that really matters is first in time, first in right. Frankly, it's all up for grabs for the first taker. If that happens to be farming—fine. I'm all for farming. But if our cities need it, and get there first, they've got it. The law is neutral. Don't worry about a thing."

"As I say, Prior, we've got a deal. Thank you for this. A lot of people will thank you."

The two shook hands and Prior moved toward the door, but then stopped and said, "And Bill, by the way, make your plans broad enough to include Mono Lake, up to the north. Your city is going to need it some day."

"Prior, you took the words out of my mouth."

And the two men laughed heartily.

Prior was wakened one morning in 1908 by a friend's loud, rapid knock. He brought news that seemed to come from Mars. "What?" Prior asked in disbelief. "Indians? Water rights? Even if they haven't diverted the water? The United States Supreme Court, you say?"

The Winters decision gnawed at Prior. He could not accept a ruling that put the Indians at the front of the water appropriation line—ahead of his miners, his farmers, his booming cities. Finally, in 1911, he got in his prized red 1909 Model T Ford and drove to the Reclamation office in Billings. He knew the people there, but even so they were taken aback by his ideas. "Take on the Winters decision? Rub out the words of the Supreme Court by real action on the ground?" But they quickly understood, and they carried out Prior's carefully drawn plan.

As the first symbolic act of a campaign that would continue for nearly the whole century, in 1911 Bureau of Reclamation officials entered the Gros Ventre-Assiniboine Reservation at Fort Belknap, the very reservation at issue in Winters. They dammed Peoples Creek, which drained most of the reservation. They diverted the flow and by canals sent the water to non-Indian irrigators in the Malta District, 150 miles away.

When Prior returned and told Ramona, she said, "Oh, Prior, those are my people."

"Damn it, this is about law, Ramona. Law protects people who use water, not those who waste it."

Two years later, Prior came up against John Muir in a fight over the damming of a beautiful valley to provide San Francisco with water. Three years later, Hetch Hetchy, the sister valley of Yosemite, was a reservoir. He railed to Ramona about Muir. "That long-haired wild man, with his talk about wilderness and beauty and animals—and flowers. He needed to be put in his place."

"But Prior, oh Prior. You used to read Mr. Muir's books. And Prior, just last night we walked by the stream and you picked me a mariposa lily, the one in the vase over there, and you told me mariposa meant butterfly in Spanish and that I was your butterfly lily."

Prior just said, "Those were books and that flower was personal, Ramona. This is about water."

By 1916, Prior had succeeded in getting the Reclamation Service to build giant Elephant Butte Dam on the Rio Grande in southern New Mexico. Traditional Hispanic farmers—1,400 farms with 50,000 acres in crops supporting 6,000 Hispanic people in all—had worked the land long before the dam. In 1936, Hugh Calkins of the U.S. Soil Conservation Service wrote a report showing that Hispanic subsistence farmers couldn't pay the charges for the big project and would not or could not convert to the new, intensive cash crops of cotton favored by the Anglos for whom Elephant Butte was built. Before the dam, Calkins wrote, "The Spanish-American population [was] largely self-sufficient and secure." Afterward the Hispanics lost their farms and became farm laborers living "at a permanently low income level and a high insecurity level." When Prior learned of Calkins' report, he cranked up his telephone and told Reclamation, "Bury it!" which Reclamation did.

"But Prior, these are my people. And aren't they living the Jeffersonian ideal?"

"This is about policy, Ramona, and progress. And policy must be color-blind."

By the 1930s, even though he was in his eighties, Prior was as energetic and effective as ever. He was ready for his last crusade: the great dam-building orgy that began in the 1930s and lasted into the 1960s. It remade the American West and it was driven by Prior's central premise: the rivers and canyons, all of them, were zoned for intensive use. First come, first served, with no holds barred.

Reservoir capacity expanded at the rate of 80 percent per decade during the boom. Ironically, Prior's greatest ally in the early 1930s was Elwood Mead, by then Commissioner of Reclamation. Although they never talked, and although each man carried a visceral dislike for the other from their 1890 meeting in Wyoming, the products of their combined activities were overwhelming. Both held a life-long love for irrigation and personally they favored the farmers. But they believed in development more, and now it was the cities, the subdivisions, the hydro facilities, and the coal-fired power plants that wanted and needed water. Prior and Mead made sure there were no obstacles.

Every river system was built up. The Columbia, the River of the West, became slack-water pools from Bonneville to Canada. The

Missouri had 85-million acre-feet impounded. The Rio Grande had 7.8 million acre-feet, twice the annual flow of the river, put behind dams. The Colorado had 72 million acre-feet in storage—nearly six times its annual runoff. And nearly all the smaller watersheds had dams, too.

It seemed not to matter that so many hundreds of places were sacrificed. Glen Canyon. The rich bottom lands of the Fort Berthold Reservation. The Hispanic settlements at Los Martinez, Rio de los Pinos, and Rosa under Navajo Reservoir on the San Juan River. Also gone were the Columbia's old falls and Indian fishing scaffolds at Celilo. On the other extreme, hundreds of rivers were drained dry by diversions.

It was an ordeal and Prior felt his age for the first time. Beginning in about 1975, he grew less and less active. His last public appearance was the closing address to an emotional, standing-room-only crowd of his truest believers. It was the 1987 annual meeting of the Colorado Water Congress and it had drawn, as usual, a prosperous audience: farmers; reasonably well-heeled public water officials; well-heeled executives from special water districts; very well-heeled engineers; very, very well-heeled real estate developers; and very, very, very well-heeled lawyers. The conclusion of Prior's famous swan song went like this:

> *Think back, gentlemen, over what we and our forebears have accomplished. We have conquered, tamed and settled the harshest land. We have made it green. We have built great cities. We have served all the people. We did it with water.*
>
> *The Bureau of Reclamation alone has built 355 storage reservoirs and 15,000 miles of canals, 1,333 miles of pipeline, and 275 miles of tunnels. More than 100,000 miles of canals divert the flows of western rivers and deliver water to irrigators and other water users. More than a million artificial reservoirs, lakes and ponds store 294 million acre-feet. This is the equivalent of 22 whole Colorado Rivers backed up behind dams, filling former canyons. It is enough to put Montana, Wyoming, Colorado, and New Mexico—an entire tier of states—under a foot of water. All of that creativity and energy was unleashed by the simple, time-proven idea that the ingenuity and diligence of the individual American should not be shackled.*

> *Progress, gentlemen, progress. That is what we have given
> to our children and grandchildren.*

Prior has now passed on. He died January 19, 1991, when his
heart seized up after receiving a fax informing him that, on that very
day, the new Director of the Denver Water Board had recommended
that the water developers not file a lawsuit challenging the
Environmental Protection Agency's rejection of the dam at Two
Forks.

In truth, however, Prior died of multiple causes.

The publication of *The Milagro Beanfield War* wounded. "It's lies,
lies top to bottom," Prior would fume. Ramona, who seldom teased
Prior, would say, "It's just fiction, love," and, she would add with a
gleam in her bright eyes, "Oh, but it's a funny book, Prior."

Carter's 1977 hit list of reclamation projects to kill also hurt. ("We
need a good conservative Republican president from the West,
preferably California," Prior ranted.) But President Reagan's
moratorium on federal funding of water projects also hurt. There
was the Mono Lake opinion and the public trust doctrine (Prior
raged, "What kind of a court is this? Talking about brine shrimp,
gulls, Wilson's Phalarope, tufa—whatever the hell that is. This was
supposed to be a case about water.") The serious illness of General
Mining Law and the ridicule he is suffering just now, in his last days,
also grieved Prior.

There were other contributing causes. The many Indian water
settlements ("They don't deserve a drop"); environmentalists—just
the mere existence of them; academics who relentlessly criticized
Prior's ideas ("The bastards wouldn't know the real world from a
beachball"); federal reserved water rights; state water planning
("We've got a plan. It's called 'first in time, first in right.' "). An
especially cruel blow was when they adopted an instream flow
program—in Utah.

But perhaps we should leave the last word to Ramona. After all,
she knew more about Prior than anybody. She had heard I was
writing this piece, and a while back she called to talk. Here is part of
what Ramona told me in her measured way:

> *Everybody knows I've never been one to criticize Prior. Lord, I
> always loved the man so. But, you know, he was wrong
> sometimes. And for me personally, the worst of it was that his
> wrong-headedness increased over the years. It seems he just*

*couldn't change—he was so set in his ways because he believed so deeply in his convictions.*

*But what people need to remember is that there were times when he was right, too. Otherwise, how could he have lived for so long? How many ideas, after all, last for a century and a half?*

*What I hope is that the reformers remember some of the good things about Prior. I hope they appreciate that Prior's real roots were in the communities he helped to build: in the Bitterroot, Gallatin, and Yellowstone valleys; the Powder River country; the Gunnison and Yampa watersheds; the Upper Rio Grande; the Verde Valley; the Virgin River country; some of the small farm communities in California's Central Valley; the Humboldt; our country out near Vale; places on the Snake River Plain; the Wenatchee Valley. And places, too, where my people have managed to thrive: the Culebra watershed near San Luis, Colorado; the Chama Valley; the Wind River Valley; the Deschutes watershed. There are many others. These are some of the finest places in the world.*

*Whatever wrong directions his hard-headedness might have taken him off in, that sense of community was what he most cared about. That was his most luminous idea.*

*I wonder whether the reformers will be able to keep the light of that idea alive and whether, now that they will have to replace Prior, they can offer up other ideas as bright. I hope they can and if they can, I wish all the reformers godspeed. I wish them 143 years also.*

*August 12, 1991*

# The Fight for Reclamation

## Marc Reisner

n *Encounters with the Archdruid,* John McPhee recounts a moment when he rafted down the Colorado River with David Brower and Floyd Dominy—and Dominy, the bullheaded Commissioner of Reclamation during the 1950s and 1960s, took the plunge into the Lava Falls rapid with a cigar clenched between his teeth. Doused by the maelstrom, the cigar, minutes later, glows again, McPhee's sly allusion to Dominy's dominance of the tempestuous river.

In August 1994, when I rode a raft through the Grand Canyon with the latest of Dominy's successors, Dan Beard, I snapped a photo of the cigarless commissioner as we hit Debendorff Rapids. When I got the film developed, Beard was invisible, for a great mound of frigid water from the bottom of "Lake Dominy" ("Powell" was Dominy's idea) covered him like an African hut. I remember Beard's reaction when he emerged from the dissipating wave. A look of cardiac shock metamorphosed into the widest grin I ever saw, from which erupted a whoop even that noisy avalanche of snowmelt couldn't overwhelm. As Beard sat there shivering, the grin never left his face. He had come not to humble nature, but to be humbled himself.

Like McPhee—like all writers—I take metaphorical license. Dominy hoped to control the Colorado River much more than he did, and Beard may never free it as much as he may wish.

The demolition of Glen Canyon Dam (which, in fairness to Beard, he would never propose) seems as unthinkable now as Dominy's mad-for-dams obsessions, two giant river plugs at Marble Gorge and Bridge Canyon. That said, the differences between these two—who as commissioners would oversee a fourth of the West's water—are almost comically extreme.

Floyd Dominy's proudest monument is the great dam that drowned Glen Canyon, an ethereally beautiful stretch of river he described as "useless to anyone." He fought ferociously for Marble

Gorge and Bridge Canyon, the Grand Canyon dams immortalized by the Sierra Club ads, whose ultimate purpose would have been to sell enough peak-hour electricity to finance a Martian-style aqueduct from the Columbia drainage into the Colorado, which he called a "river of deficit." He held secret meetings with Los Angeles' water kleptocracy to map this and even grander diversion plans and, in Zeus-like fits induced by prodigious draughts of bourbon and cigar smoke, bellowed about the "waste" of Alaskan water flowing seaward instead of southward. Dominy drove Reclamation, in McPhee's phrase, like a fast bus. Some of his passengers admired and others hated him, but both camps were scared half to death. Dominy was Patton with MacArthur's ego doing Mulholland's work, which he considered the Lord's.

Dan Beard, who is fifty-one, never spent a day at Reclamation before he was appointed commissioner, while Dominy came up through the ranks, extraordinarily fast. Before his appointment, Beard spent seven years working for George Miller, D-Calif., the deposed chairman of the House Committee on Natural Resources. In Dominy habitat—California's San Joaquin Valley, Colorado's Grand Valley, the subsidized cottonlands of Arizona—Miller is as popular as Salman Rushdie in Iran. Pugnacious and as big as a defensive end, the congressman says he takes that as a great compliment. Beard, who is less combative than Miller but an avowed environmentalist and (he actually admits this) a liberal Democrat, says he hopes he doesn't have to build any big dams, but wouldn't mind taking some smaller dams down—especially those that have ruined salmon habitat.

Interviewed in 1994 on his Virginia farm, Dominy, who was then eighty-four, said, "Now I'm sure people can survive without salmon, but I don't think people can survive without beans and potatoes and lettuce … I think the [salmon-blocking dams] were worth it. I think that there's substitutes for eating salmon. You can eat cake."

Unlike the famously autocratic Dominy, Beard is a lower-case democrat. When a Dominy loyalist in the Bureau suggests that his new boss is an environmentalist kook—and several reportedly have—Beard's typical response is an innocent "Why do you say that?" followed by a bout of Socratic debate.

Beard has the reputation of being relentlessly patient when pursuing a goal. He now runs an institution that, he readily admits, he "kicked around for years," a confederacy of engineers who couldn't wait for the next chance to build another dam. Dams have little or no place in Beard's vision. What he wants is to make the Bureau conservation-minded and, even worse, efficient. "I came to Reclamation with one purpose," he says. "To make us more environmentally sensitive and responsive to the needs of the contemporary West. Any worthwhile project we have under way I want to complete as fast as possible. Beyond that, the Bureau's future isn't in dams. The era of dams is over. I say that to my employees every chance I get."

The American West has changed tumultuously during the Bureau's ninety-two-year existence, change the Bureau has done a heroic job of ignoring until recently. Two years before the Bureau came into existence, Los Angeles had a population of 102,479. The metropolitan region is now two-thirds as populous as Canada. Las Vegas was artesian springs and a lone Mormon trading post in 1902; today it gains almost 5,000 people a month. When the Reclamation program was getting under way, the Columbia River was stirred by fifteen million salmon and the Central Valley's skies were darkened by eighty million migratory waterfowl. Their numbers have declined catastrophically, mainly because of federal dams that blocked and diverted the rivers and dried up most of California's wetlands.

By inclination and by law, the Bureau's constituency remains overwhelmingly agricultural while the West's population has become overwhelmingly urban. The Bureau sells water and power to farmers for a fraction of what it costs the taxpayers to deliver it—for a dollar an acre-foot in some project regions, like the Umatilla Basin of eastern Oregon. By contrast, urban users typically pay $400 to $800 an acre-foot. Even if you discount the higher cost of urban infrastructure, the disparity is staggering. Meanwhile, according to some project authorizations, the fish and wildlife have no legal right to water and no legitimate status as beneficiaries. And, though conserving water diverted for agriculture is the simplest and cheapest way to offer more to cities and nature, most older Reclamation contracts fix the subsidized price for forty years or longer. In many cases, it is much cheaper to waste Reclamation water than to save it.

Beard is convinced that Reclamation can supply more water to overspilling urban regions and disappearing natural areas with minimal harm to agriculture—without building dams. Not building dams may be the easiest piece of the puzzle. In the 1930s, Hoover

Dam was completed, power plant and all, for less than $49 million; today; the environmental impact statement could cost almost that much, and might be large enough to serve as the dam. Inflation, diminishing returns, and environmentalism have made new dams almost impossible to build. In a number of cases, economics favors tearing dams down. Conjunctive use (falling back on groundwater pumping during drought years) and wastewater programs, as well as off-stream storage (pumping water to created storage basins) hold some promise. However, the likeliest new water sources are conservation, crop shifts, or farmland retirement.

"The greatest challenge facing state and federal water leaders," Beard said recently, "is how we can effectuate transfers from agriculture to urban and environmental uses in a politically acceptable fashion. I don't have any specifics on how we can guide these transfers. I just know they will happen. Los Angeles, Las Vegas, San Diego, Tucson—urban regions in the desert West will not run out of water. If ag interests say, 'Sorry, but we need to keep using all this water to raise hay and alfalfa,' well, that's just not going to happen. As some sage said, water does run uphill to power and money." Beard is short on specifics because, in a region where frontier thinking still prevails, redistributing water is, to many, a sacrilegious idea. As Mark Twain noted, in the West, "Whiskey is for drinking, water is for fighting over."

In addition, water transfers are sanctioned mainly through state law, and every state has written different laws. Colorado may come closest to treating water as a free-market commodity, like pizza or pickles, but transfers to the Denver area have desolated some small agricultural regions and created a bit of a backlash. (Much the same has occurred in Arizona.) Some states recognize instream uses as beneficial, while others don't; some prescribe minimal flows while others refuse.

Ideally, water for new uses should come from conservation or crop shifts, with minimal loss of planted acreage. (Edward Abbey would have taken issue with that; his fondest wish was to re-desertify the West.) But conservation and crop shifts require incentives, which may not exist. Under hoary appropriative rights doctrine, one appropriator's conservation or lapse in use becomes the new supply of the next in line. California, among other states, has amended its water code—repeatedly—so that a farmer who conserves water retains the right to sell it. But the long, tyrannical rule of unadulterated Prior Appropriation has left a legacy of cynicism and disbelief. Several California farmers have said flat-out that the state's code revisions don't amount to anything "real," and they won't conserve water "just so L.A. can take it."

Dan Beard's Hundred Steps approach to water reform is to try to change things little by little and project by project. "The operation of each one is slowly being revised," he says. " 'Feasibility' is the operative word. Westwide revision isn't a political option. We've only seen mega-legislation affecting the whole program, or a huge piece of it, in 1902, 1924, 1939, and 1968 and 1992. Transfers will be worked out by state legislatures, in city and county governments, maybe even by Congress. But the Endangered Species Act and the changing culture at Reclamation are moving us in different ways."

Even as the "wise users," buoyed by the new Republican ride in Congress, aim to eviscerate the Endangered Species Act, the law guides more and more water policy. According to Beard, restoring the Columbia Basin salmon fishery—where a hundred salmon runs could soon go extinct—or even restoring it somewhat represents "the most complex natural resources problem in America today. Nothing else approaches it." With so many petitions for new listings, however, the Bureau has to do something, and not just on the Columbia. In California, it has lately managed releases from Folsom Lake to help flush juvenile salmon out to sea and maintain brackish water quality in the delta, at the expense of flatwater recreation and carryover storage. Meanwhile, on the Colorado River, the Bureau's biologists are concocting plans to rescue the squawfish, whose Columbia River cousins gorge on juvenile salmon detained by the reservoirs. Diversions to nourish wildlife refuges where threatened waterfowl roost are diversions taken from threatened salmon. In the modern world of western water, conflict and irony have no end, which was exactly the case a century ago.

So far, Beard's most prominent achievement as commissioner has been to reduce Reclamation's staff from 7,500 to 6,500. More than thirty thousand were employed during the FDR-Truman heyday. Further reductions in staff are likely, but he won't say where. "Our program," Beard says, "ought to dictate the size of our staff." It's a good bet he will downsize departments staffed by a certain type of engineer who, in the words of a new Reclamation non-engineer, has "concrete for brains."

Beard doesn't believe the 1994 election results will affect his objectives much. "In water development, Reagan did what Carter set out to do: not much. It was Bush who killed the Two Forks Dam. We may see a serious effort to weaken the Endangered Species Act and to limit landowner responsibility for protection. That shouldn't interfere with our program to promote efficient water use."

Like Boris Yeltsin, who inherited a tottering Soviet empire doomed by self-destruction and Gorbachev's early reforms, Beard took over a dominion where a quiet revolution had already occurred—one, as it happens, that he helped engineer. The Central Valley Project Improvement Act legislation, signed by George Bush over the wailing objections of California's farm water lobby, was written mainly by the subcommittee staffs of Senator Bill Bradley, D-N.J., and Representative George Miller, D-Calif., which is to say, by Beard. The most far-reaching compendium of reforms in Reclamation history, it reserves up to 800,000 acre-feet for wildlife and fisheries; it surcharges water deliveries to create a Restoration Fund worth close to $50 million a year; it legalizes transfers of project water statewide; it introduces tiered water pricing, shortens contract terms, and does a host of things the irrigation lobby had managed to thwart for decades.

The main reason Bush signed the legislation was because Republican corporate interests, including Jim Harvey, the chairman of Transamerica Corporation, and the proletariat's investment guru, Charles Schwab, laid siege to the White House switchboard, urging the president on. As they did that, the Metropolitan Water District was plotting strategy with the Natural Resources Defense Council. Alliances between capitalism, urbanism (which implies growth), and environmentalism are uneasy ones, but they are no longer just a California phenomenon. Through passage of the Central Valley Project Improvement Act, Utah got funds to complete the Central Utah Project. Some of the water will be rerouted from its original destination—irrigated fields—to the Wasatch front, serving people fleeing California.

Shortly after Beard helped engineer this coup from the outside, the Clinton administration submitted his nomination as commissioner. Many thought his confirmation was as likely as Ben and Jerry running the Department of Agriculture. When he was actually in his office at engineering headquarters in Denver, having moved it from the top floor to the bottom, right behind the receptionist, I phoned in stunned congratulations.

"It wasn't that hard," he deadpanned. "I laid pretty low, and I never had a nanny problem." As the new nanny for an unruly constituency that has been spoiled for a long time, he does now.

*May 20, 1995*

# 2

# The Salmon Crisis

# How the Basin's Salmon-killing System Works

## Pat Ford

**S**almon do not swim to the ocean. Consider a chinook salmon fry as it drifts in three-foot-wide lower Herd Creek. The weather warms, the snowpack starts to melt. The rivulets feeding Herd Creek rise. The spring freshet begins moving downstream, picking up speed as it picks up water. The tiny salmon drifts near the gravel where it emerged the year before. The freshet reaches it and takes it. The fish washes down backwards, snout pointing back upstream, moving within a pocket of its home stream's water.

The surge shoots from Herd Creek into the East Fork Salmon River, and a few miles later into the main Salmon River. The fish joins others washing down backward from the Salmon's headwaters 60 miles above. Now the water really moves. The fish are 850 miles from the Pacific Ocean. They will reach it at the four-mile-wide mouth of the Columbia River, in a week or so, depending on the winter's snows and spring temperatures in the Columbia Basin. When they enter the ocean, an internal transformation from fresh- to saltwater fish will be complete.

Two or three years later, those still alive will enter the Columbia, swimming this time, and fight up to the Snake, the Salmon, the East Fork Salmon and Lower Herd Creek—850 miles—to begin the cycle again, in the same place. Somehow they do this.

Or did this. In 1938, the Bonneville Dam closed on the lower Columbia River. Since then, seven more dams have blocked the migratory path Snake River salmon must travel down as juveniles and up as adults. These dams are why Snake River coho salmon are extinct, why four other wild salmon are petitioned for listing as endangered species, and why wild steelhead may soon join them. "Many factors have contributed to the general decline of Snake River salmon and steelhead runs," says their champion, Ed Chaney. "But only one threatens their survival—the eight Army Corps of Engineers dams on the lower Snake and Columbia rivers."

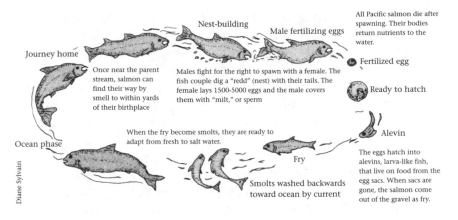

Journey home

Once near the parent stream, salmon can find their way by smell to within yards of their birthplace

Nest-building

Males fight for the right to spawn with a female. The fish couple dig a "redd" (nest) with their tails. The female lays 1500-5000 eggs and the male covers them with "milt," or sperm

Male fertilizing eggs

All Pacific salmon die after spawning. Their bodies return nutrients to the water.

Fertilized egg

Ready to hatch

Alevin

Ocean phase

When the fry become smolts, they are ready to adapt from fresh to salt water.

Fry

Smolts washed backwards toward ocean by current

The eggs hatch into alevins, larva-like fish, that live on food from the egg sacs. When sacs are gone, the salmon come out of the gravel as fry.

Diane Sylvain

Juvenile salmon are killed at the dams: shredded, shocked, and lost. They also die between the dams, where slackwater reservoirs have replaced the river and the week's trip now takes thirty days. As the fish drift in the currentless pools, they succumb to reservoir-bred predators, to high temperatures, disease, and premature saltwater transformation. Millions are taken out of the river at two of the dams, put in barges, then dumped back in the Columbia below the last dam. But salmon take handling poorly; delayed mortality is extremely high.

Returning adult fish are also killed at and between the dams. They fail to find the fish ladders, fall back from above the dams, or lose their way in the reservoirs. Oregon's Department of Fish and Wildlife estimates that each dam claims from 5 to 14 percent of the adults that reach it. Cumulative estimates of juvenile losses are 90 percent or more.

For the four Snake River salmon petitioned for endangered species listing, fishery agencies estimate that food harvests—commercial, sport, tribal, both ocean and in-river—account for between 2 percent (for spring chinook) and 4.7 percent (for fall chinook) of total human-caused mortality. From 95.3 to 98 percent of the deaths result from the dam harvest.

This massive annual slaughter occurs for a simple reason. The Army Corps of Engineers designed adult fish ladders for all eight mainstem dams, but none were designed so juvenile fish could migrate safely downstream. This fundamental engineering error was made not once but eight times over forty years. It was not made in ignorance—fish advocates pointed it out from the beginning. It was made despite laws, policies and repeated assurances that anadromous fish runs would be preserved. Because the salmon stubbornly refused to die out quickly, more than a billion public dollars has since been spent to patch around that design flaw. Turbine screens and juvenile fish bypasses were tacked on at half the dams, with varying degrees of ineffectiveness. Hatcheries were built to throw ever more millions of fish into the killing system. Water was thrown at it to achieve slight flow increases. Predator control was launched against the squawfish hordes created by the dams and fed by the hatcheries. A transport program now collects over 90 percent of the juvenile salmon from the river, barges them down, dumps them below the last dam—and virtually none ever return.

Ed Chaney sums it up: "Over fifty years we've built a Rube Goldberg artificial life-support system that simply doesn't work. The risk of total collapse has increased with each new whistle and bell added to 'help the fish.' That money could have fixed the real problem: design and operation of the mainstem dams."

The real problem hasn't been fixed for another simple reason. Changing the dams would require altering the uses they are built and operated to serve: hydroelectric generation, navigation, and irrigation.

The eight dams between Idaho salmon and the ocean—Lower Granite, Little Goose, Lower Monumental, and Ice Harbor on the lower Snake, and McNary, John Day, The Dalles, and Bonneville on the lower Columbia—are part of the world's largest coordinated hydroelectric system. More dams, higher in both basins, fill out the system, which produces an average 19,000 megawatts and gives the Northwest the lowest electric rates in the nation. Fifteen Northwest utilities, the Corps of Engineers, the Bureau of Reclamation (which operate the dams), and the Bonneville Power Administration (which markets their power) generate money as well as power. Fifty years of construction, and the WPPSS nuclear plant fiasco, have left the Bonneville Power Administration $15 billion in debt. To avoid raising power rates, the system maximizes hydrogeneration—and thus revenues from its sale—even when the region doesn't need power. During the spring salmon migration, Bonneville sells as much electricity to California as the four lower Snake dams generate.

The reservoirs also created a navigation industry. Farm and forest products from inland ports are barged down to Portland, many destined for Pacific Rim markets. Finished goods are barged up through locks and waterways built and maintained free of charge by the Army Corps of Engineers. Lewiston, Idaho, is now a seaport from which Montana wheat and Idaho paper products head overseas.

Irrigated agriculture is the third beneficiary. Huge pumps suck water from some of the reservoirs onto thousands of acres of croplands in Oregon and Washington. Recreation development—marinas, warm-water fisheries, shoreside parks—has grown up on the reservoirs as well.

It is a tight-fitting system. At the lower Snake projects, maximum generation from the turbines, necessary barge clearances, intakes for the irrigation pumps, and watering of adult fish ladders all occur within a five-to-seven-foot range of reservoir elevations. Drop below that range—for instance, to create current for juvenile passage—and each use either ceases or is substantially affected.

A system so big generates another kind of power. Its users and customers—utilities, bargers, irrigators, ports, aluminum companies—create a familiar politics of inertia. This is distinctively magnified by a mega-bureaucracy unique to the Northwest: Bonneville Power Administration and the Army Corps of Engineers, publicly financed, wielding public powers, yet publicly unaccountable. Bonneville and the Corps have built a Columbia Basin kingdom. These agencies were instruments of a great New Deal dream—public development of the Columbia Basin. While giving much, it has left two terrible wounds. The region's greatest natural gift has been ravaged, and the autocratic, self-perpetuating bureaucracies that did it grind on, largely immune to market discipline or democratic control, shackling today's dreams in yesterday's chains.

How can Snake River salmon get safely down to the sea so they will return in productive numbers? Two basic approaches are contending for favor in the Endangered Species Act process and for the newly attentive hearts and minds of Northwesterners.

The first avoids killing fish at the dams by removing the fish from the river. Juveniles would be collected and barged down past the last dam. Because 97 percent of all fish reaching the dams over the last six years were transported, this plan can fairly be called business-as-usual. (There is one new element: at least double the current flush of stored water from Idaho would be used to augment natural spring flows, to move more fish faster through the first two reservoirs to collectors at Lower Granite and Little Goose dams.)

The second approach would return the river to the fish, emulating pre-dam conditions as much as possible during the peak migration from mid-April through June. In the long term, the lower Snake dams, then the Columbia's, would be rebuilt to allow simultaneous juvenile and adult fish passage. In the short term, the four Snake reservoirs would be dramatically drawn down to create much faster flow velocities for juveniles, with adult ladders modified to keep operating.

The plans betray their chief sponsors. The first—replacing natural with engineered migration—is radical for salmon but conservative in its effects on the federal hydrosystem. Bonneville and the Corps are its major champions. The second is conservative for the fish but radical in its effects on Bonneville and the Corps. Idaho Governor Cecil Andrus is its architect. During the six months of Senator Mark Hatfield's Salmon Summit, the Idaho plan gained steady if often grudging ground by the force of its logic. Northwest fish agencies and tribes have recommended flow levels young salmon need to pass the dams in-river with reasonable survival rates. But creating those levels in the lower Snake reservoir pools would take half the river's total annual flow, delivered over three months. Even if one-third of Idaho's farmers agreed to quit farming, the river could not deliver that water unless a string of dams disappeared. The Idaho plan sponsored by Governor Andrus, however, would instead draw down the reservoirs 30 to 40 feet to create the velocities needed to move the juvenile fish through the reservoirs and down the river. The drawdowns would reduce power generation at the four dams over the two-to-three month migration period, probably ending it entirely for two months. But the advantage is that the juvenile salmon would not have to be barged at all.

In a January speech to the Salmon Summit, Andrus told about how he once blew up a dam. In 1964, he pushed the plunger to dynamite Idaho's Grangeville Dam, and a salmon run into the river was restored. Today the run is again threatened by dams, those down on the lower Snake. Andrus smiled as he told the story, but no one missed the edge. He is serious, and so are the Indian tribes, fishers, conservationists, fish agencies, and even some utilities who agree with him.

In May, the Boise engineering firm of Morrison-Knudsen will unveil the first-ever technical analysis of how (and for how much) the lower Snake dams could be modified to allow safe in-river passage of juvenile salmon. (Punching big holes in the dams, then gating them, is one option.) The work is being funded by the state of Idaho and Idaho Power Company. No institutions with any direct or indirect authority over the projects—the Corps, Bonneville, the Northwest Power Planning Council, Congress—are involved. This

says much about Northwest salmon politics, about where leadership
does and doesn't exist, and about the obstacles ahead. More than
concrete will have to be breached. Whether the Endangered Species
Act will finally provide the detonator remains to be seen.

Will salmon ever again have free migratory passage in the
Columbia Basin? Ed Chaney thinks so:

> The Northwest once had vision. It built the first high-voltage
> transmission line, the largest hydroelectric project in the U.S.,
> the largest single utility transmission system in the world, the
> world's largest coordinated hydroelectric system and a seaport
> 500 miles inland. We need to recapture that can-do attitude.
> We can figure out how to let water run downhill without
> killing most of the fish.

What would it cost to restore the salmon of the Snake River?
Since the filing of endangered species petitions last year, the
conventional wisdom prophesies dire consequences for the region's
economy that "make the spotted owl's impact look tame." The
Bonneville Power Administration said Northwest power rates could
rise by 30 percent or more; bargers predicted the end of their
industry; irrigators said farming in southern Idaho and Washington
could be devastated. Senator Mark Hatfield talked of fifty thousand
jobs at risk.

As analysis slowly replaces conditioned reflexes and sound bites,
the conventional wisdom is retreating. Early studies of the most
dramatic recovery proposal—the Idaho Plan—suggest its energy
impacts may be a wash. Hydrogeneration at the four lower Snake
River dams would cease for the spring salmon migration, but the
energy (that is, the water) wouldn't be lost, only shifted to other
parts of the year. The Columbia River dams—the backbone of the
hydrosystem—would not be shut down by the Idaho Plan. During
spring, the hydrosystem produces a surplus of energy, which is sold
to California. So managing a lower Snake spring shutdown is a
problem of marketing, energy exchanges, and perhaps short-term
replacement generation (for instance, a gas-fired combustion turbine
that could operate two months a year). Bonneville's threats to the
contrary, expensive new coal, nuclear, or hydro plants—plants that
operate year-round—would not be needed.

Impacts on agriculture also seem manageable. If anything, Idaho
farmers would make money on endangered-species listings, since the
listings would create a steady market for water lease sales by upriver

farmers to federal agencies trying to augment flows downriver. Farmers' water rights are not threatened. Washington farmers' irrigation pumps in the lower Snake reservoirs would need extending or boosting if reservoir drawdowns occurred each spring.

The Idaho Plan's major negative effect would be on lower Snake navigation; with reservoir drawdowns, barges would not be moving in the spring months. Mitigation seems possible. Montana wheat that now is trucked to Lewiston, for example, could be trucked 100 miles farther for a few months to Washington's Tri-Cities, whose port will remain open. But no overall mitigation plan has been developed by Idaho or the industry, so unavoidable impacts and mitigation costs are still unknown.

The economic benefits if Snake River salmon are restored to harvestable levels also are unknown—but undeniable. The Snake River once supported roughly half the spring and summer chinook salmon of the Columbia Basin. These millions of fish supported fisheries in Idaho and helped support fisheries in Oregon, Washington, British Columbia, and Alaska. "Restoring these fish is going to create jobs, not cost them," says Ed Chaney.

The largest economic impact will probably be the overall cost of any salmon recovery plan. Bonneville estimates its proposals would cost $150 million annually. The Idaho Plan would have very high (but as yet unknown) capital costs—to modify the mainstem dams for free juvenile fish passage—but few continuing costs. Both plans would create some jobs; the Idaho Plan in particular is a large public works project.

A financing mechanism already exists for any recovery plan. The 1980 Northwest Power Act directed that salmon restoration costs be paid, via Bonneville's wholesale rates, by electric ratepayers of the Northwest. Since 1980, perhaps $400 million has been spent (albeit without much payoff) for that purpose. Spread across several million ratepayers, the annual cost to each has been modest. Some federal appropriations, notably for the Corps of Engineers, may also be part of the mix.

"I keep thinking that a light bulb's going to suddenly go on in this region, and we will realize that a businesslike investment made now to restore these fish will create more jobs, more dollars, more stable communities for the region," says Ed Chaney. "We've got an economic opportunity here, not a threat."

*April 22, 1991*

# The Salmon Win One: Judge Tells Agencies to Obey the Law

## Paul Larmer

In what one salmon advocate describes as a welcome "slap upside the head," a federal judge in Oregon ruled that the agency responsible for recovering three endangered salmon species in the Columbia River Basin must go back to the drawing board. On March 29, 1994, Judge Malcolm Marsh told the National Marine Fisheries Service that it had been "arbitrary and capricious" when it determined in 1993 that federal dam operations on the Columbia and Snake rivers posed "no jeopardy" to the Snake River sockeye and two Snake River chinook salmon species. The judge initially told the agency it had sixty days to consult again with state and tribal biologists and produce a plan that could pass scientific muster.

The ruling, according to fish advocates and power proponents, is a landmark. Environmentalists hope it will eventually force the Bonneville Power Administration to dramatically alter the way it operates the dams. That, in turn, could force BPA to raise its electricity rates, a scenario which the aluminum, barging, and agricultural industries say could devastate them.

The decision may also signal the beginning of a court-dominated era in which lawsuits become the driving force behind salmon recovery throughout the Pacific Northwest, much as they have in the region's spotted owl forests.

Early in 1994, it looked as if the federal government's current management policy would go unchallenged. That policy relies on releasing water stored in Idaho to push the newly hatched salmon through reservoirs to collection sites. There they are pumped onto barges or trucks by the U.S. Army Corps of Engineers and transported around the dams to a point below Bonneville Dam, just east of Portland, Oregon.

As it did in its last two annual reviews of the federal hydropower system, a requirement under the Endangered Species Act, the agency determined in February that the hydropower dams pose "no jeopardy" to the salmon. It reached that conclusion even while acknowledging that the dams' turbines could still chop up nearly three-quarters of the juvenile salmon heading to the ocean.  And, as expected, environmentalists and Idaho Governor Cecil Andrus, D, immediately criticized the Fisheries Service for going after water stored upstream in Idaho while ignoring the lethal dams. "It's just unbelievable that a group of scientists will ignore all science and make a political decision," Andrus told the Idaho Falls *Post Register*.

A month later, Judge Marsh turned Andrus' words into prophecy. He ruled on a lawsuit brought by Idaho, Oregon, Alaska, and the Yakima, Umatilla, Nez Perce, and Warm Springs Reservation tribes against the federal agency's 1993 biological opinion. In his 38-page opinion, Marsh attacked both the agency's science and politics. He said the Fisheries Service was wrong to use the drought years of 1986 to 1990 as a basis for determining jeopardy. Salmon numbers were too low during that period, he said. "It is clear that a longer base period which includes higher abundance levels ... would have resulted in a higher goal." In a stinging conclusion, Marsh said the federal agency's decision making

> is too heavily geared toward a status quo that has allowed all forms of river activity to proceed in a deficit situation—that is, relatively small steps, minor improvements and adjustments— when the situation literally cries out for a major overhaul.
>
> Instead of looking for what can be done to protect the species from jeopardy, National Marine Fisheries Service and the action agencies have narrowly focused their attention on what the establishment is capable of handling with minimal disruption.

Although the judge didn't say what actions were needed to ensure salmon survival, he didn't rule out modifying the dams. Environmentalists and Andrus support major changes so that the reservoirs behind the four federal dams on the Snake River can be drawn down to speed young salmon to sea. "The idea that dams are immutable and uncontrollable like the weather ignores decades of fish protection improvements (such as bypass facilities and fish ladders) and other structural and operational enhancements," Marsh said. "... Thus, operational changes as well as systemic or facility changes to the dams' existence may well be available."

At a follow-up meeting April 8, Marsh approved a settlement plan that calls for face-to-face negotiations between high-level federal officials and state and tribal representatives, says Eric Bloch, an assistant attorney general for the state of Oregon. Under the settlement, which extends the deadline given in Marsh's original decision from sixty to ninety days, Bloch says the parties will revise the 1994-98 biological opinion, rather than the 1993 opinion Marsh ruled on, because the current plan is similarly flawed. Bloch says Marsh also told federal lawyers he wanted regular updates on negotiations and explanations of why ideas for protecting fish presented by the state and tribes are rejected.

For environmentalists, Marsh's ruling represents their first major legal victory in the battle to save salmon from extinction. "This is the crack in the dike of political corruption," says Ed Chaney, who has been fighting to save salmon for thirty years. "I intend to crowbar this baby until the whole thing comes tumbling down."

Chaney says since 1980, when the Northwest Power Council was created to give fish and wildlife equal footing with power production in the Columbia Basin, he has watched one effort after the next fail to address the fundamental problem posed by the dams. "We've blown our chances," he says. "That's why we're all in federal court." Chaney says his Northwest Resource Information Center plans to file new lawsuits in the coming year in hopes that Judge Marsh will take over the operation of the river system, much as federal Judge William Dwyer has taken over management of the region's forests west of the Cascades.

Andy Kerr, conservation director for the Oregon Natural Resources Council, also sees parallels with the spotted owl debate. Judge Marsh's decision is like the initial spotted owl ruling, which found that the Forest Service was breaking the law, he says. "It took a while for spotted owl litigation to work," he says, but eventually it strengthened the resolve of the public and the agencies to protect the owl and the forests. The same phenomenon may now be happening with the salmon, he says.

Bruce Lovelin, executive director of the Columbia River Alliance, a trade group representing aluminum companies, irrigators and the river transportation industry, agrees Marsh's decision signals a growing role for the federal courts. "We're clearly on the spotted owl track," he says. "It's really unfortunate." Lovelin says his alliance is particularly concerned about language in Marsh's conclusion that describes steps taken so far to protect salmon as minor adjustments. The National Marine Fisheries Service's current 1994-1998 biological opinion calls for an increase of water flows for fish from 10.4 million acre-feet per year to 11.5 million acre-feet per year, he says. "If that's minor tinkering, what's it going to take?"

Lovelin, however, sees signs of a political backlash. He points to a meeting in February where Governor Marc Racicot, R-Mont., and 250 supporters tongue-lashed federal officials over plans to take water from two Montana reservoirs to aid salmon recovery downstream. Racicot got a promise from the Bonneville Power Administration and the National Marine Fisheries Service that Montana's water wouldn't be touched this year. The Montana situation, says Lovelin, shows that people are beginning to feel that all the money BPA is spending on augmenting flows—$140 million by his estimation—is going down the drain because salmon populations continue to plummet. "The solution to recovering the salmon is not reservoir drawdown," Lovelin says. "The Corps of Engineers says it would take fourteen to seventeen years to do that." What remains, he says, is providing more water for the fish, and that means Idaho water. "I'm afraid Andrus may be shooting himself in the foot."

Environmentalists say the Corps' fourteen-to-seventeen-year drawdown estimation is an exaggeration. "We could begin drawdowns now," says Andy Kerr. "Once the body politic shows that it wants to save the salmon, we're going to find that drawdowns aren't as tough as we thought."

Will Whelan, a deputy attorney general for Idaho, agrees that Idaho water will have to be part of the salmon solution. "This decision may not mean less burden on Idaho irrigators, but we want a real solution." Whelan says he hopes Marsh's decision will force the Fisheries Service to reconsider its current policy of relying heavily on Idaho water to create a current through the downstream reservoirs. "You've got to wonder about a policy where the upstream tail wags the downstream dog," he says.

Marsh's decision comes at a dark moment for salmon regionwide. Salmon counts along the coast from California to Canada are so low that the Pacific Fisheries Management Council decided early this month it had no choice but to close almost the entire ocean salmon season. The ban sent shock waves through coastal communities. "We've gone from anger to denial to resignation," says Thane

Tienson, a lawyer for Salmon For All, a group representing the Columbia River salmon fishing industry. Tienson says many coastal fishers are calling it quits because "even if major efforts were begun today to restore the salmon runs, it would be a long time coming."

Scientists have known for some time that the Pacific Northwest's ocean-going fish stocks were in trouble. In 1990, the American Fisheries Society identified 106 already extinct populations of 214 endangered stocks of salmon and steelhead. But a confluence of factors, both natural and the result of human activities, seems to be accelerating the decline faster than anyone expected. Scientists point to everything from the El Niño current and overfishing in the ocean to drought, dams, overgrazing, and clearcutting inland. "I'm afraid we've pushed the system a little too far this time," says Katherine Ransel, a Seattle-based attorney with American Rivers.

The dismal condition of anadromous salmon and steelhead runs has prompted environmentalists to petition the federal government to list new salmon stocks under the Endangered Species Act. The National Marine Fisheries Service must already decide within the next few months whether to list every coastal coho salmon run in the region and three chinook salmon runs on the mid-Columbia River as endangered species. Now, under a petition recently filed by the the the Oregon Natural Resources Council, the Fisheries Service must consider listing more than one hundred steelhead (sea-going trout) stocks. Acting on their own, nine biologists from the Washington Fish and Wildlife Department asked the agency in March to add nine Puget Sound salmon stocks to the list.

The ocean ban and the rash of petitions heighten the drama taking place in the Columbia Basin, where just six male and two female Snake River sockeye made it back to Idaho's Redfish Lake last year.

The key player in the debate, the Bonneville Power Administration, continues to soft-pedal the dams' contribution to salmon decline and to tout the resources it is pouring into salmon recovery. BPA has increased its spending on salmon from $150 million in 1991, to $350 million in 1994, says spokesperson Dulcy Mahar, while flows for salmon have increased from 3 million acre-feet per year in the early 1980s to 11.5 million acre-feet per year in 1994. "There have been huge changes," Mahar says. "But we have seen no increase in survival, and in some cases the runs have declined."

Environmentalists say BPA's salmon protection efforts look good on paper, but not in the water. Lorraine Bodi, co-director of American Rivers' Seattle, Washington, office, says out of the $350 million BPA says it spends on salmon, only $80-90 million is really out-of-pocket money. "The rest is their calculation of foregone power revenues," she says. In addition, Bodi says, the agency has a bloated staff of fifty which spends an inordinate amount of money on reports and little on the priorities identified by the state agencies and tribes. One of those priorities is modifying the dams so fish can survive in the river, without having to be sucked into barges. But BPA's Mahar says focusing too much on the dams would be a mistake. "It would be unfortunate to just look at the dams just because that's where the deep pockets are," she says. What's needed, she says, is a comprehensive plan that looks at all the causes of the Snake River salmon decline, including ocean fishing, predation by other fish species, the role of hatcheries, and the destruction of spawning habitat.

Andy Kerr says reservoir drawdown is the only rational choice. "Call me a radical," says Kerr. "I think fish belong in the river, not in iron coffins (barges)." Besides, says Kerr, saving the salmon will help the Northwest's economy. "What's killing the salmon are economic activities that are being done inefficiently," he says. "Saving the salmon should force us to stop our wasteful use of water, electricity, trees, grass, and minerals."

Kerr's group has targeted the aluminum industry as the most wasteful of those dependent on cheap hydropower. "We ought to destroy the aluminum industry," he says. "It uses 20 percent of the region's electricity and provides one-quarter of one percent of the jobs." Kerr says Pacific Northwest ratepayers subsidize the industry to the tune of $325 million a year, approximately the amount of money BPA says it is spending on salmon recovery.

Dethroning the Columbia Basin power system's vested interests will be anything but easy. The aluminum industry, farmers, and commercial barging interests constitute a powerful coalition with powerful allies in Congress—none more so than House Speaker Tom Foley, Democrat of Washington state.

But environmentalists, with one legal victory under their belts, say they now see a glimmer of hope for saving one of the Pacific Northwest's most enduring natural legacies.

*April 18, 1994*

# Salmon: The Clinton-Babbitt Trainwreck

## Pat Ford

In 1991, at the Citizens' Salmon Congress in Hood River, Oregon, Michelle DeHart of the Fish Passage Center spoke eloquently about the death of salmon. The center is the tribal and Northwest states' office that monitors the Columbia River, requesting changes in hydropower operations to aid salmon migration. Its requests are routinely ignored by the Army Corps of Engineers, which runs the dams. The Bonneville Power Administration, the agency that markets electricity from the dams, regularly tries to muzzle DeHart. She knows and says as well as anyone how the eight federal dams and reservoirs slaughter salmon, and what must be done to change that.

Her message at the salmon congress was simple. Stop tinkering with the federal hydrosystem; only major overhaul will help Snake and Columbia river salmon. On March 28, 1994, U.S. District Judge Malcolm Marsh said the same thing. He carries more clout than DeHart, the states, the tribes, and the fish. Still, I believe the Army Corps will try to ignore him, too, and that BPA and its preferred clients will try to dodge his ruling.

Have you heard of "the federal family"? The notion is that federal agencies should speak with one voice on large matters of policy. The spotted owl-Northwest forest policy is an example, for on this issue President Clinton pushed federal agencies to end their bickering and speak with one voice. The federal family for Columbia Basin hydro and salmon includes four cabinet departments and six agencies. One salutary effect of Marsh's decision will be to make it harder to maintain the pretense—the fiction—that those federal agencies have a single voice and are working together to recover Columbia Basin salmon.

There are deep fault lines under the federal family surface, between and among the hydro and fish agencies. The hydro agencies—Bonneville Power Administration, Army Corps of Engineers, and Bureau of Reclamation—are not committed to or

concerned about salmon survival, whatever the law, the people, or
their public relations machines say. They have been and are in
charge of federal Columbia River salmon policy—both the phony
single voice ("we will restore salmon with a balanced approach") and
the real general thrust ("keep the hydro status quo in place"). They
have kept their dominance into the Clinton years via the support of
House Speaker Tom Foley, D-Washington, and the status quo politics
of both parties.

The fish agencies—National Marine Fisheries Service and U.S. Fish
and Wildlife Service—have been bottom dogs for decades, as the
condition of salmon testifies. Both have grown more assertive since
Snake River salmon were listed as endangered in 1992. But the
Fisheries Service's assertiveness, under "new" leadership installed at
Speaker Foley's behest, has been timid and tied closely to
hydrosystem convenience rather than the needs of salmon. Judge
Marsh has now precisely identified that hydro-first, salmon-second
bias within the Fisheries Service, and he has ruled key
underpinnings of it illegal. This gives more leverage to good people
in the agency and makes it harder for Fisheries Service leaders to
meet their patrons' desire that they rock the boat as little as possible.
It gives more leverage to those in the Interior Department—many in
the Fish and Wildlife Service, some in the Bureau of Reclamation,
and perhaps in the Bureau of Indian Affairs—who want to speak
louder on Columbia salmon but have been muted by Bruce Babbitt's
decision to avoid the issue as much as possible. Federal trust
responsibility for Columbia Basin Indian tribes, in regard to salmon,
has been as invisible under Clinton/Babbitt as under Bush/Lujan.

The judge's decision should widen some rifts among the hydro
agencies. So far the Army Corps has done next to nothing for
salmon at its eight mainstem dams while the Bureau of Reclamation
has made—by its lights—major and continuing changes at its
upstream reservoirs to provide more flows for salmon. Perhaps the
bureau will begin at least privately to ask whether the Corps'
stonewalling of any structural modifications at its dams is in the best
interest of the federal family.

Those tracking salmon action in court know that internal dispute
among BPA and other federal lawyers in Idaho's lawsuit contributed
to a poor federal performance in this case. (BPA, though not a
plaintiff in Idaho's suit, is not shy of asserting its alpha role within
the family.) As litigation continues, perhaps Janet Reno's Justice

Department will consider asserting itself with a focus on the law rather than hydro system self-interest.

My guess is the family feud will intensify, but that hydro agencies, clients, and patrons will be able to keep the lid on yet longer. The federal family will maintain the fiction and keep hydrosystem convenience largely in the saddle. BPA and the Army Corps are as dug in on hydro-salmon as the Forest Service was on timber-spotted owl; they are institutionally incapable of telling salmon truth and obeying salmon law. Judge Marsh will have to hit them more and harder before he gets their attention.

Unless ... the overarching player I haven't mentioned intervenes to force change. But I don't think the White House will at this point. Pretending there is a federal commitment to Columbia Basin salmon, while letting the hydro agencies roll on behind that pretense, is a whole lot easier than leadership in the face of Tom Foley, et al.

Where does that leave salmon advocates—both the guerrillas within the agencies and those of us without? I think we must find the shortest path to explosion, by legal and political means. Fomenting gridlock and chaos does not sound responsible, but I think it is responsible—to the fish. No one else is paying much attention to them.

A final word for observers of this issue. You will know something real is happening for the fish only by one event: an end or sharp reduction in juvenile salmon barging. Only when Judge Marsh, or the White House, or the people (I am sadly convinced it will not be the Fisheries Service) force the hydro agencies to leave salmon in the river will the major overhaul Judge Marsh says is needed be under way. Barging is the linchpin of the status quo.

*April 18, 1994*

# Northwest Is Asked to Give up Eighteen Dams

## Paul Koberstein

Interior Secretary Bruce Babbitt has said he wants to blow up a dam. Andy Kerr of the Oregon Natural Resources Council (ONRC) aims higher: he wants eighteen dams destroyed across Oregon, Idaho, and Washington—a drastic measure intended to save salmon runs now teetering on the edge of extinction. "Many people believe dams are engineering wonders that provide cheap electricity, irrigation, and drinking water and flood control," says the council's twenty-four-page study, titled *Damnable Dams* (1993). "We are taught from an early age that dams are awesome examples of people's ability to control nature. The truth is, dams are all of those things—and unfortunately, a lot more."

Experts often cite overfishing, agricultural abuses and the destruction of spawning beds by logging as reasons for the decline of the mighty salmon, a species once so bountiful in the Northwest that it was treated as a trash fish. But the same experts almost always place the primary blame on dams—the engineering marvels that have provided the Northwest with abundant, cheap, and clean energy. And since 1992, when certain runs of chinook and sockeye salmon were placed on the endangered species list, pressure to do something about the dams has escalated. No one, however, has gone so far as Kerr—to propose that eighteen dams be torn down or never built. Nor has anyone gone the next step either, as Kerr has, by suggesting a way the region could accommodate the loss of the dams' electricity.

Kerr, a thirty-eight-year-old ONRC political operative whose rounding belly and graying beard and hair make him resemble a spotted owl, says we should simply close the aluminum industry's ten giant smelters located in Oregon, Washington, and Montana. Kerr's proposal would create an energy surplus since the region's aluminum smelters consume more than twice the power produced by the dams that Kerr has put on his hit list. (The dams on his list do not include such Columbia River behemoths as the Bonneville and

The Dalles dams.) Forty-three percent of the aluminum made in this country is manufactured in the Northwest; in turn, the aluminum industry is the single largest user of electricity in the region. It consumes more than one-fifth of the region's power—but pays reduced electricity rates.

According to Tacoma economist Jim Lazar, the average household in the Northwest pays $3.75 a month to subsidize the aluminum industry's electricity rates. Eliminating the dams and smelters, Kerr says, makes environmental and economic sense. (The aluminum companies have not always enjoyed a subsidized rate for their power. The rate is pegged to the world price of aluminum; when the price goes down, the rate goes down.)

"This is a radical proposal," Kerr acknowledges. "But just because it is radical does not mean it is not reasonable. The aluminum industry is killing salmon. We ought to let the dinosaur die." Few think Kerr's proposal has a chance. But that is not because the plan is based on bad science. Most experts agree that, on scientific grounds, the proposal has great merit. The trouble with Kerr's plan is it violates the political and economic status quo of the region.

Kerr's struggle to save the salmon has striking similarities to his earlier fight to save the northern spotted owl. To Kerr, both cases involve the declining stock of a species that has been ravaged by an industry that receives enormous federal subsidies.

It's not that there haven't been efforts to save the salmon. In the past twelve years, for example, the Northwest Power Planning Council, an interstate planning agency that is supposed to oversee the Bonneville Power Administration (BPA), has supervised the spending of more than $1.3 billion in taxpayer and ratepayer money on three salmon recovery plans. By any measure, the first two failed, and few give the third—a plan that would barge fish around dams and marginally increase river velocities—much of a chance. This third plan, enacted in December 1991, has yet to be fully implemented. A federal team is preparing a fourth plan, and it too will emphasize barging.

Idaho Governor Cecil Andrus doesn't think it will work. "It's bull! Look at the numbers. They've been barging fish for seventeen years, and the salmon are nearly extinct." Instead, Andrus wants to drawdown the reservoirs during salmon migration season. That would turn the reservoirs temporarily into quasi-rivers, carrying the fish more swiftly downstream. But the cost of rebuilding the dams

would be immense—$1 billion to $5 billion—and the Army Corps of
Engineers says drawdowns still might not help the salmon.

Kerr and the ONRC believe that Andrus is on the right track, but
hasn't gone far enough. Kerr says a number of dams need to be fully
drained, turning their reservoirs back into rivers. The latest computer
models at the Northwest Power Planning Council and the BPA
suggest he may be right. The computers say allowing the Snake River
to flow naturally is the most reliable and least risky way to revive its
threatened salmon runs. But last October the team that is preparing
the fourth recovery plan rejected the natural river option without
serious analysis. "There is no way to return to the natural river
without major cultural changes in the region," the team's report
says.

Kerr claims that the only act necessary to return the river to a
partially natural state would be to end subsidies to the aluminum
industry—and watch it go belly up. "We can still produce a hell of a
lot of power and still save the fish," he says.

Ever since the beginning of World War II and the birth of the
nation's airplane and shipbuilding industry, the aluminum industry
has been a force to be reckoned with in the Northwest. Though now
less a factor than in its prime, the Northwest aluminum industry
today employs about eight thousand workers at middle-class wages
and generates about $2.5 billion a year in revenues. It is owned by
such household names as Reynolds and Alcoa, companies whose
campaign contributions help U.S. senators such as Mark Hatfield of
Oregon, Slade Gorton of Washington, and Larry Craig of Idaho.
Aluminum's biggest booster may be House Speaker Tom Foley of
Spokane, Washington, who has several smelters in his district.

The industry's clout has gained it subsidized power prices. Over
the next two years, for example, BPA expects to sell more than $1.4
billion worth of juice to the smelters but get paid barely $1 billion
for it. As a result of this and other factors, BPA itself is in a financial
straitjacket. Over the last two years, the power agency lost $750
million, and its annual revenue shortfalls could reach $800 million
within a few years.

BPA is now promising welfare reform for the aluminum industry.
Current contracts with the smelters run through 2001, but the
agency may not be able to carry the industry that long. BPA
spokeswoman Dulcy Mahar says the agency is reviewing all its rates.

The cheap rates paid by the aluminum companies, she says, "are on the table" and could increase in late 1995.

Despite the current rate discount, the industry is struggling. Rising aluminum exports from the former Soviet bloc are flooding the world market, forcing prices into a tailspin. In 1988, the price of aluminum shot above $1.10 a pound. At that time, the Soviet Union exported 200,000 metric tons of aluminum annually. Today the price hovers around 50 cents a pound, while exports from the former Soviet Union exceed 1.6 million tons.

"Anyone you ask in the industry will tell you the next year or two will be key to our survival," says Jim Dwyer, a spokesman for the Intalco smelter near Bellingham, Washington, the Northwest's single largest user of electricity. For one plant near Portland, however, economics have already spelled the end of business. Since 1991, the Troutdale Reynolds Metals Co.—which at its peak in 1980 employed almost a thousand workers—has been closed.

Other smelters are moving quickly to cut their losses. In January, Reynolds (owner of the Longview smelter) cut production nationwide by 10 percent, laying off 800 workers. It declared losses of about $200 million for the fourth quarter of 1993. Alcoa (which has a plant in Wenatchee) took a $70 million loss last quarter and laid off 1,600. Recycling has also compounded the industry's troubles. Every year, the United States recycles sixty billion aluminum cans, or about 70 percent of the total.

Confronted with a subsidized, electricity-guzzling industry that contributes to the destruction of an entire species, Kerr says the solution is clear: pull the dams, remove the subsidies, and watch the aluminum industry collapse under its own weight. To his supporters, Kerr is an environmental Dr. Kevorkian, helping to put an ailing industry out of its misery and conserve a valuable resource.

"Where are you going to replace the aluminum smelters and the high-paying jobs?" Intalco's Dwyer asks. "Another factory discount mall?"

Others, including economist Lazar, doubt the idea will ever win public support. "Don't waste my time talking about removing dams," Lazar says. "You're not going to tear down those dams. Because the public doesn't value the fish that much. That's why not."

The idea could spark a congressional backlash against the Endangered Species Act. House Speaker Foley said in 1993 the high cost of saving salmon is a good reason to weaken the act when it comes up for reauthorization this year or next. "I think the act needs to have some element of review so that other values in addition to protection of species can be considered," Foley says. Even Representative Peter DeFazio, the Eugene Democrat who headed a task force that recently examined the salmon issue, would be skeptical, an aide says. "Our operating assumption at this point is that neither the region nor the federal government or anyone else is going to choose to remove dams from the Columbia system."

But some environmentalists agree with Kerr, including Bill Bakke, conservation director of Oregon Trout. "These dams were built without regard for fish," he says. "If you are going to restore the ecosystem, it may well be the logical conclusion is to remove some of these dams. But I would caution Kerr not to quit there. If we don't control other causes of mortality we aren't going to get anything of value back."

Kerr is undeterred and points out that the obstacles he faces are similar to the ones he faced in the timber industry—a changing economy, a threatened species and an unwillingness of people to come to grips with reality. "My job is to speak for the fish, because they can't speak for themselves," Kerr says. "The question is: What is necessary to save the fish, and do we want to pay the price? If society doesn't want to do that, they can make that choice. But I'm not going to sugar-coat it."

*October 31, 1994*

# Changing Times Force Agency to Swim Upstream

### Paul Larmer

Three lobbyists in suits strode down the marbled halls of the Senate office building one day in fall, 1993. Their mission: to convince the Northwest's congressional delegation to fight a bill requested by the Bonneville Power Administration. The bill would exempt three runs of imperiled Snake River salmon from federal protection.

The men turned into a senator's office and extended their hands to the staffers: "Hello, Tim Stearns, Save Our Salmon Coalition; Hi, Gary Barber, representing Portland General Electric; Hello, Steve Weiss, Salem Electric Co-operative."

"We would walk in and their jaws would just drop," recalls Weiss with a chuckle. It is indeed an alliance to make jaws drop. It may also be good news for salmon. For years, salmon advocates have waged a lonely battle against the federal dams BPA controls on the Snake and Columbia rivers, and the economic and political clout it wields as a result of the cheap power the dams generate. The entire region has prospered on the agency's cheap electricity. But the salmon have been driven to the point of extinction.

So why would traditional BPA allies—utilities—join the environmentalists? The short answer is that BPA is struggling for its life, and to survive it is trying to cut programs that benefit both salmon and utilities.

The BPA's woes began back in the 1970s, when it began to build nuclear power plants. Escalating costs and a drop in power demand led BPA to abort the project, leaving it with a $7 billion debt and rate increases during the 1980s that mounted to 400 percent. Then, in the early 1990s, the bill for the dams' destruction of salmon started coming due, and was handed to BPA. The obligation grew each year, topping $400 million in 1994.

Accumulated debt and imperiled fish weakened BPA. But it took price competition to send it into a financial panic. Cheap natural gas and new technology have allowed gas-fired plants to produce energy as cheaply as the big federal dams. And thanks to the 1992 Energy Policy Act, BPA and all other utilities must let anyone use their transmission lines to sell power to companies within their territory. Suddenly, independent power producers, investor-owned utilities, and deal makers are competing for BPA's customers, just as Sprint and MCI compete for AT&T customers.

In response, BPA last year started to downsize, letting middle managers go and slimming programs. Then early this year it asked Congress to cap its fish-saving costs and grant it immunity from costly environmental lawsuits. BPA also cut payments to public utilities for energy conservation and suggested axing a program aimed at investor-owned utilities that reduced residential bills an average of $8.33 a month per household. Investor-owned utilities said the loss would force them to raise their rates 14 to 30 percent.

BPA's once-tranquil kingdom was suddenly in disarray. "BPA used to make so much money that it made political peace in the region," says Weiss, who also serves as a policy analyst for the Northwest Conservation Act Coalition, a consortium of seventy utilities and environmental groups. Now, the once-flush agency had to choose between a long list of competing interests.

Nothing better illustrates BPA's struggle than the agency's battle this fall to hang on to a group of aluminum company customers known as the Direct Services Industries. BPA knew that other power producers and marketers were courting the aluminum smelters, so in early spring it offered them five-year contracts with a 12.7 percent rate cut. But the DSIs didn't bite. In fact, three of the sixteen signed contracts with competitors.

A stunned BPA regrouped. At the top of its proposals was a provision that would free the Direct Service Industries from any responsibility for the nuclear debt should they leave BPA in the future. In late September, the agency held a public hearing in Seattle to explore the possibility. Lori Bodi, who was there as co-director of American Rivers' Northwest office, said the aluminum companies played hardball. "They said, 'If you don't give us reduced rates and grant us immunity from your debt, we won't sign and we will leave you with a huge financial problem,' " Bodi recalls.

Shortly after, BPA offered the DSIs five-year contracts with both reduced rates and debt-exemption. In response, environmentalists and investor-owned utilities whipped out almost identical press releases. "BPA wants to let its biggest customers off the hook while leaving farmers, small utilities, residents, and fish holding the bag," said Charles Ray of Idaho Rivers United. "It appears that BPA is attempting to shift its (nuclear) debt costs to residential customers," said Gary Swofford, a vice president of Puget Sound Power & Light, an investor-owned utility serving the area outside Seattle. "That is unfair and unjustified."

The alliance caught BPA by surprise. "That was a first," admits BPA spokesman Perry Gruber. It also surprised Northwestern lawmakers, including Oregon Republican Senator Mark Hatfield. As chairman of the Senate Appropriations Committee, he was trying to pass a bill capping spending on salmon. The new coalition urged Hatfield and the Clinton administration to make BPA obey environmental laws protecting the salmon and to reject the five-year contracts with the aluminum manufacturers. The administration listened.

In late September, 1993 the Department of Energy officials summoned BPA administrator Randy Hardy to Washington, D.C., and scolded him for offering the aluminum companies debt immunity, says Pat Ford, a Save Our Salmon coalition activist. A press release drafted by the DOE and BPA announced September 30 that BPA was withdrawing the contracts.

The next day, Republican senators Mark Hatfield, Slade Gorton of Washington, Larry Craig of Idaho, and Conrad Burns of Montana called a meeting with DOE Secretary Hazel O'Leary. "They read her the riot act," says Ford. And BPA's friends had clout: Hatfield chairs the Senate Appropriations Committee and controls DOE's purse strings. That night the Energy Department and BPA announced the latest deal the senators had won. BPA would sign contracts with companies that would use BPA power for at least 80 percent of their energy needs. The nuclear debt immunity clause would remain. To date, nine of the DSIs have signed the contracts, which begin in October 1996; Gruber says the agency hopes to nab the remaining four soon.

Though the coalition of environmentalists and utilities struck out on the industrial contracts, they got a few hits elsewhere. Hatfield and the administration agreed in October to limit BPA's annual costs for fish to $435 million, about what the agency spent in 1994. But the agency's request for an exemption from environmental laws was removed under a veto threat, and the administration agreed to kick in another $325 million if more money is needed to restore the salmon. The deal also provides $145 million in 1996 so that customers of private utilities continue to see low rates.

All this leaves BPA on solid financial ground for the next five years. But its political base has been fractured, and its future is uncertain. Energy experts say that if natural gas prices remain low, all hell could break loose in the year 2001. The industrial contracts come up then, as well as BPA's contracts with dozens of public utilities and co-operatives. Many could decide to leave BPA.

But there are other scenarios. David Marcus, an energy consultant in the San Francisco Bay area, says if oil prices go up again, so will gas prices, forcing BPA's competitors to raise their rates. Industries that have left could come running back to BPA's cheap, reliable hydropower. Zach Willey, an economist with the Environmental Defense Fund, says the legislation capping BPA's fish costs frees BPA to sell power outside of the Northwest. If more utilities and industries leave BPA in the future, "I say good riddance," says Willey, since BPA can then sell that power for more money to California, the Southwest, and the Intermountain West. The salmon will benefit, Willey says, because Northwest utilities now need most of their energy in the winter to produce heat. That sends water downstream in the winter, when salmon aren't migrating. But utilities farther south need the juice for air conditioning, Willey points out, and summer flows would help the fish migration.

Because BPA has wide-ranging impacts on residents, industries, and salmon, the governors of Oregon, Washington, Idaho, and Montana have called for a regional forum next year. The goal is federal legislation that would restructure BPA to meet the challenges of a competitive marketplace while preserving the public purposes for which it was created. That will be not be easy.

*December 25, 1995*

# An Idaho Daily Breaches the Northwest's Silence over Tearing Down Dams

## Susan Whaley

The *Idaho Statesman* likes to think its editorials are felt far beyond the modestly populated Boise metropolitan area in southwestern Idaho where the paper is headquartered. We were never sure just how far, however, until late-1997. That's when the six members of the editorial board, which includes the publisher, top editors, and a community representative, called for tearing down four earthen dams downstream from Boise on the Lower Snake River in eastern Washington. In a three-day series of editorials called "Dollars, Sense & Salmon," the board concluded that allowing the river to function more like a river again would recover endangered salmon and steelhead, the majority of which now die during migration trying to get past the dams or through the slack-water reservoirs above them. A revived fishery would contribute significantly to the economy of Idaho and the Northwest.

The response was swift. Some thought we were lunatics; after all, an entire economy has developed in the twenty-two years since the dams were completed, including a port at Lewiston, Idaho, some 400 miles from the Pacific Ocean. Others called us geniuses. The truth, I'm pretty sure, lies somewhere in between.

In a nutshell, here's what we said:

• Breach the four Lower Snake dams—Ice Harbor, Lower Monumental, Little Goose and Lower Granite—which currently create continuous slack water for about 140 miles from Lewiston, Idaho, to where the Snake joins the Columbia River near Pasco, Washington. Breaching would involve removing the earthen portions of the dams. The navigation locks and power turbines would remain in place but be unusable for now.

• Put a regional governance board—composed of state, tribal, and federal representatives—in charge of river operations.

• Cut spending for salmon recovery efforts—$317 million in 1995—to offset the costs of breaching (estimated by the U.S. Army Corps of Engineers at $500 million) and lost power revenue from the non-functioning dams (which provide only 7 percent of the region's power-producing capacity). Full recovery of a wild fish population also would allow the closure of at least nine hatcheries, at a savings of $12.7 million a year.

• Invest some of the savings in economic development for the Lewiston-Clarkston area, which will be most hard hit by the loss of the reservoirs.

• Stop the harvest of wild salmon and steelhead in the Columbia River for five years—one salmon life cycle—to allow fish populations to build quickly. Continue water quality and spawning habitat improvements.

Within a week, the Portland *Oregonian*, the *Tri-City Herald* in Pasco, Washington, and the Lewiston *Morning Tribune* in north Idaho all editorialized—predictably—on the other side. "Bad science. Bad economics. Bad timing. Bad politics. Bad neighbors. Bad stewardship. Bad biology," thundered the *Tri-City Herald*.

Some sympathized with our conclusion but said that political realities make breaching impractical. Since when is political reality the issue? The people of this nation overcame the deeply entrenched political realities of segregation more than thirty years ago to usher in a new era of civil rights because it was right. Surely we Americans can summon the will to do the right thing with four dams in eastern Washington.

Other downriver critics suggested that if we were so gung-ho for breaching, we should also support taking out Lucky Peak Dam, located 10 miles up the Boise River from the capital city. Then see how you like breaching, they cried.

Our response is simple: Fine, let's take a look. Every dam should be able to withstand close scrutiny. The benefits should outweigh the costs. The environmental trade-offs should be well understood and widely accepted. The editorial board argued, for instance, that the four large hydroelectric dams on the Columbia River— Bonneville, The Dalles, John Day and McNary—are too important to the Northwest's growth and prosperity to lose, despite their problems for fish.

Still, critics charged that the *Statesman* has created a slippery slope that will lead to the removal of every last dam in the West. Wrong.

We did a cold-eyed study of just four dams whose costs outweigh their benefits and whose removal offers a good chance to restore fish and jobs.

Breaching is good for Idaho and the region because:

• It will work, with science offering a high probability that economically useful numbers of fish could be restored in no more than twenty years.

• It will put money that now goes toward failed fish recovery and subsidies back into the pockets of taxpayers and electricity ratepayers.

• It will ultimately create a $248 million fishing-related economy, much of it in ailing rural communities hit hard by losses in timber and mining.

• It will lead to the removal of the fish from the Endangered Species Act list, which lightens the heavy hand of the federal government on loggers, miners, outfitters, and ranchers.

• It will allow Idaho to keep more of its water for agricultural and other useful benefits instead of sending it downstream to flush fish through reservoirs; and

• It will restore balance to our environment and culture.

We believe we have put the dam issue where it belongs—squarely on the table of public debate. The editorials will have done their job if they move readers—everyday citizens—to pressure their political leaders for smart, bold action that is right for Idaho, the Northwest, and the nation.

*September 1, 1997*

# Unleashing the Snake

## Paul Larmer

A stiff wind blows from the west on a blustery fall day in 1999, but it doesn't bother John McKern. Wearing a hard hat with his name in black letters across the front, the clean-cut, burly fifty-four-year-old looks like a sea captain as he leans against a railing and gazes down at the dark blue waters below. But McKern is nowhere near the ocean. Rolling hills of blond and chocolate wheat fields surround this "ship," which is in fact an immobile concretion known as the Lower Granite Dam. It is the uppermost of four federal dams that block the Snake River in eastern Washington on its way toward the mighty Columbia River. Built in the 1960s and '70s, the dams produce some of the Pacific Northwest's vaunted cheap electricity and create deep waters for barges to carry grain and lumber from this interior outpost to the world beyond.

McKern is a fish biologist with the U.S. Army Corps of Engineers, and, in a way, he is the captain of the Snake River dams. For in this brave new post-dam-building age, biologists have an increasing say in how federal dams are run. They have taken over because the famous salmon and steelhead runs that have used this stretch of river for tens of thousands of years on their way to and from the ocean continue to spiral toward extinction, and the dams have proven to be one engine of their destruction. The Snake River run of coho salmon has already vanished, probably in the mid-1980s. In this decade, Northwestern tribes and conservationists convinced the federal government to give the four remaining stocks of Snake River salmon protection under the Endangered Species Act. The listings have pushed the federal agencies in charge of the river to make all sorts of adjustments to the four dams to help fish survive, and McKern, a thirty-year veteran of the Corps, has been in on all of them.

Today, he and Nola Conway, a public-relations specialist with the Corps' Walla Walla District, descend into the bowels of Lower Granite to show off one of twelve enormous, 60-ton fish screens.

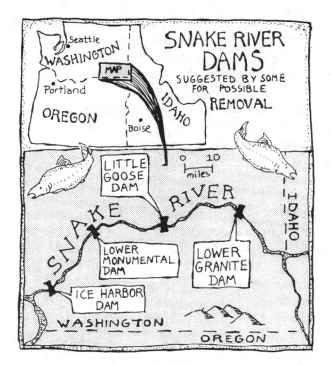

The screens deflect more than half of the juvenile salmon, or smolts, away from the dam's turbines and into a narrow pool of water, where they are sucked into a pipe and carried hundreds of yards below the dam. Most of these collected fish are piped onto a fleet of barges and trucks, then floated or driven past eight federal dams to the waters beyond the Bonneville Dam, on the Columbia River, 50 miles west of Portland.

The Corps started transporting fish in 1968. This year it spent $3.5 million to barge and truck 19.3 million fish, and McKern says 98 percent of those fish survived, a rate that "might be as high as when the river flowed naturally." Fish barging may have saved some of the Snake River runs from extinction already, McKern claims, especially during the drought years of the 1970s, when flows were very low and temperatures in the reservoirs were high enough to kill fish. If he had his way, the Corps would be allowed to barge every fish it could catch. But these days McKern and his barges sail against a strengthening headwind, even within his own agency. He and the communities and industries that rely on the federal waterway are being forced to envision the day when the dams will stand functionless, like mothballed battleships in a harbor. Many scientists and conservationists believe the dams still kill inordinate numbers of young salmon, because the number of returning adults continues to drop. All the technological tinkering in the world won't bring the runs back, they contend, and only one bold approach will: bulldozing the earthen portion of the four dams so that this 140-mile stretch of the Snake can once again flow as a natural river.

Conservationists call the concept "partial breaching," because the dams will still stand. But the term makes McKern bristle. "Partial breaching is sort of like being a little bit pregnant," he says. 'The fish-passage system and the turbines will be left high and dry," and the river will flow around the dams.

Five years ago, breaching was considered so radical few environmentalists would touch it. Today, it is center stage in a natural-resource debate more fierce and complex than that over the spotted owl.

A deadline drives the issue. This spring, the Clinton administration must decide which measures are needed to restore the runs under the Endangered Species Act. The federal agencies that run the hydrosystem—the Army Corps, the Bonneville Power Administration, which markets power from federal dams, and the National Marine Fisheries Service—are racing to finish a couple of massive studies on the various options to recover the fish and assess their potential economic impact on the region. With each passing day, the tension builds in places like Lewiston, Idaho, an inland "seaport" 30 miles above the Lower Granite Dam and 465 miles from the Pacific Ocean. Industries that rely on the dams run ads in the local paper, touting the wonders of barging and the plight of wheat farmers who will suffer without cheap barge transportation. Conservationists, Native American tribes, and fisheries organizations counter with full-page ads in *The New York Times* condemning the dams as fish killers and calling on presidential candidate Al Gore to take a stand. Both sides bury reporters in a blizzard of scientific and economic papers. As crunch time approaches, the Clinton administration and the federal agencies are looking for a way to delay the dam-breaching decision, at least until after the 2000 presidential election. No one can predict what kind of bounces election-year politics will bring, but, thus far, the tribes and environmentalists have not succeeded in making salmon a national issue, the way "ancient forests" became national in the late 1980s and early 1990s.

However, the lack of a national constituency doesn't mean the dams won't be breached. While some in the Pacific Northwest fiercely oppose breaching, and have much to lose if it happens, others in the region have much to lose if the dams continue to stand. Electricity users, Alaskan fishers, loggers, and ranchers will pay a heavy price if the burden of recovery falls on them instead of on those who benefit from the dams. Ultimately, Congress must authorize the removal of federal dams, and that won't happen unless there is a consensus within the region, or a national push that breaches local opposition. Neither exists now.

But, unlike the spotted owl, the salmon is loved by almost everyone in the Pacific Northwest, and no one has said they want to see it become extinct. If the Snake River runs don't show any signs of recovering—and soon—the region's leaders may accept breaching as the only option. That's a possibility even the dam-building Army Corps now recognizes, says Nola Conway. "It's not a matter of if we breach, but when we breach," she says, standing next to McKern. "These dams won't be here forever, and I can foresee a time when there isn't such polarization and we can agree on how to do it."

The road toward breaching has been long and painful. Scientists estimate that sixteen million ocean-fatted salmon once entered the mouth of the Columbia River yearly, heading toward spawning grounds scattered across four states and a sliver of Canada. But soon after the first salmon cannery was built in 1866, the numbers began to plummet. Early fish advocates sounded the alarm. "Nothing can stop the growth and development of the country, which are fatal to salmon," wrote Livingston Stone, a member of the U.S. Fish Commission, in 1892. "Provide some refuge for the salmon, and provide it quickly, before complications arise which may make it impracticable, or at least very difficult. Now is the time. Delays are dangerous." The warning was accurate. Fisheries collapsed, and hatcheries pumping out millions of salmon each year didn't help, and may have even hurt the wild runs. Scientsts now recognize that hatchery fish dilute the genetic purity of the wild fish and compete with them for limited food resources.

The drive to develop the Columbia River basin intensified with the industrial age. Historian William G. Robbins notes that mechanized farming and logging, large-scale industrial mining, and numerous small dams may have destroyed as much as half of the basin's fish habitat before the 1930s. At the heart of the development drive lay the vision of a tamed Columbia River, irrigating arid basins, lighting cities, running factories, and transporting goods. With the onset of the Great Depression, regional boosters capitalized on Franklin Roosevelt's massive public-works program to kick off a federal dam-building era. The first dam, Bonneville, was completed in 1938, followed in 1941 by Grand Coulee, which alone blocked off 1,100 miles of fish-spawning habitat. The building of the dams consolidated the Army Corps' position as the dominant waterway agency in the region, and created a new federal entity, the Bonneville Power Administration, which sold the electricity produced by the dams. Together, the two agencies would dominate the Northwest.

Fish advocates stood little chance against dam-building, so they focused on trying to make the dams fish-friendly. They forced the Corps to build a fish ladder at Bonneville, which got adults past the dam. But the bigger problem, and one that historian Keith Petersen says Corps officials knew about from the start, was how to get smolts heading downriver safely past the dams. Not only did the pressure generated by the dam's whirling turbines kill the smolts, but fish that were fortunate enough to get sent over the dam's spillway away from the turbines suffered from a form of the bends caused by the supersaturated gas created by the plunging waters. And without a current to push them through the reservoirs, the usually swift fourteen-day journey was extended by weeks, making smolts more vulnerable to predators such as pikeminnows, which thrive in slack water.

The U.S. Army Corps of Engineers maintained that its dams were benign. One Corps official told Congress in 1941 that Bonneville Dam's turbines were "absolutely incapable of hurting the fish. If you could put a mule through there and keep him from drowning, he would go through without being hurt."

Congress authorized the four lower Snake River dams in 1945, but for a decade Oregon's and Washington's increasingly vocal fisheries agencies helped delay the construction of the first Snake River dam, Ice Harbor. But, as Keith Petersen notes in his 1995 book, *River of Life, Channel of Death*, fish advocates could not outflank the Cold War: a call for more power at the Hanford nuclear complex in central Washington eventually convinced Congress to fund the dams.

For the Inland Empire Waterways Association, a coalition of
farmers and entrepreneurs in eastern Washington, the new dams
were a ticket to prosperity. The chain of reservoirs created by the
dams—Ice Harbor, Lower Monumental, Little Goose, and Lower
Granite, in ascending order—turned the Snake into a river of
commerce for farmers; entrepreneurs hoped that new industries
would soon gather on its banks to take advantage of cheap electricity
and cheap transportation.

But fish advocates did not give up. In 1970, the Northwest
Steelheaders Council and seven other conservation groups sued the
Corps to stop the fourth dam, Lower Granite, and a fifth dam
planned farther upstream. Larry Smith, a Spokane-based lawyer who
represented the Steelheaders, says, "We never expected to win, but
we hoped to raise awareness about the impact of dams. In some ways
we succeeded, because that was it for dams—the fifth dam was never
built." Smith, an avid fisherman and bird hunter who used to haunt
the rich bottomlands of the Snake before the dams flooded them,
says he is happy to see fish advocates once again aiming their sights
on the dams.

"I'm all for breaching," he says. "Those dams should never have
been built in the first place."

That's a sentiment also held by Michelle DeHart, who heads the
Fish Passage Center in Portland, which monitors the number of
returning Columbia River salmon. "How do we admit that we went
too far in developing this system?" DeHart asks. "How do we admit
that we need to undo something we've done?"

Steve Pettit remembers well the day in 1975 when the waters
behind Lower Granite Dam backed up into Lewiston. "I cried my
eyes out," says the bearded, curly-haired fish biologist for the Idaho
Department of Fish and Game. "I was in a jet boat and we went
down the river below Lewiston to where the slack waters were
surging and we just rode them back toward Lewiston. I was thinking
of how the beautiful stretches of water where I had caught steelhead
after steelhead on a fly the year before were now a hundred feet
underwater."

Pettit didn't know it at the time, but his professional life was
destined to become intertwined with Snake River salmon. He
became the state's fish passage specialist in 1981, when there was
great optimism for the Snake River salmon. Congress had just passed

the Northwest Power Act, granting the native fish equal footing with power production at the federal dams. To strike a balance, the law created the Northwest Power Planning Council, composed of two governor-appointed members each from the states of Washington, Oregon, Idaho, and Montana. One of the first things the planning council did was endorse the Army Corps of Engineers' growing fish-barging program led by John McKern. Biologist Pettit was an early convert. "The federal agencies predicted that with barging, Snake River runs would double in ten years," says Pettit. "I believed them."

A decade later, when the first of the Snake River stocks were listed under the Endangered Species Act in 1991, the bottom had fallen out. The number of sockeye salmon making it back to Lower Granite Dam dove from a high of 531 fish in 1976 to zero in 1990. (The number has hovered in single digits ever since, despite a captive breeding program, leading scientists to call the sockeye "functionally extinct.") Wild fall chinook had tumbled from 428 adults at Lower Granite in 1983 to just 78 in 1990. Wild spring/summer chinook had dipped from a high of 21,870 fish at Lower Granite in 1988 to 8,457 in 1991.

Nonetheless, barging remained the central fish-recovery tool, along with providing more water from upstream dams in Idaho to "flush" the smolts more quickly through the filled reservoirs. Flushing stung Idaho hard. Not only had the dams been the coup de grâce for its salmon runs—by 1978 the number of returning adults was so low that officials closed the general fishing seasons—but the federal agencies kept demanding more of the state's water for their unproven flush technique.

When the National Marine Fisheries Service determined in its annual Biological Opinion that the Corps' 1992 plan for operating the dams would not jeopardize the listed stocks, Idaho took the agency to court. In 1994, federal judge Malcolm Marsh ruled that the federal agencies were taking little steps "when the situation literally cries out for a major overhaul." He ordered federal biologists to work on a new plan with state and tribal biologists. The judge's decision created an opening for an idea that had been first floated publicly in 1990 by then-Idaho Governor Cecil Andrus. It was called drawdown—the rapid lowering of reservoirs to recreate riverlike conditions. Fish advocates rallied to the new cause, and in the late winter of 1992, the Army Corps of Engineers conducted a month-long test drawdown of Lower Granite Dam.

"We were left with a stinky hole filled with twenty years' worth of mud and muck and trash," recalls David Doeringsfeld, the director of the Port of Lewiston. But the idea wouldn't die. In 1995, the NMFS (pronounced "nymphs") directed the Army Corps to further study drawdown and make a recommendation by the end of 1999. The Corps' initial studies showed that lowering the reservoirs for part of the year would destroy the barging industry, seriously reduce power production, and require $5 billion to redo the dams, McKern says. The cost of breaching all four dams, on the other hand, was around $900 million. Suddenly, breaching didn't seem like such a wild idea. Breaching gained more credibility in 1996, when a group of independent scientists commissioned by the Northwest Power Planning Council released its *Return to the River* report. The report advocated restoring more "normative" ecosystem conditions to rivers as the best way to help salmon and steelhead.

Meanwhile, a multi-agency team of scientists convened by NMFS released studies showing that breaching was the surest and quickest way to restore Snake River salmon. The PATH team (named for the model it adopted, Process for Analyzing and Testing Hypotheses) found that breaching has an 80 percent probability of recovering spring/summer chinook, and a 100 percent probability of recovering fall chinook, within twenty-four years. The PATH team's conclusions rested on comparisons with other Columbia River salmon stocks that must negotiate the four lower Columbia River dams, but do not face the four lower Snake River dams. This includes the vigorous run of chinook in the Hanford Reach section of the Columbia. "Our fish in Idaho are performing three to ten times worse than lower stocks, even though they face the same environment below the Snake River, including the lower dams, the estuary, and the ocean," says Charlie Petrosky, an Idaho fish biologist on the PATH team. "What is it that is selectively killing the Snake River runs? It's got to be the dams."

In July of 1997, the scientific case for breaching spilled onto the pages of the *Idaho Statesman* in Boise, the largest paper in the state and part of the Gannett chain. In a brash, three-day series of editorials, the *Statesman* became the first in the region to advocate breaching. Not only would breaching recover fish, the editorial staff said, but it would benefit the region's economy.

It would be hard to convince Roger and Mary Dye that breaching will help the economy. The Dyes, third-generation wheat and grass-seed farmers, live on the rich uplands south of the Lower Granite

Dam, and, like most of the dryland wheat farmers within 50 miles of the lower Snake River, transport their wheat to market via river barge. Most of it ends up at the factories of noodle makers in the Far East, especially Japan, India, and Pakistan. These days, the price of wheat is at a twenty-year low, and Mary Dye says dam removal would force her family to truck its wheat to the Port of Pasco on the Columbia River. "I called a local trucker and he said our costs would go up 35 cents a bushel," she says. For the Dyes, that translates into an extra $20,000 a year.

Roger Dye says the breaching debate has caught most farmers by surprise. "Farmers around here used to laugh at dam breaching—'Ha! ha! what a stupid idea. It will never happen,'" says Dye. "But we're not laughing now." Dye says he has no doubts that environmentalists will go after other dams if they succeed in breaching the four on the lower Snake. Why did they start with this 140-mile stretch of river? "Because there are only 1,500 people in Pomeroy and 2,000 in Dayton," Dye speculates. "This is the easiest place for environmentalists to target."

The wheat farmers are part of a larger economic community that relies on the Snake River waterway. Five ports handle roughly 3.8 million tons of grain bound for deep-water ports on the lower Columbia River. Farther downriver, another group of farmers pipe water from the Ice Harbor reservoir to irrigate some 37,000 acres of land reclaimed from the high desert steppe country in the 1960s. And the Potlatch Corporation's pulp and paper mill in Lewiston, with more than two thousand employees, also sends one-third of its chips, paper products, and lumber downriver via barge.

David Doeringsfeld, who oversees 250 employees at the Port of Lewiston, says a University of Idaho study commissioned by three of the ports showed that breaching would cost the Lewiston-Clarkston area between 1,580 and 4,800 jobs. "Breaching would send this community back three decades," says Doeringsfeld.

In its mammoth draft Lower Snake River Juvenile Salmon Migration Feasibility Study, due out by Christmas, the Army Corps is expected to show that the economy in the vicinity of the dams and the reservoirs, as well as the port town of Lewiston, would be hit hard. But fishing and tourism industries upstream and downstream would prosper with a revitalized fishery. Overall, the region would lose 492 jobs over twenty years, according to Corps projections.

The loss of power production from the dams—about 4 percent of the region's supply—would cost the region $251 million to $291 million annually, according to the Corps. That could mean residential electricity bills climbing anywhere from $1.50 to $5.30 a month. The large aluminum companies that sit on the Columbia River could see their monthly electric bills rising anywhere from $222,000 to $758,000 a month.

Conservationists say the Corps' analysis needs to be compared to the $3 billion the region has already spent over the last decade to restore salmon and the billions more it will likely spend if the fish are not recovered. Also missing from the current debate, they say, is a discussion of how federal and state monies could ease the economic pain.

One conservation group, American Rivers, has hired economists to figure out how investments in transportation alternatives to barging—namely railroads and trucks—and water pumps at Ice Harbor could "keep farmers whole." One of the studies estimated that transportation rates for farmers would not go up if the federal and state governments invested $272 million in rebuilding railroad tracks and upgrading roads. "We've postulated the question: If you could have all the benefits that you receive now from the dams without the dams, is there any reason we can't proceed with fish recovery?" says Justin Hayes of American Rivers, who grew up in rural Idaho. "We'd love to sit down at the table and figure all of this out."

"I don't think American Rivers knows anything about farming or the transportation of grain," says Doeringsfeld.

Frank Carroll, a former Forest Service employee who now works for Potlatch Corp. in Lewiston, says most of the mitigation ideas "are coming from a group of people that have never produced anything." But he says he has met informally with Hayes, and gives American Rivers muted praise for acknowledging that "it's not OK to hurt people to save fish." "If that message spreads," says Carroll, "then we might be able to have a different kind of discussion."

Most economic players, however, aren't giving an inch, even those who are potentially big winners of a free-flowing lower Snake. The ports of Kennewick, Pasco, and Benton on the Columbia River could see a substantial increase in business if farmers can no longer use the ports on the Snake. Yet in an essay in the Seattle *Post-*

*Intelligencer*, the directors of the three ports slammed the American Rivers plan as unaffordable and based on one unproven assumption: that dam removal will actually save fish. "Recent analyses by the National Marine Fisheries Service have indicated little value to fish recovery associated with dam removal," the directors wrote. "To date, the case has not been made."

Two years ago, the scientific case for breaching laid down by the PATH team appeared to be unshakable, but sometime in 1998, with the 1999 decision date for breaching drawing near, the federal agencies "went into their own little world again and started throwing some curve balls," says fish biologist Charlie Petrosky. The first break appeared last April, when NMFS released an appendix to the Corps' EIS which cited data—the same touted by John McKern—showing that barged fish are surviving the ride down the Snake and Columbia much better than ever. If that's true, the report said, then something else must be killing a lot of the fish. Fix these other problems and breaching might not be necessary.

NMFS recommended another five to ten years of study to help it figure out whether the barged fish were really surviving, or whether many were dying quickly after being released, as the PATH science predicted. "We'll continue to triage these species for a period of time while we continue to answer the unanswered questions," Rick Illgenfritz, NMFS' director of external affairs, told the Associated Press.

"What's another ten years of study going to do for the salmon?" asks Steve Pettit. "I'm convinced the federal government didn't think breaching would gain as much momentum as it has. All of a sudden it's staring them in the face, so they come up with new science to say we need more time to study the situation." The step back from dam-breaching pleased Northwest politicians, not one of whom has come out for breaching. In July, Oregon Senator Gordon Smith, R, pronounced the dam-removal discussion "essentially over."

The Clinton administration denied that it had made up its mind, but in November it released the first draft of a long-awaited report that once again raised the possibility that breaching was unnecessary. The so-called 4H paper, a precursor to the Biological Opinion expected in April, examines the four main causes of salmon mortality: hatcheries, harvest, habitat and hydropower. It lays out several scenarios for fish recovery, including one that calls for improvements in habitat without breaching. "We've already improved the hydrosystem and reduced the harvest about as much as we can," says Lori Bodi, a BPA policy expert who sits on the team of federal agencies that produced the 4H paper. "We would ask: Where are the comparable improvements in habitat?"

Fish advocates agree that habitat degradation is a huge problem for salmon, but they say the 4H paper is slim on science and details. "Nowhere does NMFS say what projects it would do to improve habitat," says Justin Hayes of American Rivers. "Will we stop timber and grazing in the Snake River Basin, or stop irrigation to control water pollution? If improving the Columbia River estuary is important, how will that be achieved? Will the Port of Portland have to stop dredging?" Conservationists and tribal leaders note with irony that NMFS is being asked to give its approval to a Corps plan to dredge the channel of the lower Columbia River, even as it builds its case for improving habitat in the same stretch of river.

NMFS director Will Stelle says his agency would only recommend against breaching this April if it thought other steps the region takes would be sufficient to save the salmon. "Are the governments of the region willing to make commitments necessary to recover these stocks without removing the dams? That's an open question," Stelle said at a November news conference. It was a remark some interpreted as putting pressure on the states to lay out what they'd do to improve habitat.

What those commitments will be has many in the region worried, and it's these worries that keep breaching alive. "Is it sensible for taxpayers and ratepayers to maintain dams that deliver only 5 percent of the region's power and the nation's cheapest power rates, while continuing to pour millions of dollars into technological fixes that have so far resulted in $3 billion worth of failure at the dams?" asked a November 18 *Idaho Statesman* editorial. "That's the economic tradeoff the region faces." Bruce Lovelin of the Columbia River Alliance, a group representing a wide range of river users, told the Seattle *Post-Intelligencer*, "Frankly, this could mean a regional civil war."

Fish advocates say they are prepared for the Clinton administration to punt on dam breaching this April. But they remain optimistic about their longer-term prospects, because they see the playing field shifting in their favor. For one thing, the Indian tribes are getting more aggressive, and some of them have gambling wealth to give them legal and political clout. Four Indian tribes—the Umatilla, the Warm Springs, Nez Perce, and Yakama—say they may sue the federal government for breaking treaty rights if it makes a no-breach decision. "In 1855, we gave away more than 40 million acres for the right to keep fishing as we always have," says Donald Sampson, an Umatilla Indian who now heads the Columbia River Intertribal Fish Commission. "If the fish aren't there, then the treaty is broken." Sampson says he has a team of fifteen lawyers working on a "war plan." Damages owed the tribes could run into the "multiple billions," he says.

Then there are the Alaskans, whose powerful fishing industry fears that if the federal agencies avoid dam breaching, they will compensate by further restricting the harvesting of salmon in the Pacific. In a letter to Washington Governor Gary Locke and Oregon Governor John Kitzhaber, Alaska's Governor Tony Knowles urged the Pacific Northwest to get on with the task of making the rivers safe for salmon. Snake River salmon "face a 'killing field' of dams, turbines and reservoirs," he wrote. "As we all know, Alaska fisheries barely scratch this salmon population, accounting for only three-tenths of one percent of the human-caused mortality. Clearly, fishing is not the problem." Backing Knowles is the state's congressional delegation, which has never hesitated to flex its muscle to defend Alaska's fishing industry.

The federal agencies are also changing. The Army Corps now looks at river restoration as its future, says Corps spokeswoman Nola Conway, pointing to the Corps' work in Florida to restore the channelized Kissimmee River. And the Bonneville Power Administration, which supplies close to 45 percent of the Northwest's electricity, may well find it cheaper to lose a small portion of its power generation capacity than to continue spending hundreds of millions each year on a black hole of salmon recovery, says Pat Ford, the director of the Save Our Wild Salmon coalition.

Some utilities that buy power from BPA have already started to worry that if the salmon don't recover or go extinct, Congress—led by delegations in the Northeast and Midwest, where electricity rates are high—will take away their very low preferred-customer rates. One is Oregon's Emerald People's Utility District, which serves customers outside the Eugene area. Last May, Emerald shook the power establishment by supporting dam breaching. "Should the U.S. Government ... fail to take steps necessary to protect the biological integrity of the Columbia and Snake rivers, the benefits that BPA has afforded the people of the Pacific Northwest will be taken away," the utility's board of directors wrote to President Clinton. While other nonprofit public utility districts, co-ops, and municipalities that buy BPA power have not followed Emerald's lead, several, including Seattle City Light, have said that breaching should be an option.

Five months is not much time for the region and the federal agencies to come up with a solution that everyone can live with. Longtime salmon combatants say that what's needed is fresh leadership. Oregon's Kitzhaber has made some efforts to bring the region's governors together to take on the salmon issue. But so far the other governors have shown little enthusiasm.

"Ever since the fish were listed under the ESA, people have retreated to their trenches," says Lori Bodi, who was the executive director of American Rivers before taking her current job with the BPA. "We've forgotten how to work together." But, as every journalist knows, nothing motivates like a deadline. "People are so worn out that maybe they're ready for a solution," says Bodi. "If not, we'll be back in court."

Fish advocates say any solution must eventually include breaching. "We have a window of five to 10 years," says Scott Bosse, a biologist with Idaho Rivers United. "Breaching is not only possible, it is inevitable."

*December 20, 1999*

# 3

# Taming Glen Canyon

# How Lake Powell Almost Broke Free of Glen Canyon Dam

T. J. Wolf

As a Bureau of Reclamation brat growing up in Denver in the 1950s, my favorite critter was the beaver, my contributions to "show and tell" at school were Bureau scale models of dams, and my idea of a vacation was a family trip into the desert where I could see the river kicked in the teeth by one or another dam. I knew about Chuck Yeager and the other heroes of *The Right Stuff*. But my heroes weren't flyboys or cowboys. They were engineers. That was only natural since my father was the Bureau engineer (in my world, there was only one "Bureau") who designed the powerplant at Glen Canyon Dam on the Colorado River. It was also natural that I would grow up thinking Glen Canyon Dam was a thing of beauty and a joy forever.

"Just think of it from an engineer's point of view!" my father would say. Six hundred feet of acutely angled, dazzling white concrete walls arching up from the frothy white and deep green Colorado running in its red sandstone bedrock, up into the cloudless blue sky that caps the desert. What a dam! What a site for a dam! With its crest at an elevation of 3,715 feet above sea level, the dam backs up the river to create a marvelous hydropower head. From that human-made height the water zooms down stainless steel tubes to drive $200 million worth of turbines—enormous, delicately balanced turbines housed in the powerplant nestled in the shelter of the dam's arch. Smoothly spinning turbines, pollution-free power, a blooming desert. What more could anyone want? And to cap it off, as if to defy the Sierra Club's sensitivities, my father and his friends threw in a surrealistic twist. Between the base of the dam and the powerplant there is a fertile crescent—a flat, football-field-sized area sown with the finest Kentucky bluegrass, thriving on cold Colorado River water, and carefully tended by Bureau personnel. It's the meticulous touch of the engineer. The sign that everything, but everything, has been thought of and is under control.

The symbolism of that grassy field was put to hard use this summer. For a time, there was a man haying that peculiar meadow all day, every day. It was a war-time routine calculated to keep everyone calm; to show that everything was under control. But above that calm and scripted scene, above the putt-putt of the two-cycle Briggs and Stratton lawnmower engine, Glen Canyon Dam was shaking, vibrating madly. Tremendous rumblings from the galleries—the hollow passages in the dam's otherwise solid interior—sent security guards scurrying to close the top of the dam to visitors.

The shuddering had its origin in Glen Canyon's spillways. Most dams spill their excess water over the top, over specially designed concrete waterfalls that present onlookers with a show when a reservoir fills and spills. Glen Canyon Dam is different. It spills inside, down spillway tunnels that take the water from upstream, pass it beneath the dam itself, and discharge it downstream from 41-foot diameter spillway mouths. For two decades, those spillway mouths gaped dry and empty, ever since Lake Powell had begun to fill. But on June 28, 1993, early in the morning, those spillway tunnels were at work—work that was not going well. You could hear loud, fearsome noises in the left gallery within the dam and also on top, where the rising sun was warming the white concrete.

If you were on the bridge that spans the canyon below the dam that June morning, perhaps worrying about what the spillage would do to your river-running friends downstream, you would have seen a sight terrifying enough to put the fear of God into anyone, but especially into an engineer. You would have seen the steady sweep of the spillway mouths suddenly waver, choke, cough, and then vomit forth half-digested gobbets of steel reinforced concrete (bad, very bad), spew out blood-red water (my God, it's into bedrock), and finally disgorge great red chunks of sandstone into the frothy chaos below the dam. You would have seen the Colorado River going home, carving rock, moving deeper, as it has always done. If we can say a river is wrathful, then we can say Glen Canyon Dam was the object of the Colorado River's wrath last summer, when flow into the Colorado River basin grew from the normal 6.96 million acre-feet to 14.6 million acre-feet during the April to June runoff.

That doubling threatened to spell not just the end of the dam, but also the end of hundreds of professional careers. The engineers who designed Idaho's infamous, failed Teton Dam were forced into retirement because the dam's failure was actually their failure. Some of them died soon after. But if the Bureau lost Glen Canyon, it would be more than a dozen or so engineers forced out in disgrace. It might be the end of the agency. The flooding Colorado was posing the same question to the Bureau engineers that space posed to those who would navigate it. Did they design their technology correctly? Assuming their design is right, do they have the skills, the knowledge, the coolness, and the guts to operate it under extreme conditions? Do they have the right stuff?

It can be argued that more than a dam, a federal bureau or professional careers were at stake. The Bureau of Reclamation stands for an approach to nature that says rivers, forests, resources of all kinds are there to be changed, transformed, and reworked, until they respond to flicks of switches, until they go on and off at will, until they produce exactly what we want. Glen Canyon Dam provides a clear example of this dominance over nature. Glen Canyon and Hoover are where the undisciplined "useless" rushing of the river is turned into electricity—a form of energy that can do all the things engineers want energy to do.

The Bureau's approach to rivers is as opposite as can be to that of the river runner or kayaker. Those who ride rivers, who go with the flow, want to master a river without breaking it. They want to experience the river without putting their mark on it. The river people, and those who share their world view, had as large a stake in the drama that played out this summer in Glen Canyon Dam as the Bureau did. At stake was the way our society looks at nature. If that had been known, all sorts of people would have been standing on the bridge below the dam—a bridge that provides a wonderful view of the dam and its spillway mouths, the grassy crescent, and the powerhouse. It would have been a great place for the river runners to stand and cheer on the river. And just as great a place for those who feel they and society lost at Three Mile Island or Teton Dam to stand and cheer for the Bureau to show it has the right stuff.

If you had stood with me and my father on that same bridge at its dedication in 1959, you would have been peering down into the narrow canyon as he explained why the river disappeared from view for a stretch. You would have heard him say that the Bureau engineers had routed the river in a tunnel around and under the damsite so that they could pour concrete for the dam's foundations. Carefully boring through the soft red sandstone that must do here for bedrock, Bureau engineers had designed two concrete-lined diversion tunnels that led through the canyon walls, around the places where the dam would be married to the canyon walls (the abutments), and down into the canyon below, where the tunnels spilled the Colorado back into its accustomed bed.

If you had returned with us four years later, in 1963, to witness Lady Bird Johnson dedicate the completed dam, you would have seen a different sight. The diversion tunnels were plugged now, and the dam had already trapped enough of the Colorado's flow to create an infant Lake Powell—small, but showing signs that over the next two decades it was going to become a very large reservoir indeed. This time, you would have heard my father explain how the engineers had not wasted the diversion tunnels. They had poured concrete plugs into the upper section of those tunnels, cutting them off from the river. But then they had made the downstream sections of the two diversion tunnels part of the new spillway system. They had built new tunnels down from above. They had married the downstream part of the diversion tunnel to these new slanting concrete tubes coming down from above, with the connection point upstream of the dam, right below the concrete plugs.

Those new slanting spillway tunnels rise at a 55-degree angle from their merger with the old diversion tunnels at the bottom of the reservoir. Then they open out into the reservoir, 600 feet upstream from the face of the dam, up against the canyon walls on each side. Water gets to the 41-foot-wide tunnel intakes by flowing through concrete approach-channels. The lips of the spillway tunnels are at an elevation of 3,648 feet above sea level. But even when Lake Powell reaches that height, the spillways don't necessarily take on water. They are each guarded by two curved radial gates, 52.5 feet high. Those gates are raised and lowered by booms anchored into the canyon walls. When the gates are down, the water level must rise another 52.5 feet before it can flow over the gates and get to the spillway. That means Lake Powell can rise to 3,700.5 feet before it can spill. If water flows into the reservoir faster than the spillways can take it away, and the reservoir continues to rise, the ultimate spillway is the dam itself, which is at 3,715 feet of elevation.

The Bureau engineers are sure the dam can spill without suffering any damage. But the $200 million powerhouse and turbines at its base, to say nothing of the fertile green crescent, would be washed away like a log.

In addition to the tunnel spillways, the dam has two other ways to release water. One is through the river outlet works (ROW, if you like acronyms)—four steel conduits, each 8 feet in diameter and controlled by huge valves. The other way is the only one the engineers ever want to use—through the steel tubes that lead to the turbines themselves. For water that goes through the spillway tunnels or the river outlet works does not generate electricity. The Bureau tries to only use the power plant, so that every drop of water produces a bit of electricity.

In the summer of 1983, the Bureau had to waste water. It had to send water through the tunnel spillways and the river outlet works—water that didn't produce a watt of energy. In normal times, that would have been a scandal. But this summer, waste was the least of the Bureau's worries. The real worry was that, because of this peculiar design, the Colorado River came close to beating the Bureau, close to showing that it and its people didn't have the right stuff, by getting in at the ground floor and blowing out the dam's soft sandstone foundations.

The underground spillways came close to providing a route for the reservoir to rush under the dam and down the river, to overwhelm Hoover Dam, and to continue the process, toppling the other dominoes in the system—the dams at Davis, Parker, Headgate Rock, Palo Verde, Imperial, Laguna, and Moreles, each of which was already dealing with desperate conditions. Suddenly, the Salton Sea in extreme southern California could be some 50 million acre-feet bigger. Or the Colorado River might find a new outlet, a new way to the sea. A river once more.

Ironically, the chaos Glen Canyon could have caused might have spared the visible part of the dam itself. The river might have carved itself a new path downstream by ripping open the diversion tunnels, but the dam might have stood, whatever was going on beneath it. Certainly, it would stand if water spilled over it, or piled up behind it in even greater quantities than it did this summer. Glen Canyon is a tough structure, a gravity dam that is also curved. Most gravity dams, such as the Grand Coulee on the Columbia, are straight and set at right angles across the river. The straight dam depends on its weight to keep it from sliding downstream. It sets there, squat and ponderous, pushing back against the water behind it. But Glen Canyon is curved like an eggshell, with the convex part of the eggshell pointing upstream. The result is that the downstream force of the water is transmitted along the eggshell to the places where the dam abuts the canyon walls. Instead of resisting the water's force by its own brute force, it enlists the rock of the canyon to hold back the water.

So the dam isn't simply a heavy irrigation rock set into the canyon. It is more like a bathtub plug; the harder the water pushes on it, the more it pushes back. And in a sense—a sense the river runners might appreciate—the Glen Canyon Dam is made to go with the flow. It is built of enormous concrete blocks that are designed to shift, to settle, to drop into openings, should they appear, as the pressure on the dam face shifts or changes.

Because of the dam's design, the Colorado River came close to beating the Bureau in 1983. The defense against such a technological disaster, or victory of the river, whichever you choose, was the lining of the spillway tunnels—a barrier of concrete reinforced with heavy steel bars. Although the steel tubes of the river outlet works and of the power generating system were designed to take the beating of tons of water falling at 120 miles per hour, the concrete spillways were never meant to withstand such conditions.

When water rushes over concrete, no matter how smooth the concrete, it will erode. The erosion can cascade and multiply when grains dug out upstream become grinding, tearing agents downstream, ripping out ever larger chunks under the double push of air pressure and water pressure. And beyond the concrete tunnels was something worse—soft Jurassic Navajo sandstone, composed of quartz grains and a little feldspar. It is both moderately porous and highly absorptive. Not the best bedrock to hold back millions of tons of water, as the Colorado has been proving by millennia of downcutting. But Glen Canyon was the best physical site for a dam—a site so narrow and with walls so high that Bureau engineers had to put their spillways through the rock because there was no room for them elsewhere.

Spillway damage is nothing new. It even has a special name— cavitation. Hoover Dam's own tunnel spillways had experienced it in 1941 and Montana's Yellowtail Dam had experienced a 1967 episode which provided the data for designs to correct the potential problem at Glen Canyon. The correction was airslots built into the tunnel walls to bleed off the air trapped with the water and reduce pressure.

Cavitation is Bruce Moyes' specialty. An engineer at the Bureau's Engineering and Research Center in Denver, he headed the special team assigned to monitor and manage Glen Canyon Dam last summer. His job now is to make engineering sense out of last summer's near-disaster and to propose design solutions that can be put into concrete before next spring brings an equally high runoff. Working in a building at the Denver Federal Center so functionally ugly it has to have been designed by engineers, Bruce cultivates a beard, a sense of humor, and a respect for the power of the Colorado River. When you call Bruce's office, a voice answers, "Concrete Dams!" in a tone reminiscent of one of my father's favorite sayings: "I like people and technical problems, not necessarily in that order."

In addition to his cavitation work, Bruce has a long-term assignment. He keeps track of the evolution, the aging, of Glen Canyon Dam, which he talks about as if it were a living thing, a moody critter that moves and changes, keeping time with the moves and moods of the Colorado.

In the course of the day I spent with Bruce, I related to him some of the charges made by Bureau critics concerning last summer's record spills. He replied, "Hell, we could have just run 100,000 cubic feet per second down the Grand Canyon during June and flushed everyone and everything out. That would have solved our technical problems and saved the dams too. But our goal was to save the dams and the people downstream in the floodplains. Not easy. But we believe we succeeded as far as possible under the circumstances."

What were those "circumstances"? According to Bruce it was an ever-mounting flow of water into Lake Powell that required the Bureau to balance off imponderables. The chronology that follows draws on his account of the summer and on Bureau documents.

**June 2, 1983.** This day can be taken as the start of the crisis. The level of Lake Powell exceeds 3,696 feet above sea level and Bureau officials decide that powerplant discharges alone can no longer control the reservoir rise. They raise the left spillway gates and dump an additional 10,000 cubic feet per second (cfs). Over the weekend, they increase the spill to 20,000 cfs.

**June 6.** Dam personnel hear rumbling noises and see material shooting out of the left spillway mouth. Engineers fly out from Denver. But before they arrive, the dam manager has shut down the left tunnel and opened both the right spillway gates and the river outlet works. The Denver team boards a contraption called the cart, which is lowered over the left radial gates and down into the intake.

They observe some cavitation damage close to the point where the tunnel from above joins the horizontal diversion tunnel—right at the elbow.

That leaves them with nasty choices. If they reduce flow through the left spillway tunnel, the reservoir will continue to rise. If it rises until it overtops the closed gate, it might jam the gate shut and water will spill uncontrollably over the gate into the tunnel. If there is too much water even for the spillway tunnel, the reservoir will continue to rise and might overtop the dam, washing out the powerplant at its base.

To the engineers on the scene, the maximum reservoir height seems to be 3,700 feet—the top of the radial gates. But higher authorities in the Bureau overrule them just as the river is overruling the dam. Under orders, the engineers arrange for the installation of 4-foot-high sheets of plywood, called flashboards, onto the tops of the radial gates. In effect, the radial gates are now 56.5 feet high, and the reservoir can rise another 4 feet without flowing over the gates and into the spillway tunnels. It buys time by creating a surcharge pool in Lake Powell.

Along with the flashboard installation order comes disturbing news from the National Weather Service: inflow forecasts for Lake Powell are accelerating. Other disturbing news comes from closer by. The team descends into the dam itself, into its hollow insides, the galleries, on the trail of the rumbling noises heard earlier. Since the left tunnel is temporarily down, the noise has ceased. But it doesn't take a close inspection of the watery confusion in the galleries to show that the river outlet-works couplings are leaking, and that manhole covers throughout the dam show increasing signs of pressurization. Everywhere, like corks in shaken champagne bottles, various systems are responding to increasing pressure from the rising wall of water behind the dam and the huge flows through the dam.

Meanwhile, on the 225-mile stretch of the Colorado that winds from Glen Canyon downstream to Lake Mead, Park Service helicopters drop the news about the increasing releases to river runners: "Camp High! Be cautious!"

The Bureau was taking its own advice on "caution" as this report summarizing the early summer apprehensions shows: "The initial concern upon the June 6 report of noises from the left tunnel was for the safety of the dam and its foundation. This concern predominated throughout the spill period."

**June 7.** The team brings the powerplant flows up to 28,000 cfs—20 percent over normal capacity. They hold the river outlet works to 15,000 cfs. That keeps water speed down to only 50 miles per hour. And they hold the right spillway to 4,000 cfs. They want to keep it low because it occupies a dangerous position upstream from the dam's foundation. If the right spillway tunnel broke through to bedrock, it would threaten the dam's foundation.

They also get organized. They set up twice-daily inspections of both spillway portals, of dam abutment leakage (water flowing through joints where the dam meets the canyon), and a more technical evaluation of dam noises. They have been using: "Scares the hell out of me!" for serious sounds. From Bruce Moyes' account, you imagine the team members like men in battle, experiencing feelings of elation and camaraderie alternating with convictions of isolation and doom. Noah and Jonah jokes abound.

**June 8.** The left radial gates are fitted with their flashboards. Attention turns to the right radial gates. Hydraulic computations give additional reasons to baby the right spillway. So long as the water erodes straight down, everything is safe. But damage patterns, the computations show, also like to spread out laterally, or horizontally. Since the right tunnel elbow is near the dam, horizontal damage spreading out from the tunnels could threaten it. A related worry is that damage to the concrete plug in the right tunnel could create a direct connection between Lake Powell and the river via the old diversion tunnel.

**June 9.** Total discharge is at 48,000 cfs and the National Weather Service revises its predictions upward. The team decides that the river outlet-works couplings are going to hold.

**June 10-11.** The right spillway radial gates have their flashboards. Total discharge is held at 48,000 cfs.

**June 11-12.** The river outlet works are discharging 17,000 cfs with no problem. But the reservoir continues to rise.

**June 13.** The National Weather Service ups its predictions by 500,000 acre-feet and the team thinks that its forecasts will always err on the low side. They also realize that they can't totally shut down the spillway tunnels by lowering the radial gates. That would put too much pressure on the jury-rigged plywood flashboards atop the gates. But Bruce Moyes says there was one comfort: "The inherent stability of the dam and its ability to bridge openings in the foundation gave us confidence that no sudden loss of reservoir was possible. But any direct connection (of the reservoir through the spillway tunnels to the river downstream) could lead to erosion of the sandstone and the potential for uncontrolled release into Lake Mead was a real concern." In other words, the dam could hold but the tunnels could give way.

**June 15.** Discharge is up to 53,000 cfs, but the reservoir is still rising 6 inches a day. Babying the crucial right tunnel, the team increases the left tunnel by 7,000 cfs, up to 12,000 cfs, and the reservoir as a whole up to 60,000 cfs.

**June 16.** Someone figures that only 200 feet of soft Jurassic sandstone separate the spillway tunnels from the dam abutments.

**June 17-21.** Anticipating lawsuits and congressional investigations, the team establishes a memo system to document how decisions are being reached. That system comes quickly into use when the left spillway discharge falters on June 18 and disappears on June 19. They take a chance and lift the left radial gates further, hoping more water will blast out the obstruction. It works and the water discharge downstream of the dam resumes.

**June 22.** Bureau Commissioner Robert Broadbent and all the big Bureau chiefs decide in Salt Lake City to go from the present 61,000 cfs up to 70,000 cfs at Glen Canyon and to begin spilling at Hoover. The team is told: "We strongly recommend that discharges from Glen Canyon Dam be immediately raised to 70,000 cfs to protect the safety of the structure. It is imperative that discharges from Hoover Dam be raised to 40,000 cfs as soon as possible. If the extreme forecast of the NWS becomes operational, the discharges from both dams must be increased."

The team, and the dam, is between a rock and a hard place. If the increased flow of water begins to destroy the spillway tunnels, they will have to shut the gates. That will knock down the wooden flashboards and cause a tremendous, uncontrolled surge of water into the already damaged spillways, possibly destroying them. As if to underscore this concern, the left tunnel's discharge fails again, even at 21,000 cfs, which should sweep blockages away. And noise levels in the dam and spillways are high. So the team lowers the left spillway to 10,000 cfs and increases the right to 15,000 cfs. Noise drops and the left discharge becomes smooth again.

A June 23 memo answers the question: Would overtopping of the radial gates be serious? "The answer must be a qualified yes ... expansion of the damaged area could affect the stability of the canyon walls. This is even more critical in the right tunnel since its elbow is further upstream" and therefore closer to the dam abutments.

**June 27.** Heavy rains and high temperatures in the upper Colorado River Basin force the team to go from the already high 70,000 cfs up to 80,000 cfs. But raising the spillway gates and actually getting the flow are two different things. The discharge from the left spillway is very weak. And there is booming and vibrating throughout the galleries on the left side of the dam.

Put yourself in the control room that June 27 morning, when you feel frantic about the left spillway discharge, and you are under orders to reduce the dam's noise and vibration before the turbines start to wobble on their axes and spin themselves into destruction, just before the spillways also self-destruct. You can't shut down the power system, and you dare not shut down the river outlet works. So you turn the dials regulating the left spillway not down, but up—up from the 25,000 cfs rate that is already performing a tonsillectomy on the left spillway, up to 32,000 cfs. Your other hand revs the right spillway (the one you are really afraid to use) up, up from 10,000 to 15,000 cfs. Counting everything, your dials tell you the total discharge is 92,000 cfs. What the discharge really is you have no idea. There are no flow gauges down in the bedrock.

While you play with the dials, maybe your inner video flips far up the channel of the Colorado, far upriver where the waters of the apocalypse creep towards Rainbow Bridge, some 8 feet higher than the previous all-time high water mark. Maybe that is where the environmentalists are on this day of doom, saying: "We told you so!" Prophesying from Rainbow Bridge, crying forth in a loud voice to the empty desert, to the rising reservoir: "Make straight the way of the Lord. Let the river flow." Maybe such voices sound in your mind back in the control room, as you increase the flow in the right spillway up to 27,000 cfs, and wait. Then you hear it. Outside, the little two-cycle Briggs and Stratton lawnmower engine labors on, shaving the bluegrass down to putting green quality. Comforting, especially as you realize you can hear it because the terrible thundering and vibrating has stopped. For now.

Downstream from this sudden peace, the new Colorado has turned deadly serious. Since normal flow is 25,000 cfs, a release at 92,000 cfs moves like a tidal wave through the Grand Canyon. Pontoon rafts 40 feet long capsize at Crystal Rapids, providing some passengers with 8-mile-long lifejacket rides through seven other major rapids before they reach shore. Though helicopters evacuate around 150 people from the Canyon, dozens are hurt and one drowns. Also drowned out and scoured away is the new (since 1963) riparian habitat made possible by Glen Canyon's once steady releases. The Park Service is mad. River runners are mad.

If the unregulated Colorado was something that had to be controlled with dams, what do you call this?

**June 29.** Good news. Forecasts say flow into Lake Powell is peaking. So the team drops the Glen Canyon discharge to 87,000 cfs.

**July 2.** With both spillway tunnels at 20,000 cfs, the right discharge falters. It is upped to 24,000 cfs in an attempt to sweep it clean. But inside the dam, in a gallery, drainholes begin to bubble violently. Great sighs of air and water surge from the drain holes in the gallery nearest the right tunnel—the tunnel that comes closest to the dam's foundation. The team cuts the right spillway to 15,000 cfs. The surges calm, but no one knows what has happened. Until the plywood flashboards are replaced with 8-foot-high strong steel ones—a job in progress—they don't dare shut the radial gates. And until they shut the gates, they can't go into the tunnels and inspect the damage.

**July 4.** Holiday visitors to the dam can watch the construction company working around the clock to install the steel flashboards—which will be stronger and four feet higher than the plywood ones.

**July 6-7.** The steel is in place and the left tunnel shut down. The team is swung into the tunnel over the radial gates on the cart. There they find much more damage than expected. In fact, the cart cannot proceed through the tangle of twisted steel and concrete. The water still in the tunnel prevents an exact evaluation. But they know there's a lot. Most disturbing, they find damage much higher in the tunnel than expected. This suggests that rockfalls have occurred in the tunnel due to horizontal, or sideways, damage toward the dam.

**July 8.** Today they ride the cart into the now-closed right spillway. They find the damage on this side starts lower down than it did on the left. So they proceed down the slanting elbow of the tunnel into the horizontal section. There they attempt to launch a rubber boat over the small lake filling an eroded portion of the concrete. But they lose the boat to strange currents and decide it makes more sense to return to the surface. They have no desire to be swept out of the tunnel and into the river. Back at the surface they open the radial gates, sending a modest 5,000 cfs down each spillway. "Damage (to the left spillway) includes a massive hole into the sandstone to about 36 feet below the tunnel invert. The upstream-downstream length of this hole was about 150 feet. It extended laterally (horizontally) to about 15 feet beyond the full tunnel width." In the right spillway tunnel, a large hole extended 10 feet horizontally beyond the full tunnel width, according to a report.

**July 15.** The reservoir finally peaks at 3,708.4 feet—some 60 feet above the spillway tunnel crest of 3,648, and a mere seven feet below the crest of the dam itself. Discharges can now be dropped from 61,000 cfs to 51,000 cfs, where they remain.

**July 23.** With the reservoir at 3,707.8 feet above sea level, the spillway gates on both sides are slammed shut. The 8-foot-high steel flashboards hold. It is 8 a.m. Crews prepare for immediate descent into the spillway tunnels to begin planning repairs.

*December 12, 1983*

# The Grand Canyon Is Just Another Turbine

## Dennis Brownridge and Steve Hinchman

**F**ew structures heat up environmental emotions as much as Arizona's Glen Canyon Dam, a wound in the flesh of conservationists since it was completed in 1963. Most of their ire has focused on the dam's upstream impacts—the drowning of Glen Canyon's haunting redrock walls under Lake Powell. But over the years, the focus has shifted to the dam's ongoing downstream impacts—the scouring of the Colorado River through Grand Canyon National Park.

Since the mid-1960s, river runners, environmentalists and lovers of the Grand Canyon have vainly sought an environmental impact study on the dam's operation. They charge that daily tides created by the dam are wreaking havoc on the park below, eroding beaches and banks, stranding boaters, cutting endangered fish off from spawning zones, and forever altering the canyon's riparian ecosystem.

But the federal agencies that manage the dam—the Bureau of Reclamation (Department of Interior) and the Western Area Power Administration (Department of Energy)—have usually refused to deal with those impacts, arguing that their job is to produce kilowatt-hours, not save beaches. Supported by a consortium of utilities that use the dam's power, the federal agencies have blocked every move environmentalists and others made to gain a voice in Glen Canyon Dam's operation. But in the summer of 1989 the feds broke. Faced with evidence of severe environmental degradation, mounting public pressure both in the U.S. and worldwide, and concerted lobbying from Congress, Interior Secretary Manuel Lujan on July 17 ordered Bureau of Reclamation officials to begin an environmental impact statement (EIS) on how dam operations affect the canyon.

Two months later, on Sept. 29, the environmentalists scored an even bigger victory. Utah Federal District Judge J. Thomas Greene ruled against the Western Area Power Administration (WAPA) in a

lawsuit filed by the National Wildlife Federation, Grand Canyon
Trust and rafting groups. Greene found that WAPA's sales of Glen
Canyon Dam power had clearly caused "irreparable injury" to the
Grand Canyon river corridor. He revoked several recent WAPA power
contracts and told the agency to write a second EIS on how its power
sales affect the canyon.

These first official recognitions that Glen Canyon Dam has
harmed and continues to harm the Grand Canyon environment add
up to a major victory for environmentalists. But it is just the first
round in what may turn out to be one of the biggest environmental
battles of the next decade.

"The Glen Canyon EIS is the most important EIS the Bureau has
ever prepared," says Representative George Miller, D-Calif., who
oversees both the Bureau of Reclamation and WAPA as chair of the
House Interior Committee's Subcommittee on Energy and the
Environment. Miller calls the Grand Canyon one of the most
treasured natural landmarks in the United States, if not the world.
He says the studies are an important precedent. "It is not the first
hydroelectric dam to be challenged on environmental grounds,"
Miller says. "Action was taken to restore salmon on the Columbia
River after it became clear that dams on that river were having a
devastating effect on fish survival. But it sets precedent for going
back and re-thinking a dam project." It will be a high profile
investigation. Putting the canyon environment on par with or even
above power production would mean a fundamental change in the
way rivers are managed in the West.

Every major environmental organization has targeted the Glen
Canyon Dam as a key issue. The National Park Service, U.S. Fish and
Wildlife Service, the National Academy of Sciences, and four
congressional subcommittees are also watching.

It is not a simple issue. Glen Canyon is the key dam in the
Colorado River Storage Project: a series of water storage and
hydroelectric projects in the Colorado River basin, which include
Flaming Gorge Dam on the Green River in Utah and the three dams
of the Curecanti unit on the Gunnison River in Colorado. The
project's primary purpose as mandated by Congress in 1956 is to
store Colorado River water for allocation among all the basin states.
But Congress also told the Bureau of Reclamation to "produce the
greatest amount of power and energy that can be sold at firm power
and energy rates." The Bureau of Reclamation has done that. Glen

Canyon's eight turbines have a combined capacity of 1,300 megawatts, which make up more than 10 percent of WAPA's power supply.

The Bureau of Reclamation built and runs the Colorado River dams. WAPA serves as the power broker for fifty federal hydroelectric projects in the West and tells the Bureau when to turn the dams on and off, based on regional power needs. However, most of the revenue from Glen Canyon's turbines does not accrue to the federal treasury. Instead it is passed on to public utilities in the form of power rates that, at 1 cent per kilowatt-hour, are among the cheapest in the nation. Those utilities, known as the Colorado River Electric Distributors Association, or CREDA, serve an estimated one million retail customers in six states: Colorado, Wyoming, New Mexico, Arizona, Utah, and parts of Nevada. David Conrad, a water specialist with the National Wildlife Federation, says cities and counties with CREDA power pay about one-fourth of market prices.

CREDA depends heavily on that subsidy, and WAPA and the utilities have found ways to increase its dollar value. For the first decade or so of production WAPA marketed the power as baseload supply—around-the-clock electric generation—and the river flowed relatively smoothly. But over the last fifteen years, WAPA has increasingly used the dam for peaking power—generation when electricity is at its highest demand and highest cost—which sends the river downstream in pulses that chew up the environment but save the utilities tens of thousands of dollars. Despite environmental concerns, the Bureau of Reclamation, WAPA, and CREDA continue to increase the economic value of the twenty-five-year-old dam's hydropower operations. In the early 1980s, the Bureau rewrapped Glen Canyon's turbines, increasing its peaking power capacity by 16 percent; and over the last few years WAPA has begun to blend its power with other federal hydroelectric dams and non-federal power plants to increase the peaking power available to CREDA customers.

The gradual integration of Glen Canyon Dam into the West's energy machine has sparked a growing movement to save the river corridor downstream. Balanced against the view of the dam as a power station and cash register is the overpowering experience of the Grand Canyon, regarded as one of the world's premier whitewater runs. It winds 240 miles through the longest de facto wilderness in the contiguous states. Recreational river running was born there, half a century ago. But the Colorado in the canyon today

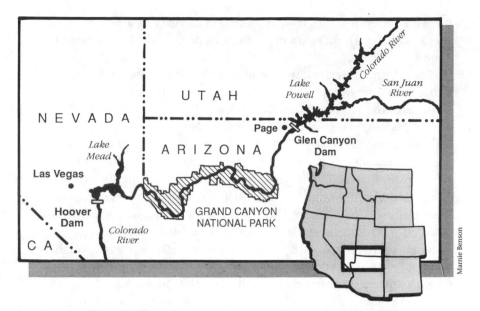

is very different from the virgin stream. The dam replaced the great
spring floods and low summer flows with daily tides that ebb and
flood as the generators follow hourly demands for electricity. In
narrow stretches, the river can rise and fall as much as 13 feet in a
day. "The river's being operated like a flush toilet," says Dan Dagget,
conservation chair of the Sierra Club's northern Arizona group.

Rafters say the unnatural fluctuations are damaging the canyon
environment and degrading visitors' experience. "At some rapids,
when the flow is low, boaters have to stop and wait until higher
flows come along," says Rob Elliott, vice president of Western River
Guides Association, who has been running the river since 1965.

The old Colorado was the nation's muddiest river: "Too thin to
plow and too thick to drink," as the saying went. Let a cupful stand
and you might get a third of a cup of mud. The reddish silt and clay
gave the river its name—El Rio Colorado, the red-colored river. Sixty
million tons of it were carried down the river each year, replenishing
the beaches scoured away by annual floods. Now that sediment
settles behind the dam, veteran river runners say beaches have
shrunk noticeably, especially in narrow stretches like Marble Gorge
and Granite Gorge, where they were always scarce. "Our primary
concern is the erosion of the beaches, because it's irreversible," says
Elliott. "It's getting so there aren't enough quality campsites to go
around."

Despite several years of study, sediment transport through the canyon remains poorly understood. But some hydrologists think the beaches would eventually stabilize if it weren't for the large daily fluctuations. They are particularly concerned about the rapid ramping rate, the speed at which the river is raised and lowered.

The dam's effects on the river's sediment load and water quality are so thorough—filtering out sediments, suspended solids and nutrients—that 300 miles downstream Nevada has had to begin fertilizing Lake Mead to keep its trophy sport fishery alive.

The dam has also had enormous impacts on vegetation and wildlife. Spared the annual floods, new vegetation has taken hold on the river banks. Some species, like the introduced tamarisk, now dominate, and are pushing out the native plants. While some regard the "tammies" as buggy pests, they have also attracted five times more birds than used to live in the canyon.

The dam's clear, cold waters have spawned a fabulous rainbow trout fishery, but simultaneously extirpated half of the eight fish species native to the canyon and reduced the rest to endangered or threatened status. The rapid fluctuations have also been known to cut off the remaining native fish from spawning areas in warm side canyons. "The river is so artificial now, I don't think we can ever really restore the native fish," laments Dagget.

The impact on recreation, however, is a mixed bag. In summer, the natural river was warm enough to swim or paddle across on an air mattress. Now the water comes out of the depths of the reservoir at a frigid 45 degrees. Boaters who fall in are as likely to die of hypothermia as from drowning, and several do each year.

Cross-canyon foot travel has been effectively banned (except at Phantom Ranch, where there is a bridge). Nevertheless, most summer rafters say they like the cold water, which "air conditions" the hot canyon floor and lets them chill their drinks. "We've improved the recreationist's opportunity," contends Lloyd Greiner, WAPA's area manager. "Prior to 1963, only a thousand people had gone down that canyon. Now 15,000 to 20,000 go down every year. They would not be going down there without that dam." He says the clear, cold water has made the river more attractive, and the dam has lengthened the rafting season by eliminating dangerous spring floods and providing higher summer flows.

"That's baloney," responds Elliott. "In the late 1960s river running was exploding all over the West. We could have run trips (on the virgin river) all year. We'd just use different equipment, a different style in different seasons. We'd use big motor boats in the spring and small oar-powered boats in the late season."

Environmentalists concede that many of the dam's impacts can't be changed and that some may be perceived as desirable. But they want to minimize the negative effects. "Nobody's talking about removing the dam," says Liz Birnbaum, a lawyer with the National Wildlife Federation. "The issue is, should we operate it solely for a relatively small group of people who use the power, or for the international resource which is the Grand Canyon?"

Ed Norton, president of the Grand Canyon Trust, a regional conservation organization, adds, "The 1968 Colorado River Basin Act makes it very clear that other priorities—recreation, fish and wildlife—are at least equal to hydropower."

The groups want to see higher minimum flows, with the flow regimen smoothed out to let the river regain its balance. While the environmental impact studies are being prepared, the National Park Service has called for interim minimum flows of at least 5,000 cubic feet of water per second. Environmentalists would prefer an 8,000 cfs minimum and rafting concessionaires say they would like to see steady daily flows, which in most months would be even higher. Current minimum flows are 3,000 cfs in the summer and 1,000 cfs in the winter.

Recently, Bureau of Reclamation officials have kept quiet on the minimum flow and fluctuation issue, instead letting WAPA fight the battle. WAPA contends, categorically, that power production comes first and resists changing operations. Lloyd Greiner says, "We don't think it has been substantiated that daily fluctuations are having an adverse effect on the canyon."

WAPA estimates that power revenues from the dam total about $80 million and officials say increasing minimum flows to 5,000 cfs would cost their customers $5 million a year. The park's twenty commercial river companies gross about $15 million. Environmentalists contest WAPA's figures and say the impact on individual customers would be small in any case. "Nobody really knows the value of the dam's power, since it's usually mixed with other sources," says Birnbaum. "But there are other values— intangibles—you've got to consider in the equation. After all, this is the Grand Canyon."

The dam's critics note that the Bureau of Reclamation, WAPA, and the Colorado River dams were authorized by Congress to attract settlers to the West by supplying plentiful irrigation water and, later, cheap electricity. Now, they say, that mission is outdated and continued federal subsidies are fueling the destruction of the region's scarce resources.

"Reclamation encourages the profligate waste of both water and power," says Bob Witzeman, conservation chair of the Maricopa Audubon Society in Phoenix. In addition to consuming some 85 percent of the West's water, farmers use prodigious quantities of electricity to pump that water onto their fields (although agriculture accounts for only a small fraction of total electricity use in the region). Witzeman adds that 68 percent of western farmlands are used to grow surplus crops heavily subsidized by taxpayers. He cites the case of Arizona, where the dominant crop is cotton. "The two thousand farmers in Arizona have an average net income of $205,000 a year," he says. "It's welfare for the rich." Cotton farmers respond that without access to cheap water and power they might be forced out of business.

The next stage in the battle over Glen Canyon Dam is the two environmental impact statements. The two documents will be coordinated but written separately, and most likely will be highly complex and hundreds of pages thick. Most observers expect the process to take at least five years. The Bureau of Reclamation, however, is only allotting two years for its EIS. Steve Robinson, who is the Bureau's project director, says Interior Secretary Lujan asked the agency to complete the EIS as quickly as legally possible. Robinson says he will hold scoping meetings next January and hopes to have a draft statement ready by 1991. "That's an ambitious schedule," says Robinson, but he notes the Bureau already has seven years of data accumulated from the Glen Canyon Environmental Studies—the $7 million study project that led to Lujan's decision to write an EIS.

The WAPA EIS will be directed by Ken Maxey, deputy area manager in the agency's Salt Lake City office, and will be wider in scope, looking at all Colorado River Storage Project dams and the effect power sales from those dams have on endangered fish and the environment.

*December 4, 1989*

# Government Tames Its Wild, Destructive Dam

## Florence Williams

**E**arly in August 1991, Interior Secretary Manuel Lujan issued a decree to alter the operation of a key faucet on the Colorado River—Glen Canyon Dam. After eight years and $15 million of studies, the dam would no longer release water just to generate electricity or deliver water to thirsty irrigators downstream. Now the dam has new constituents: the canyon's ecosystem, beaches, and boaters.

"This is the biggest thing to happen to the Colorado in thirty years," says David Wegner, the manager of the Glen Canyon Environmental Studies for the Bureau of Reclamation. "For the first time, changes have been made to dam operations to protect resources and not to make money." In a major victory for environmentalists, Secretary Lujan issued regulations beginning August 1 that reduce by three-quarters the Colorado River's fluctuations and by one-third the river's high water line. The new flows are designed to offer interim protection to the Grand Canyon's resources while work continues on the dam's environmental impact statement, due out in 1993.

"We're all very surprised," says Gail Peters of American Rivers, a group supporting the new regulations. "[The Interior Department] finally looked at our science seriously, and it finally dawned on them, 'We can do something to help these resources.' "

The Western Area Power Administration (WAPA), a federal agency that manages the twenty-eight-year-old dam and markets its hydropower, now faces restrictions on how much water it can pour through the dam's turbines, and when. In the past, WAPA has turned the Colorado River on and off like a spigot, releasing water according to the demands of its electricity consumers. This has meant that during the heat of the summer and cold of the winter, the river below the dam has fluctuated wildly to accommodate morning and evening power demands. The river level rose and fell as much as 13 feet in a day. Such extreme variations left whitewater rafters and

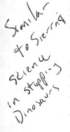

*Similar to Sierra Science in stopping Dinosaurs*

anglers stranded on banks and sand spits. The mercurial flows have also eaten away fragile beaches and the biological life they sustain. Moisture-loving plants are left high and dry one minute, and drowned the next. Two endangered fish, the humpback chub and the razorback sucker, which need steady water levels for spawning and feeding, are declining fast. "We've lost two endangered fish already, the bonytailed chub and the Colorado River squawfish, as well as endangered vegetation," says Wegner of the Bureau of Reclamation. "The goal is to take away stresses so that the canyon can heal itself."

To WAPA, an agency whose motto is "Keeping the power flowing," the new constraints on the dam are unwelcome. "We're destroying a hydrological resource," says Lloyd Greiner, WAPA's Salt Lake City manager. Changing the dam operation, he says, is expensive and of questionable benefit. Greiner says the environmental studies by the Bureau of Reclamation are incomplete. "We have not been able to see any conclusive data," he says. "The scientists had preconceived notions of what they'd find, and they did their studies based on unusual flows." Greiner says WAPA will lobby the Department of Interior to modify the regulations in November, when they will be re-evaluated.

Larry Stevens, an ecologist with the National Park Service, says evidence of the dam's impacts became apparent as early as 1987. "We have a pretty solid handle on the science." Changes to the regulations are more likely to come from political pressure than from new scientific data, he says.

WAPA dislikes the new constraints because they will affect the way the agency runs the entire Colorado River Storage Project, including twelve major dams, says the Bureau's Wegner. "(Lujan's regulations) mark the Pearl Harbor of the electricity industry," says Wegner. "You'll see a ripple effect throughout the entire upper Colorado basin."

"This will set precedents," agrees Martha Hahn, conservation director of the Grand Canyon Trust. "This will start a chain reaction of EISes. From now on, any type of dam operation will be up against this kind of scrutiny. This has already changed the way water is looked at in the West, and the Bureau of Reclamation is realizing this."

The Bureau is indeed changing, and Dave Wegner is partly responsible. A mid-level administrator for the nation's largest dam-building agency, Wegner commands a fleet of ecologists, the like of which the agency has never seen. With 140 scientists and 500 volunteers, the Glen Canyon Environmental Studies, headquartered in Flagstaff, Arizona, is making history. Dam impacts have never been studied so intensely before. For the first time, researchers are learning why the Grand Canyon's beaches are eroding and how to prevent it. A report by Wegner's top scientists last April recommended changes to the dam's operations based on a year of experimental flows. The scientists found that when the river level dropped quickly, beaches crumbled into the river. Damage increased exponentially with greater fluctuations. At the same time, Lake Powell, the reservoir behind the dam, traps sediment that used to replenish the beaches during spring floods.

The Grand Canyon's streamside habitat supports five thousand species of plants and animals. When the river banks disappear, say the scientists, so does vegetation, and, with that, the beginning of a food chain. Vertebrates and invertebrates eat the algae and other vegetation; fish, in turn, feed on insects. Predatory birds, which eat fish and other small mammals, sit at the top of the chain. When the banks are swept away, they also take precious archaeological sites with them.

To correct the problem, scientists suggested keeping water levels at a more constant level and making only gradual changes. These recommendations, with minor modifications, mirrored those issued by Secretary Lujan after much negotiation with various federal resource agencies and WAPA. Instead of the river flow varying as much as 25,000 cubic feet per second daily, it can now fluctuate no more than 5,000-8,000 cfs a day, depending on season. Flows will not be allowed to increase more than 2,500 cfs each hour, or decrease more than 1,500 cfs each hour. In addition, Lujan required a new ceiling of 20,000 cfs rather than the usual 30,000 cfs, eliminating the high flows needed to generate peak power. A new minimum flow of 8,000 cfs from 7 a.m. to 7 p.m. will accommodate boaters. The level can drop to 5,000 cfs during the night.

The flows will be re-examined in November, when more information becomes available on the economic costs of the change. "Essentially, we got 95 percent of the whole enchilada," says Duncan Patten, the study's senior scientist and an ecologist with Arizona State University. "I'm pleased with the regulations, and was really surprised when it came out."

WAPA has fought hard to maintain its flexibility to produce peak power. Administrators fear the clamp on high flows could cost $23 million a year. Instead of using the dam's turbines to generate peak power, the agency will have to purchase power from elsewhere to accommodate times of very high demand. "Now we can produce 1,200 megawatts at 30,000 cfs," says Lloyd Greiner, the Salt Lake City area manager for WAPA. "If we have to operate at 20,000 cfs, they're cutting 400 megawatts out of our capacity. It's going to be expensive."

But last week WAPA scored a small victory. Lujan issued draft "exception criteria," which would allow WAPA to violate the dam restrictions 3 percent of the time, or about twenty hours per month, plus emergencies. The criteria, opposed by resource managers, would save WAPA an estimated $20 million, according to deputy area manager Kenneth Maxey.

Final criteria will be released in mid-September after further negotiations with the National Park Service and the various wildlife agencies and Indian tribes involved.

The power produced by Glen Canyon Dam is valuable because it can be abruptly changed. By comparison, the power output from coal-fired power plants can only change slowly. As a result, the coal-fired plants in the West are run at a relatively steady, "base-load" rate, with Glen Canyon Dam being turned on and off to follow changes in demand for electricity. The system makes great sense from an economic and electric utility sense: power from Glen Canyon Dam is cheaper than from anywhere in the country.

The beneficiaries of WAPA's cheap electricity are mostly small municipalities and publicly owned rural cooperatives throughout the West. Serving sixteen million people in fifteen states, the agency generates $590 million in annual revenues. Glen Canyon Dam is the keystone of WAPA's electric empire, producing 80 percent of the power out of the Salt Lake regional office. Under the new regulations, manager Greiner predicts the price of power may increase from 1.4 cents to 1.8 cents per kilowatt. The difference may be enough to drive some of WAPA's customers elsewhere.

"These regulations ignore the responsibility WAPA has to utilities," says Carolyn McNeil, manager of the Intermountain Consumers Power Association, a group representing WAPA's customers. "We may have to go to more coal-burning facilities to get the power we want, and that's not a good environmental tradeoff."

Furthermore, says McNeil, "The small utilities may go out of business or will have to sell out."

Environmentalists have argued that the energy is replaceable while the Grand Canyon's ecology is not. "[WAPA's] purpose in life is to supply the cheapest power," says Hahn of the Grand Canyon Trust. "But that's not the purpose of the dam, which is to store water. WAPA might have to go back and look at their objectives." Hahn also says legislation may be introduced to subsidize the power further and protect it from rate increases. "There are ways you can respond to this economically," she says.

Does this mean the Bureau of Reclamation is finally assuming its much-trumpeted role of resource protection agency?

Says rafting outfitter Rob Elliot: "We're cautiously optimistic that this is a step in the right direction. They've come a long ways. I'll be looking and hoping for other indications."

*August 26, 1991*

# Indian Tribe Pushes for a Natural River and Canyon

## Florence Williams

According to Indian legend, the Hualapai people sprang from the clays, willows, and reeds of the banks of the Colorado River. Since the beginning of time, the Hualapai, hunters and gatherers, lived along the river and performed spiritual ceremonies there. Today, the Hualapai Reservation borders the southern bank of the Colorado for 108 miles below Glen Canyon Dam. Directly across on the north side is Grand Canyon National Park.

The Hualapai have watched their river change. Since 1963, when Lake Powell began storing water, the river water has been cold and clear, instead of warm and muddy. Daily fluctuations replaced the annual floods that once raged through the canyon. "We have documented evidence that flows from the dam adversely affected our resources," says Clay Bravo, a Hualapai wildlife technician. "Our cultural concerns are of utmost importance to us. We contend that nature is our culture." Bravo says native species of plants have been driven out, and that cultural artifacts and ancient skeletons have washed away with eroding beaches. The desert bighorn sheep, an animal of both religious and economic value to the tribe, has lost valuable habitat.

The Havasupai, Hopi, and Navajo tribes also claim ancestral ties to Grand Canyon and consider it sacred. The National Park Service has placed Hopi salt mines off limits to the public, since the Hopi use the site for religious ceremonies. Other ancient burial and dwelling sites abound. Countless remain unknown. The extent of the canyon's archaeological riches was only guessed at until a flash flood in a side creek exposed a major site, the Furnace Flats, in 1987. But the Park Service barely had time for excavation before releases from the dam washed away the exposed artifacts, according to Martha Hahn, a former park resource manager now with the Grand Canyon Trust. After the flash flood, the Park Service began cataloguing sites for the Glen Canyon Environmental Studies. So far it has found 470 sites along the river, says Jerry Mitchell, the park's natural resources supervisor. "I don't think the number of sites is as important as the fact that these sites have a tremendously high value to the tribes," says Mitchell.

The tribes played an integral role in persuading the Bureau of Reclamation and Interior Secretary Manuel Lujan to implement strong flow regulations. Six Hualapais work full time on Dave Wegner's Glen Canyon Environmental Studies staff out of Peach Springs, Arizona. "We haven't been very political in the past, but now we are being heard," says the tribe's Bravo, who was among the delegation of Native Americans that met with Secretary Lujan a week before the dam regulations were announced. "I feel the secretary was very receptive to our pleas," says Bravo. "I don't know how much consideration he gave our efforts, but it was good timing."

The presence of important cultural sites helped sway Lujan's decision, says Mitchell of the Park Service. "There are very clear mandates and legislation to protect these resources, as much as the endangered species," he says. "Lujan takes very seriously his trust responsibility to Native Americans."

Meanwhile, says Mitchell, the park and the tribes are working together to inventory as much of the remaining sites as they can. The new flows will go a long way to preserve what is left. "The interim measures are almost everything we asked for," he says. "We're delighted."

*August 26, 1991*

# Welcome, Floaters, to River City

## Daniel McCool

nterior Secretary Manuel Lujan announced in August 1991 a significant change in the policy that determines release flows from Glen Canyon Dam on the Colorado River. Maximizing hydroelectric production is no longer the only consideration; wildly fluctuating release flows will be mitigated somewhat to reduce the damage to riparian habitat and the impact on river recreation. But after an eighteen-day raft trip through the Grand Canyon during that fall, I am skeptical that a new era has arrived.

The Colorado River is still dominated by commercialism. Eighty-five percent of the 22,000 people who float the Colorado are paying passengers. As a non-commercial, non-motorized party—we were running the river for fun rather than profit, rowing small rafts—we were overwhelmed by motorized commercial rafts. These huge boats passed us by the dozens, their motors echoing up and down the river and leaving a trail of oily exhaust. Below Lava Falls, many commercial passengers were helicoptered out of the canyon so they would not have to spend an extra day on the river. The competition for campsites is tremendous, but the big rigs can turn on the power and take the best beaches. Because the dam stops virtually all sediment flows each year, there are fewer and fewer beaches. The new regulations do nothing to solve these problems.

Because of the large number of commercial passengers, unique attractions along the river are overrun with tourists. In "remote" places such as Shinumo Falls and Thunder River, we encountered as many as seventy-five to a hundred boaters who had been suddenly disgorged from large motor craft. At Deer Creek Falls and Havasupai, there were at least two hundred people crowding together for a look at the wilderness of Grand Canyon. At each place, the vegetation was trampled and the bare ground eroded, giving it the look of an overused city park. The new regulations will not solve these problems.

They also ignore another serious problem. As well as altering the flow of water, the dam altered its character. The river flows out of the depths of Lake Powell cold and clear; it is the water of a mountain lake, not a desert river. It fits into the Grand Canyon like an iceberg in the Amazon. With the water temperature at 45 degrees, and the air temperature usually in excess of 100 degrees, boaters are in danger of both hypothermia and hyperthermia. After five minutes in the water you become immobilized; after twenty minutes you can die—despite the Number 40 sunscreen you are wearing.

Are we really making headway against the threats to the Grand Canyon? Lujan's new policy will certainly have an impact, but of far greater importance is the environmental impact statement (EIS) currently being developed by the Bureau of Reclamation. For the initial phase of the EIS, the Bureau generated ten alternatives.

To solve the problem of dwindling beaches, the Bureau's EIS proposed building "sediment slurry pipelines" that would pump sand from a variety of locations, ranging from Lake Mead to the San Juan River, to locations deep in the canyon that have been deprived of sediment deposition because of the dam. To protect the few remaining beaches, the Bureau proposes jetties and rock walls. To solve problems created by cold water, the Bureau suggests adding "multilevel intake structures" to Glen Canyon so that warmer-temperature water can be drawn through the dam.

The fluctuating flows from the dam—the only problem addressed by the Lujan regulations—are also dealt with in the preliminary EIS alternatives. The Bureau of Reclamation has always strongly resisted any limits on dam releases. The agency, and its ally, the Western Area Power Administration, prefer radically fluctuating flows because it permits them to open the dynamos for peak power needs; this maximizes the amount of money they can make from the dam. The non-structural solution to these fluctuations is to limit changes. This is what the Lujan regulations attempt to do, and the Bureau included this approach as an alternative. But the Bureau of Reclamation, ever fond of building, suggests another way to reduce fluctuations. Two of the ten alternatives include constructing a "reregulation dam" downstream from Glen Canyon Dam. Curiously, this proposed dam is at the same site as a proposed pump-back storage dam that the Bureau has wanted to build for years. The river canyon between Glen Canyon Dam and the new dam would become a giant holding tank which would fill during high flow periods and empty during low flows.

Much has been said recently about the "new" Bureau of Reclamation. But of the ten alternatives it proposes for the preliminary EIS, six entail pouring more concrete. And of the remaining four, three require the Bureau to pump sand out of the river and onto beaches. Only the "no action" alternative would result in no new intrusive activities. Perhaps the "new" Bureau of Reclamation isn't all that different from the old Bureau.

Secretary Lujan and the Bush Administration have placed a band-aid on a head wound and declared the patient saved. The EIS process—and the final choice of alternatives—will be the real test of whether we have truly entered a new era on the river.

Rowing the haystacks of Hermit Rapid and fighting the hydraulics of Lava Falls is still a world-class experience. But the Colorado River through the Grand Canyon is a far cry from a wilderness. It is a tightly regulated, over-crowded urban corridor that has little resemblance to a natural stream system. Only a new management philosophy that stresses environmental integrity over commercialism and concrete will change this. Both the National Park Service and the Bureau of Reclamation will have to revise fundamental operating assumptions; only then will a new era begin.

*December 30, 1991*

# Glen Canyon: Using a Dam to Heal a River

## George Sibley

*I*n the context of the place, it was a very strange idea. In 1995, we were sitting in a boat on dark green water deep in a red-walled canyon, a few hundred yards downstream from a 10 million-ton mirage. The mirage of smooth brilliant white looked curiously fragile in that otherwise raw landscape of red sandstone, green water, and infinite sky: a 500-foot fingernail wedged between us and more than a year's worth of the Colorado River. And in that surreal place, the boatman who'd brought us there, 16 miles up the Colorado River from Lee's Ferry to Glen Canyon Dam, was presenting an idea even more surreal: he wanted to see the dam create a flood to help the river below the dam. This seemed so alien to the purpose of a dam— really, to the whole purpose and thrust of the past century, which has been so much about controlling and rationalizing nature—that it was hard not to laugh.

From the time it began to back up water in 1963, Glen Canyon Dam turned the lower basin of the nation's wildest river into a waterworks that flowed entirely according to the demands of those who used its electricity and water. For its builder, the U.S. Bureau of Reclamation, this dam had come into being as the arch-realization of that vision of political and economic rationality that sees the natural as raw material to be reconstructed to meet human needs and desires. Into this monumental stronghold of the rationalist vision, the boatman wanted to intrude a flood?—a synthetic flood? Skepticism was understandable. But, ten months later, in the spring of 1996, I stood on the deck of the Bureau's powerhouse, at the base of the 500-foot mountain of the dam, feeling through the soles of my feet the thrum of 45,000 cubic feet per second of water passing through the dam, everything in the dam that could be opened up running full out—close to a third of it not even "paying its way" by going through the generator turbines—as the dam and its managers created that most undamly thing: a flood. A scheduled, managed, controlled flood, from March 26 through April 2, 1996.

Southwestern writer Russell Martin wrote a good book about the building of Glen Canyon Dam, *A Story That Stands Like a Dam: Glen Canyon and the Battle for the Soul of the West.* But, much as I liked the book, I think he got the title backwards: it's more to the point to say that Glen Canyon is a "dam that stands like a story"—one of the deep myths that is the real scaffolding for everything that humans do. Those deep stories are tricky: we think that because we seem to be enacting them as our story, we are somehow their author. But in fact, they are stories being written about us, and they are stories about what we are actually doing, not just what we think we are doing, or hope we are doing.

The boatman on the river below the dam that day was Dave Wegner, principal architect of the flood of 1996. In 1982, Wegner, an ecologist, was hired by the Bureau of Reclamation to manage what sounded like a reasonably unthreatening new program: the Glen Canyon Environmental Studies. After twenty years of operation, the project was to study the effects of the dam on "existing river-related environments and recreational resources of Glen and Grand canyons," and to determine if there might be better ways "to operate the dam," for environmental and recreational needs, but still consistent with the dam's original purposes. The office, at that time, had no charge other than to "study the dam and its effects"; no impact statements were mandated, no deadlines set—just "study the effects of the dam."

The Bureau of Reclamation, which had had the project imposed on it as a result of a lawsuit brought by the Environmental Defense Fund, responded as though someone had thrown a dead cat through the door. Wegner was told by his superiors that he was "window dressing," a "token environmentalist"; that the less he accomplished, the better. A colleague in the Bureau told him that he had been chosen over an engineer because they were afraid an engineer might get something done. This kind of reaction is sometimes laid over deeper currents of fear, and support for this suspicion is provided by conservationist Dan Beard, who eventually gave the old guard at the Bureau a whole lot to think about when President Clinton made him Commissioner of Reclamation in 1992. "Wegner's superiors were scared to death of what he might do," Beard said. "They didn't even want him to list (his) office phone number."

Most of our conflicts over the Colorado River may stem from its reality as a construction zone, where a modestly scaled but energetic flow of water is in the process of removing a bulge from the earth's crust to construct a river. A river is not what it appears at first glance—a kind of natural storm sewer, carrying water off the land. A closer look at the way a river works indicates that the water, while unable to deny gravity's pull, creates and participates in many strategies to slow its own passage from the land. Where it flows off of steep land, the water picks up whatever it can carry—dirt, rocks, leaves, trees, animals seduced and drowned—and drops that load in front of itself as soon as it can, trying to meander, spread itself, disappear back into the land by supporting whatever plant life will grow up in its quiet places and backwaters. In its matured relationship with the land, the flow of water meanders through softly sloped valleys in great, slow, sweeping bends, depositing itself in pools and hiding out in wetlands—its departure inevitable but delayed as long as possible.

A river, seen thus, is not just a flow of water, but a whole set of strategies for interacting with whatever the water flows through. Ditches, waterworks, drainage canals, sheer canyons—those are not rivers. They are systems for water on its way to somewhere else. A river is water that already is somewhere. And a river is not just the water but everything that participates in its being there: the meanders the water makes by dropping its baggage in its own path, the floodplains whose water table it maintains, the pools it makes for the furtherance of the projects of beavers and farmers, and the workings of the beavers and farmers—all are part of, and joined by, the river.

But due to an upwarp in the North American crustal plate, the flow of water we call the Colorado River is a long way from being matured. It is a system for cutting and carrying earth in quantity, working with wind and airborne water to remove the upwarp called the Colorado Plateau, and build a river's kind of valley. By the time Anglo-American civilization reached it, it had already cut and conveyed so much earth out of the Plateau that, in its lower reaches below the canyons it has cut, it was running on a broad leveed platform of its own deposits above the surrounding desert region; it had pumped so much silt into the Sea of Cortez over the past five million years that it had run a dam all the way across it, cutting off the northern hundred miles or so of the sea, which dried under the desert sun and became the Salton Sink (now the Imperial Valley).

When we got there, the Colorado River was still in the chaotic state of all serious construction zones, as it will be for millions of years to come: running for part of its course in deep canyons as much as a mile below a high desert that it drains but does not water, and for another part of its course running above a low desert that it floods—when it has the water. A chameleon of a river, then, once out of its mountains and into the arid lands: a trickster river running either below or above the surrounding drylands, doing little for the land but eating at it, moving it around, conveying it to the sea.

The Colorado's changeable quality was enhanced by the fact that it was not nearly so large a river as it sometimes seemed. It only ran in a powerful flood for a few months each year, when the winter snowpack was melting up in the tributary region. Some years, a hellacious flood: In 1884, it came through the canyons at 300,000 cubic feet per second—enough to put water 10 feet deep on a football field every second. Many other summers it ran well above 100,000 cfs. Once the snow was gone in the mountains, it became a very modest flow, often well under 10,000 cfs for months at a time—except when thunderstorms up on the dry Plateau might bump it up to 40,000 or 50,000 cfs for an evening or a day. So it had gone for millions of years: a steep flow of water gnawing down into the ongoing uplift, trying to drop more in front of itself than it tore out—a situation similar to driving a car at full acceleration with the brakes set.

And the wind and the airborne water kept working on the walls cut by the flowing water, shaping the upper layers of the canyons to what we know today: a precipitous and vastly scaled region of beautiful desolation, a land without enough water shedding what little it gets quickly and casually off its steep slopes, and the rest of the time drying up and blowing away, or falling in on itself, while at the bottom of it all, in a green and brown strip, a flow of water and scatter of life tried to put together a river in a confined space.

That was the natural landscape into which the Anglo-Americans advanced, caught up in a movement variously called "Manifest Destiny," "Progress," and "Western Civilization." In the more general perspective of American history, this was a story of technologically reconstructing and rationalizing nature in the context of a set of economic and political ideals, a teleological tale in which all would eventually live happily ever after in a world rebuilt around human needs and desires. But as that destiny-driven story moved into the semi-arid Great Plains, and then into the driest parts of the West, it began to resonate with old stories from early religions, the story of turning a desert river into the desert, to turn the desert into a garden. "Come," said the people on the plains of Mesopotamia, "let us build ourselves a city and a tower whose top may reach unto heaven, and make a name for ourselves." Or it was, as American historian Donald Worster put it, "the myth of human redemption through irrigation technology."

I believe it serves accuracy to say that where Western Civilization met the westernmost arid West, "Manifest Destiny" broke through the limits of philosophy and ideology and became—never mind what the Constitution says—a state religion. The religion began with the belief that just the advent of American farmers onto those semi-arid and arid lands west of the 100th Meridian would suffice to turn the desert into a land of milk and honey. The incantations that "rain will follow the plow" or "rain will follow the trains" were offered up as "scientific facts." After thousands of true believers had dried up, burned out, or blown away on the Great Plains, the faith was still not questioned but modified to acknowledge the need for technological intervention, more toward the Protestant ethos of "God helps those who help themselves." Following the example of the Mormons, hardly a secular society, irrigation became the new gospel: turn the water into the desert to turn the desert into a garden, "and the desert shall bloom as a rose."

But who should do the work that God had somehow neglected? Many settlers didn't wait around for instructions but got right to it, organizing local ditch companies and moving the smaller, more manageable streams out onto their land. Others—God's truly chosen—played the capital game, creating large land and water developments onto which they lured settlers for a kind of indentured servitude. But parts of the West, like the Colorado River's vast and chaotic "construction zone," were too much of a challenge even for large capital ventures—as abortive efforts to open up the Salton Sink showed. Trying to develop the Colorado at the California end of the river (where the river ran above the land) was a little like trying to drink out of a fire hose. So prophets like William Smythe of California began to hold large "revivals" calling for intercession, not from God, but from the federal government. And in 1902, the prayers of the faithful were answered with the Newlands Act and the creation of the Bureau of Reclamation. This helps explain the Bureau's antipathy to the "imposition" of an environmental studies office. The Bureau of Redemption was not created to do science; it was created to do technological miracles. The Bureau might use science in constructing its miracles, but it didn't do science.

The incompatibility of science and religion was illustrated in the West when one strong, disciplined, and dedicated scientist took on the religion of irrigation and "Manifest Destiny." That was John Wesley Powell, who launched his career with the first exploration of the Colorado River and its canyons in 1869. He parlayed that trip into a career investment in a scientific approach to life in the West, eventually in public, and generally unsuccessful, opposition to the national religion. His dedication to the way of science and its application—the development of public policy based on the observation and experiencing of reality—led him in 1893 to Los Angeles, to attend William Smythe's "International Irrigation Congress." He knew how big the Colorado River and other rivers and streams in the West really were because he and his surveyors had measured them; he saw that the religious were deluding themselves into thinking there was enough water to spread over all the deserts of the West. So he tried to tell them what was scientifically accurate. He was booed off the stage. In place of Powell's science, the Bureau of Reclamation was created to use technology in the service of religion, and its technology has been magnificent. Which brings us back to the dam.

It's not the first time something like that has happened to the river in the canyons. A million years ago or so, volcanic activity along one of the cracks in the Plateau uplift threw a lava dam across the canyon at least as high as Glen Canyon, probably higher. It was not, however, so cleverly constructed as Glen Canyon; the lava dam just backed up the water until the water overflowed it and started cutting it down. Lava Falls is the remains of that dam. It may take longer for the river to turn Glen Canyon Dam into Concrete Falls— the Bureau of Reclamation estimates seven hundred years before the reservoir fills with silt and turns the dam into a muddy waterfall three times higher than Niagara. But it will happen, sooner or later, and the most interesting question with respect to that is whether, between now and then, we who built the dam will be telling the story of the dam as joke or tragedy or something in between.

When the diversion tunnels were closed on Glen Canyon Dam in 1963, the flow of water through the canyons was immediately affected. Before the dam, the river had been a warm, muddy flow with tremendous seasonal fluctuations—summer highs over 100,000 cfs, winter lows less than 10,000 cfs. After the dam, the river immediately became a clear flow of cold water, drawn from deep in the reservoir behind the dam, and with a much different pattern of fluctuations. Seasonal fluctuations effectively ceased, but the river in the canyons below the dam experienced daily fluctuations sometimes in excess of 30,000 cfs, from low flows as low as 1,000 cfs to flows of 31,500 cfs when the Bureau cranked open all the power-generating turbines in response to calls for "peaking power," electricity for Sunbelters.

This sudden change to a flow of cold, clear water had a major impact on the warm-water native fish of the Colorado: humpback and bonytail chubs; razorback, bluehead and flannelmouth suckers; the Colorado squawfish and the speckled dace. All those natives are now either officially endangered or considered for listing except for the bluehead sucker and the speckled dace, both of which hang out in lower canyons where sidestream inflows increase both the turbidity and temperature to something close to old-river standards. On the other hand, non-native cold-water species—primarily rainbow, brown, and cutthroat trout—have thrived, more so the closer one gets to the dam. The Glen Canyon stretch from Lees Ferry to the dam has, in fact, become a renowned trout fishery.

The dam also changed the aquatic food base—but not necessarily negatively. Before the dam, the food base in the canyons was mainly decomposing plant and animal life carried down from the whole drainage basin; after the dam, all of that was deposited in Lake Powell above the dam. The 16 miles of unprecedented clear water from immediately below the dam to the inflow of the muddy Paria River at Lees Ferry, however, now let enough sunlight into the water to grow an abundant crop of *Cladophora glomerata*, a stringy green algae that, in turn, feeds an array of diatomic life and aquatic invertebrates that become what some of the biologists call "the supermarket for the Grand Canyon."

The absence of the seasonal high, dirty flows of the past has probably had its greatest impact on the plant and animal and human communities on the sandbars and side beaches deposited by the silty pre-dam floods. The good news is that the general absence of beach-scouring flows higher than 30,000 cfs has been a boon for much of the plant life in the canyons, which grows much closer to the water than it could in the past. The bad news is that the exotic tamarisk, a water-loving shrub, now dominates the beach-plant system, undermining its diversity. Small animal life—amphibians, lizards, snails, birds, and small mammals, and at least one endangered bird, the southwestern willow flycatcher—thrive in the moderated environment.

But the plants are not enough to hold the beaches and sandbars against persistent erosion. Sediment to replace eroded material continues to come into the canyons from tributaries below Glen Canyon, like the Paria and Little Colorado rivers, but only about 20 million tons per year. Missing is the 66 million tons a year that came down the main stem before the dam—and missing also are the high and heavy flows that built up the bars and beaches. The overall trend has consequently been a shrinking of these sandbar-beaches, with the sand and silt not moving out of the canyons as on the old cut-and-carry express, but slumping down to the bottom of the channel. Projecting ahead, there will eventually be no place left for the endangered Kanab ambersnail, the little leopard frogs, the troublesome tamarisk and its nesting flycatcher, the archaeological and contemporary artifacts of indigenous Indian cultures, and the twenty-two thousand annual overnight campers from the multimillion-dollar canyon rafting and river-running industry.

That is the situation, then, in what remains of the natural environment below the dam. The challenge laid on Dave Wegner, and the small army of scientists whose work he helps fund and coordinate through the Glen Canyon Environmental Studies, is to figure out how the dam should be operated to maintain or enhance that culturally impacted natural environment for the short term—the seven centuries that the dam is expected to be operational.

In what Bureau nostalgitarians might consider a happier time, the presence of beaches and sandbars in the Grand Canyon below Glen Canyon Dam would not have been a worthy concern. They had dams planned for those canyons that would have put beaches and sandbars at the bottom of reservoirs. But Glen Canyon Dam stands on the border of a major change in the cultural environment; it marks the border, and in the opinion of many, including Dave Wegner, was instrumental in creating it. The dam stands at the end of the old religion, the breaking-up of the irrigation myth on the shoals of its inconsistencies. As Powell predicted, there was not enough water to do what was promised. An agrarian democracy did not spring up in the desert any more than it had in Massachusetts or Virginia, where water was taken for granted. Even the technology which the dam represents began to break down. The quantity of water "developed" was smaller than the prophets had foretold, and the quality of the water, as it was used over and over on the alkaloid and saline soils of the desert, became increasingly problematic. Historian Donald Worster:

> Reclamation … is a technological stunt that, as the experience of other irrigation societies shows, cannot be indefinitely sustained. As the irrigation system approaches maximum efficiency, as rivers get moved around with more and more thorough, consummate skill, the system begins to grow increasingly vulnerable, subject to a thousand ills that eventually bring about its decline. Despite all efforts to save the system, it breaks down here, then there, then everywhere.

All this began to come home to the Bureau, and the rest of the brotherhood of the water buffalo, when in 1968 they had to give up two big Grand Canyon power dams to get the Central Arizona Project through Congress. The other shoe fell in 1976 when some relatively low-level functionaries in President Carter's government simply scratched about half of the approved (but unfunded) water development projects along the Colorado River for their dismal cost-benefit analyses.

Handwriting was already on the wall in the mid-1950s, when Glen Canyon Dam was still just a proposal, part of the water buffaloes' effort to get for the Upper Colorado Basin the kind of federal commitment the Lower Basin had received through the first half of the twentieth century. This Colorado River Storage Project (CRSP) involved a number of "cash register" dams generating power that would create dollars to pay for a host of smaller water delivery projects, involving all manner of Rube Goldberg-like systems of aqueducts, pipes and tunnels and siphons to bring lots of water to—it seemed—every acre of land flat enough to be settled in the southern Rockies. Glen Canyon was the keystone "cash register," but as the vast scheme moved into the legislative process, attention focused on a smaller proposed dam in a valley on the edge of Dinosaur National Monument in far northwestern Colorado: Echo

Park Dam. The Sierra Club, under David Brower, and other national preservationist organizations chose that dam for their first real national challenge to the Bureau, and the theretofore unchallenged mission the Bureau was charged to carry out. They walked all over the Bureau, in large part because the Bureau was simply not used to having to defend its figures.

CRSP made it through Congress in 1956, minus the Echo Park Dam, and within a decade all of the remaining "cash register" dams were either built or under construction—Glen Canyon, Flaming Gorge on the Green River, Navajo on the San Juan, and the three dams of the Wayne Aspinall unit on the Gunnison. But it was not like the old days. Glen Canyon Dam began to back up water in 1963 and cracked slightly as the river began to lean into it. Nothing serious, but still ... Before the reservoir was full, the nation had: a) denied the two downriver Grand Canyon dams that would have alleviated all the pressure on Glen Canyon by essentially eliminating Grand Canyon river-running, and b) passed a National Environmental Policy Act that mandated federal analyses of impacts, thus pretty well precluding realization of the vision of water systems totally rationalized around human needs and desires. The "Carter hit list" red-lining most of the CRSP water delivery projects was never seriously challenged by Congress.

Bureau reaction to these setbacks was to preach the gospel a little louder. In the mid-1970s it began to roll the log for an upgrade of the power-generating facilities at Glen Canyon. The nonprofit Environmental Defense Fund (EDF) took the Bureau to court demanding an environmental impact statement (EIS) on the impact of power generation and fluctuating flows on the river in the canyons below the dam. The courts supported EDF. The water-buffalo brotherhood kicked in at that point, and got a rider attached to an appropriations bill prohibiting the funding of a Glen Canyon environmental impact statement. But there was no formal opposition to the creation of the Glen Canyon Environmental Studies office as a compromise, just the informal flak that Wegner had to put up with in the ranks.

Wegner kept his cool: he spread around what money he could garner to the scientists working on Grand Canyon studies, and he built networks of support for good river science within and outside the Bureau. An important supporter was Democratic Representative George Miller of California. Miller badly wanted an EIS to be done on the impact of the dam on the Grand Canyon region, and in a semi-legendary shouting match with Bureau officials right on the river during a raft trip, he promised that if the Bureau didn't do that EIS, he would introduce legislation to have Congress do it. It was a successful threat: in 1989 Interior Secretary Manuel Lujan administratively ordered a Glen Canyon EIS, to be prepared by Wegner's team. That was given more priority when Congress passed the Grand Canyon Protection Act in 1992.

The EIS was completed in March 1995. "You can go around the world," said Dan Beard, Bureau of Reclamation commissioner from 1992 to 1995, who now works for National Audubon Society, "and no place will you find such a detailed study of the downstream impacts of a dam." Beard should know. In 1993 President Clinton appointed him—George Miller's former staffer—as commissioner of the Bureau of Reclamation, and Beard wasted no time in "standing up and saying what most people in the Bureau knew we had to do." The Bureau had to "become an environmental agency," Beard said, "moving away from dam-building and into water-resource management." Under his two-and-a-half years of leadership, the Bureau decentralized the management impetus from top-down Washington bureaucracy to an emphasis on field-level operation. New hires are as likely to be biologists and ecologists as engineers, although there are not that many new hires: the organization has downsized by about 25 percent. It would be naive to think that the old-time religion has simply disappeared, and isn't just lying low in pockets and enclaves, hoping for better times.

Meanwhile, there's the flood to consider—and the Bureau's participation in that. In a historical context, what happened last March wasn't really a flood by old Colorado River standards. The official designation was "a habitat-building test flow" since most of the problems in the river below the dam come down to the problem of erosion. Some of the river scientists hypothesized that the high daily fluctuations in power-generating releases from the dam were a major factor. As a result, the preferred management alternative proposed in the EIS restricts the daily fluctuations between low flow and high flow to 8,000 cfs or less, depending on total monthly flows. While the quantity of electricity generated will not change, adhering to the preferred low-fluctuation alternative will cost the Bureau a full third of its marketable power capacity, mostly because it will no longer be able to run its turbines flat out when power is most needed and when prices are highest.

That is a significant cost for a strategy that might not work very well anyway. Following passage of the Grand Canyon Protection Act, the Bureau began experimenting with reduced fluctuations, and has already discovered that it doesn't seem to make as much difference in erosion as everyone had hoped it would. "We're learning that erosion in steep narrow canyons can't really be stopped by regulating the flow of water in the canyon," said Utah State University hydrologist Jack Schmidt, who has been studying the canyon sandbars since 1985. Down in Glen Canyon, Wegner pointed out how even the gentle slapping against the beaches of bow waves created by the big river rafts caused river sand and silt to slump into the water.

So what might work instead? The scientists hypothesized that a sustained "floodflow" (a flow in excess of the 33,200 cfs that can go through the power plant) might help to stir that sand and silt off the bottom of the main channel and get it up onto the beaches and bars again. The "flood of 1996," then, was a "habitat-building test flow" of around 45,000 cfs—what could pass through the power plant plus the four big river-outlet tubes at the base of the dam. If it could redeposit the sand and silt that had slipped to the bottom of the river channel onto the bars and beaches, it would help achieve an array of other objectives: restoring the backwater breeding pools (below the bars) needed by the endangered native fishes, preserving or restoring the camping beaches, protecting cultural artifacts on the beaches, and watering the mesquite, acacia, and other native vegetation in the high-water zone.

Two months after the flood, Wegner says he's encouraged: A lot of sand and silt—especially from two large flash-flood deposits at the mouths of the Paria and Little Colorado rivers—was definitely stirred up and redeposited on beaches. He notes, however, that they won't know for months how stable the new deposits are. Or whether they will help the endangered warm-water fish species that need warm backwater pools for breeding. The test flow was not large enough to do some things they'd hoped it might: it did not wash out any of the exotic tamarisk that is edging out a lot of the native diversity, and it was not large enough to wash any of the non-native fish that are not flood-adapted out of the canyons. On the other hand, it also did not do any significant damage to the non-native trout fishery which is popular with fishers, and it did not disrupt the "algae factory" that feeds the canyon's life. But all those very explicit scientific objectives notwithstanding, the flood of 1996 achieved something else that may be very important in the unfolding story of our involvement with the river—and of the dam that stands in the middle of the story: for a change, virtually everyone at the dam and below was doing science, rather than just using science to do religion.

For the week of the flood—and for weeks, even months before and after—more than a hundred and fifty hydrologists, biologists, geologists, and other earth scientists convened to spread out through the 250 miles of the Grand Canyon below the dam in ten base camps, interconnected by satellite links and supplied by helicopter. More scientists on rafts rode the wave of the flood through the canyons. The last I saw of Wegner, he was leading a class of Northern Arizona University graduate students down into the canyon to help with the sampling and measuring that was going on everywhere. Not only had ten fish been fitted with radio transmitters to see how they negotiated the flood, ten rocks had been fitted with radio transmitters to see how far the water might roll them.

According to one scientist, "It was the hydrological event of the century." "It was a media circus," another said. But what it might really have been, in the larger historical picture, was a changing of the guard, at least on that part of the river: science replacing the oldtime religion as the management imperative. And everyone, including the Bureau of Reclamation managers of the dam, seemed to be responding with unfaked interest. Technology was very much there, but serving science rather than religion, from the radio transmitters in the rocks all the way up to that largest technological device of all: the dam.

*July 22, 1996*

# A Tale of Two Rivers: The Desert Empire and the Mountain

## George Sibley

*"We've done our best and worst and a lot of inattentive average work in settling this our Western place."*

—Colorado Justice Greg Hobbs,
  at Bishop's Lodge 1997

*"It would be quite a remote period before (the Upper Colorado Basin) would be developed—fifty or one hundred or possibly two hundred years."*

—Delph Carpenter, testifying in 1925
  on the Boulder Canyon Project Act Bill

**W**e are so easily sidetracked, I thought, when the Sierra Club fired its shot across the bow of the western water establishment last November. We build big impressive systems, developing ideas for transportation, communications, food production, impounding water behind huge dams, what have you. Then, just when we are to the point where a system is in place but needs a lot of fine-tuning and maintenance, either we all get bored and forgetful, or some faction that didn't like the system from the start lures us away, and we abandon what has been built and go charging off after some new idea.

Take, for example, the proposal to drain Lake Powell behind Glen Canyon Dam. It seems serious enough. The Sierra Club is working with a Salt Lake City organization, the Glen Canyon Institute, to formulate and carry out a thirty-month citizens' study as "the first step in the ultimate draining of Lake Powell, the restoration of Glen Canyon, and the preservation of the Grand Canyon and the Sea of

Cortez estuaries." In announcing the board's resolution last November, Sierra Club President Adam Werbach said, "It's the job of the Sierra Club to show what being green really means, and it takes broad visionary strokes. This is that type of stroke."

I'm reminded of the old engineering school adage: "When you're up to your ass in alligators, it's hard to remember that you set out to drain the swamp." Glen Canyon looms so large in our minds and emotions that it almost obliterates the rest of the Colorado River. Nevertheless, it is important to remember that draining Lake Powell is just alligator mitigation—an attempt to deal with a bunch of relatively small problems. It may be a good idea, and it may be a way of switching one perceived mess for another mess while increasing the cultural friction that generates memberships.

Whether the draining happens or not, it should not be done all in a rush, out of revenge or out of an attempt to solve problems that loom large to us because we aren't thinking about the larger ones behind them. We should start by recognizing the Glen Canyon Dam is a physical manifestation of an historic agreement—the Colorado River Compact—among the seven states that make up the Colorado River basin. And we should not assume that the compact that gave rise to Glen Canyon Dam is necessarily in conflict with what many of us see as the hopeful, progressive ideas that crystallized in the 1960s, just as the water was rising behind the dam. Before we go tearing away at the dam and the compact, we should look at their roots. We may still decide to demolish both, but at least then we will know what we are doing, and not be surprised by the consequences of our act.

In November 1922, representatives from seven western states met at a resort called Bishop's Lodge near Santa Fe, New Mexico, to complete an interstate treaty determining how the waters of the Colorado River basin would be divided among those states. The Colorado River Compact divided the water by splitting the river. It gave half of the river and half of the water to the four states along the Upper Colorado River (Colorado, New Mexico, Utah, and Wyoming), and half to the three states along the Lower Colorado River (Arizona, California, and Nevada).

Some treaties—especially the ones that don't work—are imposed arbitrarily on a landscape and a people. The Colorado River Compact falls into a happier category. It fits the landscape, at least, like a glove.

The ancestral Colorado River rose along with the "New Rockies" out of the slow grind and crush of the North American plates in the Laramide Orogeny millions of years ago. Like the present-day streams draining the west slopes of the Wasatch Mountains in Utah, the ancestral Colorado only flowed out into the basin-and-range region west of the Rockies. There it ended in a large lake much like today's Great Salt Lake somewhere in what we call southeastern Utah and northern Arizona, blocked there by the northern edge of the Colorado Plateau—an immense uplift created by the buckling of tectonic plates.

In the same geologic time, another river—ancestor to today's Lower Colorado River—was draining the southern slope of that uplifting plateau, running through subtropical deserts down into the tectonic crack now called the Gulf of California, or Gulf of Cortez. That southern river gradually ate back into the plateau until, around 5.5 million years ago, it eroded a channel through the plateau and "captured" the terminal lake containing the flow of the Upper Colorado River.

At that point, the two rivers began the geological labors associated with becoming a single river system by removing the convex hump of the plateau in their middle section. Today, that monumental task is well under way, as the canyons of the Colorado River attest. A massive amount of the plateau has been reduced to debris and conveyed down to the Gulf of California. The emerging river has cut a mile down into the plateau, while wind and water have been taking off layers from the top and widening the gaps between the many canyons' rims. This construction process has been aided several times this past million years by immense glacial runoffs. If this were to continue long enough, the Grand Canyon and the plateau would eventually disappear. But in recent time the river has been modest in size, and the energy with which it saws at the plateau has slowed. There's a certain amount of mess involved with such a project, and that dirt and rock have all been moved downstream on what might best be described as a big, seasonally erratic conveyor belt below the Plateau canyons.

As much as the river has done thus far, it is still accurate to describe the Colorado as two rivers working diligently in a vast and desolately beautiful construction zone to become one. There are still two river basins. The upper section is a temperate zone mountain-and-valley river we call the Upper Basin. The lower section, which emerges from the canyons of the Colorado Plateau and which we call the Lower Basin, is a subtropical desert river, "an American Nile."

That was also the situation when a swarming population of Europeans invaded the region surrounding the Colorado. They were not the first humans in the western reaches of the continent, but they came in unprecedented numbers—and with culture, custom, and technology unprecedented in such migrations. Although they all called themselves "Americans," they were divided in economically brutal and often overtly violent conflict over the kind of a West they wanted to build.

Following the relatively recent abandonment of Frederick Jackson Turner's frontier thesis, historians have been trying to sort out what happened west of the Mississippi in the eighteenth and nineteenth centuries. For the Colorado River basin, it makes most sense to see the American advent as a usually civil war (I am not counting the conquest of the Native American peoples here) between a mass of people successfully advancing a revolution, or a pro-development agenda, and a kaleidoscopically changing coalition attempting to assemble a counter-revolution around rural or agrarian ideas.

The revolution being advanced was the Industrial Revolution. It was a coming-together of economic ideas (corporate capitalism and individualism), the primacy of property rights, technological advances (steam power followed by electrical power and advances in applied chemistry and metallurgy), and new socio-political structures (bureaucracies and industrial cities).

Because of the twin barriers of geography and aridity, this attempt at industrial development, and the opposing attempt to craft a non-industrial way of life, came last to the Colorado River region. For example, my adopted town of Gunnison, Colorado, on one of the Upper Colorado River's main tributaries, was not settled until the 1880s; the most recent town in our valley, the industrial ski village of Mount Crested Butte, was not incorporated until 1974. Initially, at least, it went even slower in the desert regions of the Lower Colorado River. Hit-and-run industrial mining towns came and went, and stable agricultural settlements were precarious along the lower Colorado River, where irrigating was like trying to drink out of a fire hose that either ran in huge bursts or put out only a muddy trickle.

In my Upper River valley, the valley of the Gunnison River in western Colorado, both the revolutionaries and the counter-revolutionaries arrived at the same time. A company of relatively serious agrarians came into the valley in the late 1870s, just as gold and silver were discovered up the valley above the subsequent mining camps of Crested Butte, Irwin, and Gothic. The agrarians—high-minded, sober, religious but not driven by religion—settled "West Gunnison," while, about four blocks to the east, main-street "Gunnison" grew as a standard mining-region railhead. Gunnison and West Gunnison soon enough grew over and through each other; what was unusual was having the dichotomy so distinct at the start. In most of the start-up places of the Colorado River region, the two cultural strains mixed from the start in tension and contention. Knots of agrarians and socialists and just-folk who lacked the genes for accumulation shared mud streets and raw-wood walls with the mob of fortune-hunters wanting only to get in on a "ground floor" in time to high-grade it, get rich, and move on. For many, it would have been hard to say which side of the war one came down on, so tangled is the human heart. As it is hard to say today.

Although the West, even today, looks rural and downhome in places, it's a mirage. We may pine now for the Old West and its simpler life, but we fool ourselves. As early as 1890, the West was not "agrarian." There were cows and crops in fields, and farmhouses and villages with trees along the streets. But already the farmers were industrial worker bees in the same job-for-wage sense as the miners upvalley, producing raw materials to send out on city-bound trains that brought back manufactured goods—with everything, including their debt, bought and sold at the cities' prices.

The industrial revolutionaries, and the counter-revolutionaries, whom we can roughly lump together as agrarians, brought into the West very different cultural baggage. But the rules were the same for everyone. The basic law for the distribution of land, water, and natural resources of material value was "first come, first served." And as it became clear that there was a lot less water than land, the distribution of rights to water became pivotal.

Since water cannot be surveyed and corner-staked like land, its appropriation depended on "beneficial use"—anything a human wanted to do with a dollop of water so long as it involved diverting it out of the stream. "Consumptive beneficial use" used up the water.

What you "beneficially consumed" was yours—so long as you kept using it; stop using it and you lost it. To use it better and thereby conserve it, or to use it instream was not "beneficial" and you lost your claim to it. It is hard to imagine a more destructive bias. John Wesley Powell—the first counter-revolutionary to infiltrate the developers' power structure, circa 1890—argued vigorously against the separation of water from the land. But the developers successfully resisted. To cite one terrible example, in the mining regions they took the water out of the streams and turned it against the earth, using high-pressure hydraulics to reduce whole hills to gravel to get out the gold.

As the West filled, however, and ever larger ditches led ever more water ever farther from its streams of origin, the consequences of appropriation and privatization grew more complex and alarming. So alarming that some developers were forced to try to rein in their fellows.

Take the Owens Valley incident. In 1902, Congress had created the Bureau of Reclamation, ostensibly to get down on the ground with small farmers and help bring the agrarian dream into being. But the Bureau was, from the first, full of an idealistic breed called American Progressives, for whom "the greatest good for the greatest number" was an intuitive belief. It was also full of engineers who were captivated by visions of formerly unimaginable things that new construction materials and financial resources were making possible. But for a while—five years, to be precise—the Bureau did what its enabling legislation said it was supposed to: it worked on irrigation projects that were a little too ambitious for a group of local farmers.

One of the first projects the Bureau explored was an irrigation development in the Owens River Valley, a small, closed basin on the east side of the California Sierras. But Los Angeles was also looking at that valley. It was 240 miles away and downhill all the way.

The movie *Chinatown* missed the point of this drama. It wasn't the relatively quiet fuss involving urban corruption and incest that the movie portrayed. This was the biggest flare-up in America's frontier war since Shay's Rebellion. And when President Theodore Roosevelt stepped in, he resolved it in favor of the industrial revolutionaries and their urban vision in Southern California. He acknowledged some validity to the plaints of "a few" Owens Valley farmers, and their desire for a small-scale irrigation system, but he came down on the side of "the infinitely greater interest to be served by putting the water in Los Angeles."

"There it is," Los Angeles Water and Power manager William Mulholland had said, in dedicating the Owens Valley Aqueduct, "take it." And elsewhere in the Colorado River region, developers and agrarians alike shuddered. Powerful as the river was, it was clearly not so big as the dreams coalescing around it. It looked as if Los Angeles and other California dreamers would not just "take it," but would take it all. And the law of the land and river would let them, thanks to legal precedents being set elsewhere in the West at about the same time.

The most serious threat to the non-California part of the Colorado River basin was the Laramie River case between Colorado and Wyoming. Both states distributed their water through Prior Appropriation and beneficial use; in other words, first come-first served, and get it out of the stream or it's not yours. In its decision, the U.S. Supreme Court treated the Laramie as though it were a single legal river, even though it crossed state lines. Whichever appropriator in whichever state got to the water first would own the water. If Wyoming irrigators diverted the entire river first, it was theirs. It was the handwriting on the wall: if the six other states in the Colorado River region wanted a share of the river's water, then they had better negotiate some "equitable apportionment" before Southern California spread the whole river out to dry in its unlimited desert reaches.

They were encouraged to move in that direction by a case that occurred outside the Colorado Basin, when Kansas sued Colorado over the diminishing flow of the Arkansas River. The Supreme Court refused to choose between the appropriations laws of Colorado (all legal uses had to be out-of-stream) and the riparian laws of Kansas (only in-stream uses were legal, the common law in humid regions). Instead it ordered the states to negotiate an "equitable apportionment" of the river's waters between the two states.

That decision indicated a possible solution to the threat from California: an interstate agreement to limit California's ability to consume the entire river.

Which brings us, finally, to the Colorado River Compact: not, as has been said more than once this year in commemorating it, at "the beginning of the development of the Colorado River," but at the beginning of the end of the Industrial Revolution's unchallenged conquest of the West. It was the compact that first put up a barrier to the intense development of the entire West. It is not so simple as saying that a line was drawn, with the industrial revolutionaries on one side and the agrarians on the other. If anything, it was one set of industrial revolutionaries, mostly but not entirely in the Upper Basin, who had not yet had their main chance at riches, drawing a line against their down-river competitors. The Upper Basin competitors couldn't win if they played by the dominant rules, so, almost against their wills, they had to change the rules. They had to modify the Doctrine of Prior Appropriations. They had to say that "take it" wasn't always the best rule for the West. It must have been a hard swallow, but they got it down.

Their leader was Delph Carpenter, a Colorado lawyer involved in the slow passage—from 1911 to 1922—of *Colorado vs. Wyoming* (the Laramie River case) through the courts. He was probably one of those whose heart was torn by the American Industrial Revolution; he was a native son of Greeley, Colorado, which had begun as an intelligent agrarian community. But as it grew, Greeley gave in to the industrialization of agriculture imposed by the transportation and finance networks overlaid on the West.

It was Carpenter who suggested, to a conference of governors, that the seven states of the Colorado Basin negotiate an interstate treaty for "equitable apportionment" of the Colorado River. He pointed out to California's governor that this was even in California's interest. California was relatively rich and powerful, but it still needed outside capital. If California wanted federal funding for the massive structures necessary to control the Lower Colorado River, it would have to make a deal with the other states in the basin. Besides, he predicted, even the biggest Upper Basin state, Colorado, would never be able to consume more than 5 percent of the river's water. And since California was downstream of all the Upper Basin states, it would inevitably get their water.

The governors cautiously agreed to discuss a treaty, and each appointed a commissioner to represent it. Secretary of Commerce Herbert Hoover represented the United States, chairing what came to be known as the Compact Commission. The first meeting was held in Washington, D.C., in January 1922, with subsequent meetings in Phoenix, Los Angeles, Salt Lake City, Grand Junction (Colorado), Denver, Cheyenne, and, finally, Santa Fe. The future of much of the river might have been predicted from the locations of those meetings—only the Grand Junction meeting was in the river's natural basin. The rest took place in Colorado River basin states, but outside of the river's watershed.

The meetings took place in what Carpenter called "semi-executive session," with each commissioner entitled to one legal or engineering advisor. The press was excluded. The commission began with fruitless efforts to divide the river based on the amount of irrigable land. But these power-suited guys were not gathering in the emerging cities of the West to dicker over farmland, and that effort went nowhere.

The breakthrough came from Carpenter, who suggested something unprecedented: look to the natural geography of the region, and divide the water between the two obvious and distinct "regions of settlement" above and below the canyons. Chairman Hoover agreed, and he drafted a memo worth quoting from:

> The drainage area falls into two basins naturally, from a geographical, hydrographical, and an economic point of view. They (the two basins) are separated by over 500 miles of barren canyon, which serves as the neck of the funnel, into which the drainage area comprised in the Upper Basin pours its waters, and these waters again spread over the lands of the Lower Basin ... The climate of the two basins is different; that of the Upper Basin being, generally speaking, temperate, while that of the Lower Basin ranges from semitropical to tropical. The growing seasons, the crops, and the quantity of water consumed per acre are therefore different.

Carpenter's "broad visionary stroke" was what the commission agreed upon. The Upper Basin states (Colorado, New Mexico, Utah, and Wyoming) and the Lower Basin states (Arizona, California, and Nevada) would each be entitled to consumptive use of no more than half of the river's water; the states in each basin would then allocate their half of the water among themselves.

California asked for some more definite quantity of water to work with than "half the river," so an effort was made to quantify the amount. Around the turn of the century the United States Geological Survey (USGS) had begun measuring the river's flow near the Lee's Ferry access in northeastern Arizona, just above its descent into the Grand Canyon, but below most of the river's major tributaries. The USGS "long-term" measurements (two decades) indicated that the river was averaging 17 million to 18 million acre-feet of water a year at Lee's Ferry. So the Commission based the division on 15 million acre-feet, leaving what appeared to be a healthy margin for low-flow years and other demands (i.e., from Mexico, which held the bottom 90 miles of the river and which they knew might eventually obtain a claim on the river). The Upper Basin was thus charged with assuring that an average of 7.5 million acre-feet flowed past the Lee's Ferry gauge every year.

It was also necessary to take other legitimate but complicating claims into account. For example, they acknowledged the possibility of future claims from the Indian nations—since the Supreme Court had already declared in 1908 (*Winters vs. United States*) that the reservation of lands for the "civilizing" of the Indians implied the reservation of sufficient water to accomplish that purpose.

At the eighth meeting of the Commission in Santa Fe in November 1922, six states signed the compact. The Upper Basin states were happy because Los Angeles, the thousand-pound gorilla, had been caged by the compact. But the compact put Arizona and Nevada in with the gorilla. Nevada was little more than a hangover from mining booms. Arizona, harboring its own California dreams, found itself in the cage with the gorilla and refused to sign something that might let Southern California appropriate all of the Lower Colorado River share. California and the Bureau were eager to begin reconstructing the river, so, to get around Arizona's boycott, California got a rider added to the Boulder Canyon Project Act (Hoover Dam was initially called Boulder Dam) that finally passed Congress in 1928, saying that six out of seven states were enough to make the Compact binding. In return, California had to agree to limit its claim on the Lower River's 7.5 million acre-feet to 4.4 MAF (with 2.8 MAF for Arizona, and 0.3 MAF for Nevada). More than half of the Lower River for California—but less than all of it.

With the Boulder Canyon Project through Congress, the Bureau of Reclamation and Southern California's Metropolitan Water District began their great works on the river. There is certainly more to be said about the development of the Lower River these past seventy-five years, but I'm not going to say it here. The story of the Desert Empire and its plumbing system has dominated past discourse over the river, and would, if we let it, tie us up in the details of water development.

So at the seventy-fifth anniversary of the Compact, we will practice "cultural triage": we will concede the Lower River to the Industrial Revolution, to those who would turn everything into cities, factories, and high density, and regroup around the other river, the Upper Colorado River, and its role in the ongoing saga of the fragile, incipient, but increasingly necessary counter-revolution.

> *While this America settles in the mould of its vulgarity,*
> *    heavily thickening to empire,*
> *And protest, only a bubble in the molten mass, pops and sighs*
> *    out, and the mass hardens,*
> *I sadly smiling remember that the flower fades to make fruit,*
> *    the fruit rots to make earth ...*
> *But for my children, I would have them keep their distance*
> *    from the thickening center; corruption*
> *Never has been compulsory, when the cities lie at the monster's*
> *    feet there are left the mountains.*

— Robinson Jeffers, *"Shine, Perishing Republic"*

                    The Colorado River below the canyons has been a recognizable kind of landscape for five or six thousand years now, going back to the Nile and Euphrates. In a desert region with a river running through it, you can add water to sunblasted earth, stir—and voila! Food in unprecedented quantities—food enough to supply an army of accountants and managers and soldiers to protect the farmers, keep the neighbors in line and keep the society organized—civilization, in short.

But an inland mountain river, like the Colorado above the canyons, was different. These kinds of places have always been home to those on the fringe of civilization: the Scots of the British Isles, the Israelites in the desert, the Appalachian people in their "hollows." At once spectacular and intimate, mountain valleys like those through which the secondary and tertiary streams of the Upper Colorado flow seem made to fit the Jeffersonian dream. But his is not an easy dream. Long winters made general agriculture possible only up to around 6,500 feet altitude; hay and grass farming was possible above that to about 8,500 feet. Higher yet, it was pasturage only—or urban-industrial sports like mineral mining, timber mining, and neo-Paleolithic indulgences like hunting, fishing, and playing around outdoors.

Moreover, the counter-revolutionaries in search of a rural way of life retreated into the mountain valleys after 1880 to find the spreading networks of the Big Business-Big Government industrial juggernaut already in place. There were cut-and-run factories for mining and rough-milling everything from gold to grass to trees, railroads to haul it all off to the city for the real value-added work, and by the early 1900s great blocks of undistributed land put into forest preserves by Roosevelt and Gifford Pinchot and—so it appeared from down on the ground—held for development by corporations like Weyerhaeuser, that could work on an urban-industrial scale.

With some exceptions, the Upper Basin slumbered from the compact signing in 1922 through the Great Depression. Roosevelt's New Deal barely touched the Upper Basin, and even World War II bypassed it. Then in 1948, the four Upper Basin states finally met to divvy up their half of the Colorado River. The Bureau of Reclamation was pushing them to get going on river development; inflated with hubristic momentum after the conquest of the Lower Colorado and the Columbia, the Bureau had hit the ground running in 1946 with a Colorado River report. Subtitled "A Natural Menace Becomes a National Resource," it proposed 134 water developments for the Colorado River—one hundred of them for the Upper River.

A couple of things were different, however. A treaty during World War II had ceded 1.5 MAF a year of water to Mexico. More ominously, the river had been running less water than it was "committed to" by the compact. In 1934, it had dropped below 10 MAF, and the best light the Bureau could put on the four-decade average was somewhere between 15 and 16 MAF. Other estimates put the average at less than 14 MAF, and a four-century tree-ring study has since put the average at around 13.9 MAF a year.  In the first major acknowledgment of reality, the Upper Basin states decided not to divide up the 7.5 MAF the compact "gave" them. After giving the northeastern corner of Arizona 50,000 acre-feet, they allotted themselves the following percentages of whatever water precipitation the Lower Basin and Mexico made available: Colorado, 51.75 percent; New Mexico, 11.25 percent; Utah, 23 percent; Wyoming, 14 percent.

Only a few months after the Upper Colorado River Compact was signed, the Bureau put the "Colorado River Storage Project and Participating Projects" proposal on the table. CRSP was the Bureau's bid to outdo its Lower Basin Boulder Canyon Project: an integrated set of dozens of large and small water projects to develop every acre of irrigable land in the Upper River region, and to water all the growing cities in the Upper Basin states outside the natural basin. (The Upper Basin itself, as distinct from the Upper Basin states, lacks large cities.) These projects were all to be paid for by power revenues from "cash register dams," built for both storage and power generation on the main tributaries of the Upper River: Flaming Gorge Dam on the Green River, Echo Park Dam below the junction of the Green and Yampa rivers, two Curecanti Dams on the Gunnison (now the three dams of the Aspinall Unit), and the keystone of the whole project, Glen Canyon Dam just above the Lee's Ferry division point—the Upper River's equivalent of Hoover Dam.

At that point in the evolution of the American West, the cultural environment in the Upper River basin was California dreaming. An Upper River water establishment was in place: a set of Los Angeles clones—Denver, Albuquerque-Santa Fe, Salt Lake City—had water boards ready to invest heavily in out-of-basin diversions, and every watershed had its "water conservancy district" dedicated to conserving water by getting it out of local streams before someone lower down got it first. The Upper River water establishment wanted what the Lower River had; it had just needed more time to get there.

The Upper Basin champion who emerged in the 1950s and 1960s to implement the Upper Basin's desires was Colorado Representative Wayne Aspinall, a Grand Junction schoolteacher who learned the Washington system and worked his way—as honestly and capably as is possible in that power center—into the chairmanship of the House Interior Committee, which oversaw all Department of Interior activities. For two decades, Aspinall made sure that nobody got anything that didn't also involve something for the Upper River—first, passage of a Colorado River Storage Project Act (CRSP, 1956), then the funding on the big dams and larger diversion projects and planning work on the vast array of little Rube Goldberg-like water diversion projects.

But it was evident from the first introduction of a CRSP bill that the cultural environment was on the verge of a "climate change," at least at the national level. A coalition led by David Brower of the Sierra Club drew a hard line at the Echo Park Dam in the first CRSP bill, which was to flood 63 miles of beautiful valley and canyon country along the Green River and 44 miles on the Yampa. This coalition mounted the first effective national assault on the pieties of western development. The Bureau—accustomed to trumping John Muir-type aesthetic appeals with statistical cost-benefit analyses demonstrating "the greatest good for the greatest number"—now found itself up against opponents who knew how to get the public's ear and eye, and who had learned how to expose its blue-sky assumptions about costs and benefits. Brower's frontal assault on the Bureau's cobbled figures for Echo Park, coupled with Wallace Stegner's beautiful Echo Park coffee-table book, the first great piece of environmental propaganda, sent the CRSP back to the drawing boards without Echo Park.

Aspinall was eventually able to pass a CRSP bill, but it took seven years—and he had to do it in spite of the Bureau, which not even the big-man arrogance of its chief, Floyd Dominy, could restore to the confident impetus it had before being sliced and diced by Brower in the Echo Park hearings.

It is worth noting that the western water establishment split over the CRSP. California liked using that million acre-feet of "surplus water" from the Upper River, and rather than giving the Upper River support in the spirit of the Compact, "the Desert Empire" joined Brower and company in trying to eliminate the CRSP. To get Echo Park Dam out of the CRSP bill, the preservationists had to go along with the big dam in the little-known Glen Canyon. Brower—who is Dominy's equal in everything, including ego—has always taken personal responsibility for that "loss" on himself; and since Brower is again a force in the Sierra Club, as a board member, this history probably figures in the current proposal to drain Lake Powell.

The great "cash register dams" of the CRSP got built in the 1960s: Flaming Gorge on the upper Green, three dams in the Aspinall unit on the Gunnison—and Glen Canyon. A number of the "Participating Projects" also got built: the San Juan-Chama out-of-basin diversion into Albuquerque, the Central Utah Project out of the Green Basin into the Wasatch Front, and some more modest in-basin irrigation projects.

The construction of those "big pieces" of the CRSP concluded an era. As the big lake behind Glen Canyon began to fill in 1963, the Upper River region itself began filling up with an unusually concentrated and focused cast of counter-revolutionaries. The same old developers were still there—miners looking for the overlooked ore body, forest products companies looking for the last old-growth, and land speculators feeding on the tourism boom and anticipating the vacation-home rush. But for this moment, there were more people arriving in flight from the empire than advancing its interests—and they were coming with a "last stand" attitude. They were a breed that the industrial revolutionaries and agrarian counter-revolutionaries alike would be calling "hippie environmentalists" by 1970, although many of them were serious middle-aged and elderly people, troubled by the course of the urban-industrial empire.

At the same time, new laws and court decisions were putting their ideals on a more even footing with urban-industrial money. Congress passed the first endangered species legislation in 1966, modifying and strengthening it in 1969 and 1973. This has turned a number of scarcely noticed (because scarce) fishes and birds into major obstacles to traditional water developments. The National Environmental Policy Act followed in 1969, with the creation in 1970 of the Environmental Protection Agency. The national Clean Water Act came in 1972, and that same year Congress passed the Colorado River Salinity Act to answer Mexican complaints about the deteriorating quality of water in the Basin.

The change also came from within the Upper Basin states themselves. In 1973, the Colorado Legislature enlarged the concept of "beneficial use" in a powerful way, passing the first "Instream Flow Appropriations" law. This law, incredibly for a western state, empowered the Colorado Water Conservation Board (a state agency) to "appropriate minimum stream flows or natural lake levels ... to preserve the natural environment to a reasonable degree." The strange notion that water might be beneficially used in the river is still being worked out down on the ground in the Upper River Basin. Some of its impetus is biocentric altruism, but it also reflects a growing economic shift away from the out-of-stream consumptive industrial and ag-industrial occupations to in-stream recreation-industrial activities—fishing, white-water boating, and other economic uses that need the flowing water that incidentally benefits natural systems. Utah and Wyoming have since passed similar instream laws.

Colorado also pioneered, in 1974, some fairly radical land-use legislation, which gave county-level governments unprecedented authority to demand adequate impact mitigation from the developers of everything from subdivisions to major industrial projects. It was clear that a new age was dawning when these "1041 powers" (from Colorado House Bill 1041, 1974) were used by the Eagle County commissioners to stop a water diversion to Denver suburbs on the Front Range.

So, by the time the inland sea behind Glen Canyon Dam was full, the Upper River had become America's first solid base for an effective down-on-the-ground alternative to the Industrial Revolution. The water establishment was still dominant, but it was being eroded from above as well as below. In 1976, just two years after Wayne Aspinall lost his congressional seat, President Carter issued a "hit list" of western water projects that shut down funding for nearly all remaining CRSP projects. And in 1990, the EPA just said no to the Denver metropolitan region's Two Forks Project for storing water diverted from the Upper Colorado River Basin.

So the mountain-river Upper Basin region today has gained some federal protection from the L.A.-like cities outside its watershed, but within the Upper Basin states. Added to those environmental laws is the compact itself and Lake Powell—an inland sea that holds close to twice the annual flow of the river, and that can meet the demands of the Lower Basin through even a lengthy series of dry years. Those walls provide more breathing room than the counter-revolution has ever had in America.

At the 75-year mark, it is time to ask if the compact has been— and still is—useful. To some, it looks merely naive. The "river's joke"—an average flow well below the amount of water apportioned in the compact—was a bad enough mistake. There was also no mention of system losses—-the evaporation of up to six feet of water a year from desert reservoirs, the use of water by natural riparian systems, the leakage through the "solid" rock of Glen Canyon, etc. This turns out to be a healthy tax: at least 2.2 MAF, 15 percent of the river's total flow, according to published Bureau figures, and, according to other organizations, so much more than that one wonders how any water ever gets to California. And there was no mention in the compact of what happens to the quality of water when it is run over the alkaloid soils of arid lands again and again.

The California dreamers of the Lower Colorado River do not want to talk about these things, preferring instead to fall back on the myth of "surplus water" so vaguely mentioned in the compact. California admits that it has been using unappropriated water that belongs to the Upper River—but only the million acre-feet or so for which it has written Bureau contracts. The state is virtuously trying to come up with a "4.4 Plan" for living within the 4.4 MAF of its legal entitlement. But it refuses to admit that the 4.4 MAF should also include its share of the river's system losses, or a share of Mexico's water; it wants these charged to the fiction of "surplus water" above the basic 16.5 MAF of apportioned water.

According to Bureau figures that include system losses, wildlife use, Mexican water and everything, actual consumptive use of the water today is almost three-fourths for the Lower River, one-fourth for the Upper (11-plus MAF to 3.9 MAF in 1985). It means the Colorado River's flow is being fully consumed. It also means that the people of the Upper Basin have the moral and legal base for taking the Lower Basin to court to "get back our water." Any further Upper Basin water development depends on suing the downstream bastards. There is considerable enthusiasm for this in the Upper River Basin states—but not necessarily in the Upper River Basin itself. And this is where discourse on "the spirit of the compact" gets interesting.

If you are just another industrial revolutionary still looking for your main chance, then you probably believe that the compact was just about "water problems," and you would go with the Upper Basin states in calling back "our water" from the Lower Basin states. But if you are carrying the fragile flame of the counter-revolution against the developers, then you may want to think about further negotiation in the spirit of the compact. Right now, about 0.7 MAF of the Upper River's water is bled off in out-of-basin exports to the Denver metro area, the Salt Lake metro area, the Santa Fe-Albuquerque area, and other areas outside the natural boundaries of the Upper River Basin. That's about a fifth of the Upper River's consumptive use. And those cities want more; most of the agitation for getting "our" water back comes from the industrial urban clones of the Desert Empire in the Upper Basin states, but outside of the Upper Basin.

Those industrial urbs have developed a smug myth about the omnipotence of money, which is really about their power over the mountain and desert areas within the basin. "In the West," they say, "water doesn't flow downhill, it flows uphill toward money." To achieve this, however, ever larger quantities of money must flow out from our endlessly growing cities. A Denver metro county is prepared to spend a billion dollars in the Upper Gunnison Valley to take a relatively piddling quantity of water.

The more we learn about the two reconstructed rivers, however, the more it seems that a proper accounting of water and money might even advance the post-industrial agenda. In the mid-1980s, two University of Colorado economic scientists examined, valley by valley in the Upper River, agricultural productivity and farm income, the downriver salt-loading costs of upriver consumptive use, power-generation revenues and the like. They came up with compelling evidence that every acre-foot of Upper River water that flows downstream adds more wealth, by a factor of three or four times, to the region than if that water were consumptively consumed in the Upper Basin or diverted to Denver or Salt Lake or Albuquerque. (This study is in the World Resources Institute's *Water and arid lands of the western United States*.) That money of course does not come back from California and Nevada and Arizona to the Upper Basin now, and most interpretations of both appropriations doctrine and the compact preclude that happening; that may indicate that the "Law of the River" needs modification, to open up opportunities for a real "cross-flow" of money and water.

But to get hung up in water marketing issues, to get involved in figuring how to make money flow toward water—this is like getting hung up in whether Lake Powell should be drained for the sake of the long-term canyon ecology or whether the canyon ecology should become adapted to long-term river management. Instead of that argument, we should be confronting this window of opportunity for developing alternatives to a California fate. The odds are still daunting. Economically and socially, industrial culture thoroughly infiltrates and permeates the Upper Colorado region. And the current wave of refugees from California and other industrialized areas carry the germs they are fleeing. Nevertheless, there is hope in the presence of so many articulate and educated people for whom the Upper Basin is a refuge from America, coupled with a legal and moral environment that puts the Jeffersonian approach on a more or less equal footing with the increasingly rundown industrial revolution.

If an intelligent post-industrial society is going to be ecologically coherent, then the Upper Colorado River might be world enough for now, and the inland sea at the end of the river a virtue for the time being. I am not suggesting a "roll-the-rock" isolationist sensibility in the manner of The Riders of the Purple Sage; I am only suggesting that we not unthinkingly throw away the clear-cut definition of regional space and independence the dam and river afford us now. We should at least ask: is pulling down Glen Canyon Dam the most important thing we can do? Will it further, or hurt, our objectives? I would also ask that we take another look at the Colorado River Compact. We might find that it is more in step with our ideals than we think.

And what should we do—what would a society countering the excesses of the Industrial Revolution be like? It is too easy to drift into utopian mirages. I would suggest instead that we learn the following from the compact:

**Preserve opportunity.** The compact preserved the chance for other things to happen. Without it, the Upper Basin would have been forced to appropriate water as fast as possible. Development would have been even more reckless and destructive than it has been. Most probably, the surrounding cities would have rushed to drain the Colorado River before California could appropriate the water.

**Make culture congruent with nature.** Where the compact was organized around natural bounds and divisions, it helped us. Where it either ignored or did not understand natural limits, it failed us.

**Forget the broad visionary strokes.** Move in increments. Dave Wegner, one of the principal architects of the Glen Canyon Dam management plan adopted last year to restore and maintain the Grand Canyon, and who was treated shabbily by the Bureau of Reclamation, now dismisses those efforts as "Band-Aids." He has become a leader in the "pull-the-plug" on Lake Powell movement. But the biosphere works a lot more with Band-Aids than with "broad visionary strokes."

**And finally, look for strange bedfellows.** Allies exist outside the standard corridors of power—strange endangered actors like the humpback chub, or rural county commissions driven to the wall by cities within their states but outside the Colorado River Basin. Resistance to the industrialization of the Upper Basin started long before the 1960s. We may have allies we've never dreamt of.

*November 10, 1997*

# 4

## Federal Water Projects

The Central Arizona Project

# Arizona Digs Deep for Water

## Douglas Towne

**H**eat and isolation, but mainly the apparent absence of water, dominate the rugged, cactus-strewn Sonoran Desert scrublands around the town of Salome, Arizona, located about 100 miles west of Phoenix. The local motel's swimming pool is probably the area's largest body of water. Washes flow only after the rare desert monsoon thunderstorms. Even Salome High School's mascot, the Salome Frog, is a play on the region's mere 7 inches of average annual rainfall. Both the mascot and the town were founded by Dick Wick Hall, who called attention to his settlement by composing tall tales about desert living. Those tales were syndicated in the 1920s, including this one about the Salome Frog.

> *… Hatched out here by some Mistake—*
> *Three Hundred Miles from the Nearest Lake,*
> *And all the Water I can get to Drink,*
> *Is what Leaks out of the Kitchen Sink …*

But Dick Wick Hall had it wrong: Salome and surrounding La Paz County are rich in water, underground water. The five aquifers in La Paz County contain an estimated 38 million acre-feet of recoverable water. That is almost three times the annual flow of the Colorado River and 25 percent more water than either Lake Powell or Lake Mead holds when full. Hundreds of millions of gallons more lie beneath the other counties in Arizona's western deserts.

In the arid but fast-growing Southwest, that water is a coveted commodity. Over the last decade, urban growth and intense speculation in groundwater have triggered a bitter fight between Arizona's cities and rural counties over the state's underground reserves. The prime target is the underground water around Salome.

These aquifers are tapped mainly to produce cotton, but cotton growing is in trouble economically. Although a few farmers have diversified into crops with higher value, such as pistachios, pecans, and jojoba, most stay with cotton "because cotton's the only crop

*Arizona. The three aqueduct segments of the Central Arizona Project
stretch from Lake Havasu to Tucson. The Navajo Generating Station
would power the project's pumping plants. CAP would include
construction of the new Waddell and Cliff dams and some reconstruction
of the Stewart Mountain and Roosevelt dams.*

these farmers know how to grow," says Larry O'Daniel, a local water improvement district board member. Over the decades, fewer and fewer farmers have raised more and more cotton on bigger and bigger outfits. Those operations—sometimes with absentee owners— produce an energy- and pesticide-dependent crop destined for distant markets and supported by government subsidies. The place has never been an agrarian dream.

But those farms may have one last bumper crop. Despite the economic decline of cotton, farmers putting their nearly bankrupt operations on the market have gotten premium prices, often with leases that let them continue farming. The price of cotton and the condition of the land are irrelevant to the buyers: all they want is the groundwater. The buyers are municipalities and speculators. With most water supplies in Arizona claimed, or over-claimed, satisfying urban growth in the state now means converting water from agriculture to urban uses—turning cotton farms into water farms.

In La Paz County, the sudden invasion of the water market has made a few farmers rich, mostly around Salome. But it has left the rest of the county—a 4,400-square-mile stretch of desert with fewer than sixteen thousand residents—facing the threat of becoming a water colony, reminiscent of California's Owens Valley.

La Paz County straddles the Central Arizona Project canal, which brings Colorado River water to Phoenix and Tucson. That makes it attractive for water farms because the plumbing to move the water to the cities is already in place. Municipalities and speculators have bought deeds or options on nearly 60,000 acres in the county, says Gene Fisher, chair of the La Paz County Board of Supervisors. But because only 10 percent of the county's land is privately owned, that 60,000 acres adds up to half its deeded land. Fisher warns that if all that land is turned into working water farms, La Paz will become an economic and environmental sacrifice area for the future growth of Arizona's central urban corridor. Yuma and Mohave counties, La Paz's neighbors to the south and north, are in similar, though less severe, predicaments. The rural counties, Fisher argues, are endangered by a law that was initially praised as the first responsible approach to groundwater use in any state in the desert Southwest.

Arizona has far more water underground than on the surface. That water is both in the western deserts and in numerous deep basins throughout the state. The aquifers are heavily used for domestic, industrial, and agricultural needs, but recharge so slowly that they are essentially one-shot, non-renewable resources. By the late 1970s, intensive farming and exponential growth in Arizona's central urban corridor—Prescott, Phoenix, and Tucson—resulted in tremendous overdrafts under the cities. Groundwater levels dropped sharply, causing ground fissures and subsidence. State officials ignored the problem, but Congress didn't. It threatened to cut funding for the massive Central Arizona Project unless the state got its house in order.

In response, the Arizona Legislature passed the 1980 Groundwater Management Code. Technically, the code protects all groundwater in Arizona. But stringent regulations are in force only where there are significant overdrafts: the aquifers under greater metropolitan Phoenix, Tucson, and Prescott. Those basins are labeled Active Management Areas, and the cities must decrease groundwater pumping to equilibrium, with withdrawals equal to recharge, by 2025.

Many expected the code, which also requires a developer to guarantee a 100-year water supply before building a new house, to force urban Arizona to get serious about water conservation. It hasn't worked that way. In part, the cities were able to avoid conservation because the code also repealed an old law that required groundwater to be used on the land from which it was pumped. The repeal allowed the cities to try to balance their overdraft problems by raiding the countryside for rural groundwater. As Roger Manning, executive director for the Arizona Municipal Water Users Association, explains, most of the 1.8 million acre-feet a year the Central Arizona Project will bring from the Colorado River will be used to replace water the cities formerly pumped from underground. New water brought in from La Paz County and other water farms will be used as a 100-year assured supply for the cities' future economic growth.

In fact, opening rural aquifers to market forces may have been an implicit, though unadvertised, goal behind the code. "Economic development is stifled by a perceived lack of water in Arizona," comments Bill Stevens, a member of the commission that formulated the groundwater code. "(If a corporation is considering) moving an industry that requires any water, Arizona drops off the list of potential sites. We can't afford to impact the economy of the state," he says.

Manning says water transfers are a necessary and historic fact of life in Arizona. "Moving water from places of relative surplus to places of high demand is going to be a part of our water management policy for a long time." In that sense, Manning argues, "The code is working." Several of the many cities that have sprung up around Phoenix have "water farms."

But Fisher says that the 1980 code has failed La Paz County. "The intent of the groundwater law was a noble one," he says, "but it has not been practiced in a way any reasonable person would put into place. It's you against me." Cities have taken advantage of the code and a poor agriculture economy to secure a substantial amount of water from outlying areas. Any attempt to modify the law, impose regulations, or limit the cities' access to rural groundwater is strongly resisted. Fisher says, "Try it and people say, 'They'll break the code.' " As it is, he says, it's breaking the county. Fisher says there are problems with the cities over taxation and pumping schedules. But a worse problem, he says, is the speculators, who have bought up even more land than the cities.

The largest of those is AgriCom, which Stevens labels a "special interest out to make a lot of money." The company was formed by Ron Ober, a former staffer for Arizona Senator Dennis DeConcini, D., who made a small fortune buying up land in the path of the Central Arizona Project canal. AgriCom's sole business is to purchase lands in western Arizona to market the water to municipalities, especially those too small to finance their own water farms. However, instead of concentrating on farmland, AgriCom purchased 26,000 acres of mostly undeveloped, dirt-cheap desert land, says Cliff O'Neill, co-chair of the Citizens For Water Fairness in La Paz County. O'Neill says while residents were willing to work with the firm, it became greedy. "Their big push was through lobbyists towards legislators, not hydrologists to discuss the situation with the locals."

The firm helped sponsor a bill that went before the Arizona Legislature early this year. Currently there are no restrictions on groundwater transfers in Arizona, except for the protected aquifers in the central urban corridor. Outside the Active Management Areas, surface owners may extract as much water as they please and send it anywhere they like, so long as it is put to beneficial use. House Bill 2666 would have banned groundwater transfers from all the state's aquifers except for nine groundwater basins in the western desert.

While the bill also limited pumping from those nine aquifers to about 70 percent of capacity in order to conserve a minimal supply for the future, and would have required cities to pay in-lieu taxes before taking the water, it left them as the only source of new water for the fast-growing cities.

The measure, dubbed the "Bill straight from hell" by angry residents of La Paz County, nearly set off a minor war. "It is morally and ethically wrong to sacrifice any part of the state—to say that we will take your future so that another part might grow," says Fisher. "La Paz County, almost to the individual, will agree with the approach we're taking." Led by the Citizens For Water Fairness and the La Paz County Board of Supervisors, western Arizonans picketed AgriCom's corporate offices in Phoenix and delivered 1,500 tied straws to the Arizona Legislature on the eve of the vote. The bill lost, killed by La Paz County's outrage, Manning says.

The passions inflamed by the bill may have also killed chances for any negotiated reform of the groundwater management code. But in the last days of the legislative debate on the issue a new idea surfaced that may provide a solution both the cities and the counties can live with: turning the entire problem over to a state or regional water authority. That authority would have the power to eliminate speculation and competition in the water market, set rules for use of water farms, and require better conservation practices. It would also give the counties some say in municipal groundwater purchases.

The first target may be agricultural holdings—300,000-plus acres—that surround Phoenix and use massive amounts of water. "If you have a water crisis and you are going to plant houses and grow people—and agriculture takes 70 to 80 percent of your water, you can't justify keeping that land in production," says La Paz County's Fisher. Manning says the large cities would also like to be able to tap into agriculture close to home. "The question is whether or not continued investment of 85 percent of our water resource base into an activity that returns less than 2 percent of our GNP is a sound investment in economic, social or environmental terms." But at the moment, those farms are protected from being turned into water farms. Because they are within an Active Management Area, the groundwater code requires groundwater from those farms to be retired when the land goes out of production; whether their water remains immune remains to be seen. Manning says the farms control enough surface water to supply fifteen million to twenty million people—three times the projected population of Phoenix in 2025.

While the cities and counties fight over water, conservation and limits on growth are overlooked. Arizona has lost 90 percent of its riparian areas: dams and diversions have halted rivers, and groundwater pumping has dried up smaller streams and desert springs. Rather than reverse that trend, the groundwater management code marks a further failure of conservation, says Joni Bosh, a water specialist with the Sierra Club in Phoenix. "[The cities] have decided that augmentation is preferable to conservation," says Bosh, who questions the point of achieving safe yield in one aquifer by mining another. Bosh criticizes the conservation requirements in the code. The law requires the state Department of Water Resources to set conservation goals for each municipality within an Active Management Area. The municipalities must then write their own conservation plans, but are not required to enforce them. Bill Plummer, director of the Department of Water Resources, says the majority of cities in the Phoenix area missed their conservation goals in 1987 and 1988. Plummer is now in negotiations with most of those cities, trying to prod them toward water savings.

While Plummer admits the state is "not there yet" on conservation, he warns, "you cannot achieve enough conservation to take care of the growth that's predicted." To meet the needs of the six million people who are predicted to inhabit Phoenix in the next thirty-five years, Plummer says the state is also researching cloud seeding and vegetative management—thinning vegetation in selected northern Arizona watersheds to increase water production. However, Fisher says the cities' greed for more growth has gotten out of hand. He points to recent studies showing that for every three people that come to Arizona, two leave. "People come to Arizona because of clean air and open spaces. Phoenix has so many problems with traffic congestion and air pollution at this point they don't need to fuel more growth. It's a quality of life issue as well as a water issue."

*November 20, 1989*

# Arizona's Water Disaster

## Tony Davis

Farmer Norm Pretzer is a booster of the Central Arizona Project (CAP). He also calls it a boondoggle. Pretzer, fifty-nine, has gone to Washington, D.C., more times than he cares to remember to push for federal money to build CAP. At $4 billion, it's one of the biggest and most expensive water projects in the nation's history. It was supposed to keep him and his fellow farmers from running out of water.

Pretzer's got plenty of water available from CAP, but not enough money to pay for it. Late in the winter of 1991, hard times forced him to seek Chapter 11 bankruptcy protection for one of his family's two farms. He's not using all the CAP water he could, and neither is the rest of Arizona. In 1991, it used less than one-third of the 1.5 million acre-feet of Colorado River water it could have sent through a 330-mile-long aqueduct. Pretzer is president of the Central Arizona Irrigation and Drainage District, one of nine in the state that are having a hard time paying for CAP water. Cities are not doing as well at using CAP as expected, either.

Why isn't the project water selling? Largely because it costs up to twice as much as pumping groundwater. "Nobody wants the water. That's a boondoggle," Pretzer said. "If we had to do this over again, I might have done certain things differently, but I damned sure would have hated to see us not get the water in. This water is absolutely crucial for our long-term betterment. But the present way they're operating it, it's a boondoggle."

"Boondoggle" is a familiar term from critics of CAP and other water projects, but not from farmers who have benefitted from subsidized water around the West for nearly a century. Some of President Jimmy Carter's staff thought CAP was a boondoggle; in 1977, CAP made Carter's short-lived "hit list" of water projects he considered both economically and environmentally unsound.

These days, Pretzer and other farmers are fighting for their lives politically as well as economically. They want hundreds of millions of dollars in help from cash-strapped Arizona city governments to pay for this water, and there are those in the state who think farmers are over-dramatizing CAP's problems to make the case look better for a bailout. Virtually everyone in the state's water establishment, however, agrees that the project isn't working as planned, and that it will not be cheap or easy to make it work. "The project is going to go through some very difficult economic times, but it is too valuable to the state's future to permit it to fail," said George Britton, a deputy Phoenix city manager. "It's going to be Arizona's mini-S&L crisis."

The story of CAP is the story of a project that was expected to be a water rescue operation for an arid state. Instead it turned into a water planner's version of a new power plant bursting with excess capacity. It's the story of a  project that was approved and largely built during a time of boom, but came to life in a time of bust. The state's economy and population growth rates have been on the skids in recent years. Arizona's unemployment rate topped 8 percent early this year. Today, despite the project's problems, virtually everyone in the state's water establishment still expects Tucson and Phoenix to use enough water to make the project work over the long term. By the time CAP is fifty years old, those cities' metropolitan areas are expected to grow from about 680,000 people today to 1.5 million in Tucson and from 2 million today to nearly 6 million in Phoenix. For now, however, city manager Britton acknowledges that officials had "an overextended expectation" about who would use CAP water, just as real estate developers overestimated how many shopping centers people needed. "There was also a fairly optimistic calculation about the cost," recalled Britton, who worked as an aide to former Governor Bruce Babbitt during the 1980s. "We assumed the water would be cheaper. There's been a decline in demand, or at least not as fast a growth as expected. And there have been other supplies."

CAP, with its concrete canal slicing across the state's mid-section, has been the symbol of the relentless growth that hit Arizona from the postwar era until the late 1980s. The main aqueduct is nearly as wide as a two-lane road and is deeper than most swimming pools. Some water observers have called it Arizona's Holy Grail, a manifestation of the great unifying force of the state's water politics. For forty years, everyone who was anyone in the state pushed to build CAP. Trips to Washington, D.C., by Arizona farmers, miners, developers, mayors, and county supervisors to push for CAP money became an annual rite of spring.

Non-use of CAP, however, has spawned worries among some water interests that Arizona could lose some of its hard-won Colorado River water to California or Nevada; then the water won't be there when Tucson and Phoenix need it. Others fear the project's financial stability might sink with the farms, and that too few customers buying CAP water could mean sharply higher water bills for cities such as Tucson and Phoenix that are eventually expected to drink heavily from the CAP aqueduct. Many people find those fears far-fetched. They are still concerned, however, that with CAP water staying in the river, the state won't be able to stop its fifty-year-old habit of pumping deep underground aquifers.

For six months this year, the state's water interest groups—farms, cities, Indians, and others—tried to sort out solutions in a task force that meets twice a month. State water resources director Betsy Rieke half-jokingly called the task "mission impossible." Farmers wanted the project's operator, the three-county Central Arizona Water Conservation District, to raise local property taxes to bail out agriculture. That would cost $750 million over thirty years. Another proposal was to build massive, expensive underground water recharge projects to store the remaining water farms can't use until it's needed. That would cost another $15 to $25 million annually over ten to twenty-five years, with the expense dropping as cities gradually open their taps to CAP. Cities wanted farms to sell off the cheap electric power they use for groundwater pumping to pay some of their CAP bills. A fourth proposal would have taxed groundwater pumping, to make CAP a better buy by comparison. Some observers wanted to let the farms go under, and turn their unused water over to the Indians to pay off their decades-old water-rights claims. The most radical idea is one that's never been carried out in the United States: leasing the water across state lines to Arizona's old arch-enemy California. Arizona could take the water back in the future when it's ready to use it.

Despite the task force's failure, project officials remain optimistic. Only two summers ago, during a run of 110-120 degree heat, the CAP canal was full, and farms and cities wanted more than the project could deliver, recalled Tom Clark. He is general manager of the Central Arizona Water Conservation District, which operates the project. "Sometime we're going to wish we had more water to bring to the river, but now we have more water than we can use," said Clark. "You build a freeway and [if] you build it right, the first five or ten years it doesn't carry as many cars as it can carry."

A drive through Central Arizona farming country is a journey through time. It's a place where one farm-based society vanished five centuries ago and where another may soon follow. On the north edge of the farm belt, near the seven-thousand-plus-person town of Coolidge, lie the buried kalichi walls of the Hohokam people. They thrived for several hundred years on squash, beans, and corn nourished by irrigation canal water. Then their civilization abruptly collapsed around 1450. Farther south, near Eloy and Arizona City, farm after abandoned farm from the 1950s and '60s today is scrub, sagebrush, and weeds. Lying nearby is the latest batch of abandoned farms, still covered with ready-to-plant furrows, where ancient well engines—large as tanks—stand idle and where tumbleweeds collect in dry irrigation ditches.

Nobody knows why the Hohokam culture died out. For years, as Arizona struggled not to run out of water, the folklore was that the Hohokam had fallen to drought. Today, archaeologists are more likely to blame floods. For years, the smart money had it that current farmers would succumb to aridity too. Most farmers in this area can tell stories of groundwater levels dropping 300 or 400 feet in a few decades. Long, thin cracks running along nearby mountains come from subsidence, a sort of geological whiplash that causes ground to sink when water below ground is removed by pumping. One crack runs 12 miles long.

The talk of the cotton fields today is about bankers tightening up on loans, cotton prices at their lowest level in years, water prices climbing out of sight, whiteflies and boll weevils gobbling up crops, and competition from Japan, the South and even Nebraska. These farms were supposed to be a holding basin for CAP's water. They were expected to use up to two-thirds of CAP water until Phoenix and Tucson got big enough to use it. As recently as 1987, Pinal County, where many of these farms lie, was the twentieth biggest farming county in the United States, raking in $402 million in crop sales. But in the last two years, the number of acres planted in the Central Arizona Irrigation District fell from 80,000 to 40,000 acres. Pretzer, the district's president, said the district will be lucky to plant 30,000 acres this year. Other farmers predict as few as 25,000 acres.

The farms are sinking under $300 million in federal and private loans they took out to build concrete ditches hooking them to CAP's big ditch. "Now," said Bo Warren, whose family has planted cotton at B&J Farms just outside Arizona City since 1951, "it's survival from one year to the next." Sitting on the back of a pickup truck, wearing a T-shirt and sporting light brown sideburns, Warren said that when CAP arrived a few years ago, everyone in the irrigation district thought it would increase land values. Instead, the cost of building access canals drove property taxes up and land values through the floor.

Everywhere, unplowed farmland is dotted with "For Sale" signs, and nobody's buying. Bill Erwin, who does maintenance work on the farms, said he knows of a half-dozen farmers like Pretzer who have filed for Chapter 11 bankruptcy protection in the past year. "The handwriting was on the walls with the pumps. They were going lower and lower," Warren said. "We were forced to take CAP; the canal water was needed so badly. Now, what's in most farmers' minds is that we could have survived a little longer with the pumps; they were cheaper."

Back in the 1960s, farmer Jamie Gellum of Coolidge recalled his late grandfather, C.D. Shiflet, going to Washington to tell Congress that CAP would be the farmers' savior. "He died before CAP ever got on the farm. I wonder what he'd be thinking now," said Gellum, who opted to cut his losses and quit farming in 1991 after almost eleven years. "Here it is, one of the big contributors to my cash shortfall. But I still maintain it was a good thing for the area. It offers good quality water, and the guys will need that. But it probably will kill us in the long run."

Farmers love to argue, and one can get every shade of opinion about CAP here. Some say it is the cause of their problems and some say it's a blip. Some say their irrigation district leaders never told them exactly how much their loans would cost until too late; others say leaders such as Pretzer have done all they can to keep the districts afloat. Many farmers agree with Randy Edmond of the neighboring Department of Water Resources office that CAP has hurt farms in another way: by creating a "monoculture" of cotton. Besides making the land less fertile, cotton left them with no other crops to fall back on when prices crashed a year or two ago. Until CAP, about 25 percent of the crops in the Central Arizona irrigation district were grains, sugar beets, vegetables, and other non-cotton crops. Now, cotton is about 90 percent of what's grown, Pretzer said. CAP's high costs made the difference, farmers and Edmond say, by making other crops less economical.

Most farmers agree that if something isn't done to lower water costs, many farms and their irrigation districts won't last much longer than two years. In the past two years, 15 to 20 percent of the 650 farmers on CAP water couldn't get loans to plant crops, Pinal

County Supervisor Dean Weatherly said. Another 15 to 20 percent are on notice they won't be farming much longer if they don't get their houses in order. Two of nine irrigation districts on CAP are behind schedule in repaying their federal loans. "CAP will have to be restructured to work," farmer Charlie Bush said. "There have to be changes in the system, but I don't know when or where."

Unlike their corporate counterparts in California, many of these farms are family-owned. Their parents or grandparents came to Arizona during the Great Depression to escape the Dust Bowl in the Midwest or after World War II to join the boom that was about to smack Arizona between the teeth. Their farms are a world apart from the mega-farms in California's Central Valley. Like their counterparts all over the country, however, these farmers are heavily subsidized. They get low-cost, federally financed power from Hoover Dam to pump their well water. They pay no interest on the loans they took from the federal government to build their local CAP irrigation canals. City residents on CAP water pay a federally subsidized interest rate of 3.3 percent, well below what a home buyer pays a bank on his mortgage. Plus, when the U.S. Bureau of Reclamation declares the project finished in the mid-1980s, and users have to start paying back the cost of the main canal, farms will pay only $2 an acre-foot. Cities' rates will start at $5 an acre-foot and eventually hit $40 an acre-foot.

Farms also dip heavily into federal set-aside programs that pay them not to grow crops. From 1989 to 1991, three thousand farmers in neighboring Maricopa County pocketed about $200 million in subsidy payments, U.S. Agriculture Department records show. More than half the money went to these farms in 1991, when cotton prices crashed and farmers were slashing production. "I think the American farmer would rather not be involved in any type of government program, but when it comes to survival, you've gotta do it," said Warren.

Pretzer said, "It's highly unfair to say, 'Just you guys on the farms get subsidized.' Look at what cities get—transit subsidies, library subsidies, education subsidies. The real cost of CAP water to the cities is $250 an acre-foot, and they're paying maybe $130 to $140 an acre-foot. Is the other $110 a subsidy? I would say it is. It gets down to the point of, sure, I'm a whore … All of us are whores."

*August 10, 1992*

# Arizonans Quarrel over CAP while California Waits

## Tony Davis

C entral Arizona Project farmers want another subsidy, perhaps the biggest of all. In spring 1991, they tried to stir interest in a proposal to raise the property tax charged to landowners in the three counties that use CAP water. The rate would rise from 10 cents per $100 of assessed valuation today to up to 28 cents per $100. The farms coupled the tax hike request with a pledge to turn the water over to cities in twenty-five years.

Cities blasted the proposal as a massive shift of money from Tucson and Phoenix to rural Pinal County. An Arizona Municipal Water Users Association study concluded that Pinal County would get 67 percent of the new money from the new tax while paying only 3 percent of the freight. "Last year, America West Airlines (whose headquarters is in Phoenix) came to the state asking for direct financial assistance, and they had thousands and thousands of jobs, far more than the farms do," said Bill Chase, Phoenix's water resources manager. "They were asking for less money by a whole bunch than this group is asking for, and they were turned down."

In turn, the cities asked farmers to "put their assets on the table" by selling their low-cost Hoover Dam electric power. That turned farmers apoplectic. That very cheap federal power, used to pump up groundwater, has been their economic cornerstone since the Great Depression. They intend to continue pumping some cheap groundwater in addition to the CAP supplies.

To farming interests, these cat-and-dog fights with the cities are the biggest threat to the CAP's survival. While the two sides squabble, California and Nevada are asking the other five Colorado River basin states to give them additional Colorado River supplies. California, after five years of drought, says it wants a legal pact giving it more water until 2010, to give it time to get conservation programs going. It's been using 800,000 acre-feet of Arizona's unused water for years. Nevada, which expects to exhaust its Colorado River supplies by about 2008, wants its new water to be a permanent supply. Arizona and other western states have resisted these proposals, but some wonder how long Arizona can hold out. "Arizona is treading on eggs with CAP. In the West, the law of beneficial use, use it or lose it, still holds true," said farmer Norm Pretzer.

But the farmers' arch-enemy, Arizona Municipal Water Users Association director Roger Manning, said he is not worried about California. "Is Congress going to begin the practice of stealing one state's resources and giving them to another?" Manning asked. "If so, every congressman must decide and wonder if his state is going to be next." As for the farmers' irrigation districts, Manning predicts catastrophe. "As we see it, the majority of Arizona irrigation districts are on various stages of the bankruptcy court steps," Manning said. "They're economic basket cases. If you and I were in their situation, we probably would be in bankruptcy right now, and maybe even in a homeless shelter."

However, there are farming and urban interests who favor leasing water to California, as well as people in both camps who fear leased water won't return. Arizona Water Resources Director Betsy Rieke says it's short-sighted to discuss leasing until all other solutions are exhausted, and the department's task force recommended against leasing the water. "If you invite the giant into your kitchen for a week, it may be hard not to have him eat you for dinner," said Bob Lynch, a Phoenix lawyer and a lobbyist for the farmers.

In the past few months, some Arizona farming irrigation districts have explored the leasing idea. They even flew to California to discuss a possible deal with the Metropolitan Water District, the giant utility that keeps southern California green. "As a devil's advocate, I raise the issue of leasing, and as soon as I get done saying anything, everyone tells me they're opposed to it," said Dean Weatherly, a pro-farming Pinal County supervisor who sits on the water task force. "Betsy Rieke beat me up when I asked her about it; a farmer beat me up when I asked him about it. But I just don't know how you can take any option off the table."

At present, the discussion is theoretical. Arizona can't use the water, and so at least half of the CAP supply will either stay in reservoirs or continue to flow to California. Arizona cities are already starting to try to get their hands on the farmers' unused rights to CAP water, but the cities aren't ready to use that water yet. Given the sick Arizona economy, nobody can predict when CAP will start carrying out its promise to make the desert bloom, either with crops or with subdivisions and golf courses.

*August 10, 1992*

# Re:CAP

## Tony Davis

In 1993, the state's water power structure devised a solution that propped up the Central Arizona Project. CAP's governing board, the Central Arizona Water Conservation District, approved a complex, multi-tiered pricing structure for farmers that let them buy some of their CAP water as cheaply as $13 to $17 an acre-foot. Previously, they had paid $50 or so an acre-foot. Making up the cost difference were the residents of Phoenix, Tucson, and other central and southern Arizona cities and towns, whose CAP costs rose slightly. Their willingness to help the failing farmers represented a seismic shift, since they had previously scorned farmers' requests for a bailout and had dismissed the farmers' woes as irrelevant to them.

The cities reversed their stance after researchers for the project showed that a collapse of agriculture could set off a spiral in which dropping demand ratcheted prices skyward, in turn reducing demand and increasing prices still more. This reversal of the law of supply and demand would have occurred because regardless of how much water the cities and farms slurp down, the water district must repay the same debt to the federal government to cover the costs of building the vast concrete canal. The pricing shift's results were dramatic. In 1991, the state used only 400,000 acre-feet out of a total available supply of 1.5 million acre-feet. In the middle and late 1990s, the project's use topped 1 million acre-feet annually, thanks mainly to the cotton farmers.

But Tucson, the city that has signed up for the single largest block of CAP water, remains a no-show. That's largely because of what virtually all local observers now agree was an inept, careless effort by city officials to bring CAP water on line in 1992. After the Tucson Water Department plugged CAP into city water mains, tens of thousands of residents in older neighborhoods started noticing something terribly wrong. Customers said that rusty-colored, smelly, poor-tasting water started coming through their pipes and in some cases caused pipes to leak or burst. The city's water engineers later concluded that the corrosive Colorado River water did a number on their aging water pipe system, which dated back to the 1920s in some of the older parts of the city. Worse, the water department had disregarded its own consultant's recommendations to bring the CAP water on line slowly by testing its use in a few neighborhoods first, and by blending CAP water with groundwater. The city, anxious to stop pumping from its rapidly dropping underground aquifer, had precipitously switched to all CAP water without testing.

Consumer anger prodded the city council into shutting off the project entirely by 1994. A year later, residents pushed through a voter-approved initiative banning direct delivery of CAP water into peoples' homes unless it was treated to make it as clean as city-pumped groundwater.

Since then, water, in the words of the alternative newspaper, the *Tucson Weekly*, has become the third rail in the city's politics. In 1997, voters overwhelmingly rejected a local swimming-pool dealer's efforts to pass another initiative overturning the 1995 direct delivery ban. In November 1999, voters defeated another initiative to strengthen and extend the terms of the 1995 ban. But when asked when the city might start using its CAP water, Kathy Jacobs, director of the state Department of Water Resources' Tucson office, replied: "I hesitate to even guess."

*Written for this volume*

Central Utah Project

# After Decades of Trying, Opponents Get the Central Utah Project into the Ring

## Ed Marston

**A** map of the two halves of the $2.1 billion Bonneville Unit. To the east, the Strawberry Collection System intercepts mountain streams at 8,000 feet of elevation and sends them to the Enlarged Strawberry Reservoir. From there, the water is to flow through the Wasatch Range to irrigate farms in south-central Utah. The other half of the unit starts with the Jordanelle Reservoir, which will collect water bound for Salt Lake City via an aqueduct. One-third of Utah Lake may be diked and dried up to reduce evaporation losses.

On November 19, 1985, residents in twelve counties covering one-third of Utah will vote on whether to back or kill one of the nation's "world class" water projects. At stake is the Bonneville Unit of the Central Utah Project—a multibillion-dollar effort that has been under construction for about twenty years and that, if things go smoothly, will probably take another twenty years to complete.

It should be said upfront that it is impossible to understand the Central Utah Project or its Bonneville Unit. Even the physical part of the project—the system of reservoirs, aqueducts, tunnels, water swaps and lake dikings—is constantly shifting and ill-defined. A twenty-page Sunday supplement on CUP by the Salt Lake City *Deseret News*, prepared by a team of journalists "over a period of months," spent no more than a sentence on large chunks of the project's physical features. A careful reader would have been left wondering how almost 140,000 acre-feet of Colorado River water was to get west across the Wasatch Mountains to the Salt Lake City area. They would also have wondered where were the thousands of acres of arid lands that CUP is to irrigate.

Nevertheless, the supplement and a long, critical article in *Utah Holiday* magazine represent a large step forward in both Utah's and

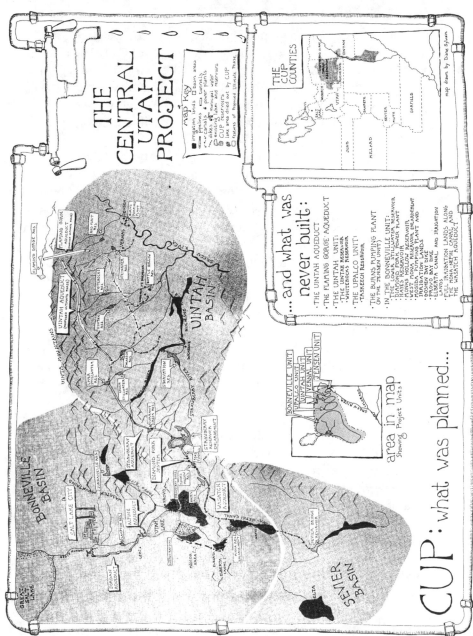

Diane Sylvain

the nation's attempts to grapple with its water future. Before the election, there was no public debate in Utah about CUP. The only battles were within CUP—struggles over which city or farm region would get what benefits, or bear what impacts. Unlike other states, which have staffed public-interest groups bird-dogging water projects, in Utah there is only the Utah Water Alliance, a one-person, one-room operation staffed by Dorothy Harvey.

At the national level, environmental groups, headed by the National Wildlife Federation, have consistently fought CUP. But given the lack of in-state opposition, and unanimous support by Utah's governors and congressional delegations, the groups had little effect until the mid-1980s. Without local concerns and opponents to bring to Washington, the national groups were told they were carpetbaggers who were telling local people what was good for them. That handicap was reinforced by a 1965 vote in which, by a 13-to-1 margin, voters agreed to repay to the federal government $158 million as their share of the Bonneville Unit. At that time, the Bonneville Unit, which completely dwarfs the other four CUP units, was expected to cost $330 million and to be carrying water through the Wasatch Mountains by the 1970s. Twenty years later, the project is still fifteen years from completion, with the cost up by a factor of six, to $2.1 billion. As a result, the old repayment contract is inadequate, and on November 19, voters must decide whether to repay an additional $335 million to the federal government. That amount, critics predict, also will prove to be inadequate.

The repayment vote has not come without a struggle. According to a Government Accounting Office report prepared at the request of Senator Howard Metzenbaum, D-Ohio, it comes years late. According to the GAO, the U.S. Bureau of Reclamation has been spending money on CUP illegally for years because it had no guarantee that Utah residents would repay their share of the project. The Bureau has spent $600 million on the Bonneville Unit's reservoirs, tunnels, aqueducts, and even a bowling alley for impact mitigation in the isolated eastern Utah town of Duchesne. But the national stake in the November 19 election goes beyond those dollars, or the $1.5 billion still to be spent. CUP is one of a few surviving major projects—the Central Arizona Project, the Garrison Project in North Dakota, the Columbia Basin Project in Washington—and has heavy symbolic and practical importance.

CUP is a key to the survival of the U.S. Bureau of Reclamation. The Bureau, which in its eighty-three-year history vigorously dammed and transformed the western states, is today a shrunken, shaken outfit. Its main hope for buying time to adapt to a new world lies with the CAPs, CUPs, and Garrisons. An adverse vote on November 19 would mean deeper cuts in its budget, personnel, and ability to promote future projects. The chance that voters will deliver a knock-out punch to CUP and the Bureau is slim. But there will be no 13-to-1 victories. Polls show CUP's margin sinking from an early 5-to-1 to a present 2-to-1.

If CUP is as illogical and wasteful as critics say, it could win the election but lose the war. Sketchy as the *Deseret News* supplement was, it laid out a huge overall cost increase due to Bureau bad luck or incompetence which led to costly overruns on individual contracts (in one case Bureau ignorance of geological conditions led to the trapping and abandonment of a $1 million tunnel mole) and enough information to provide a base for future understanding. With perhaps twenty years of congressional appropriations ahead, public understanding of the critics' side of the issue and informed debate within Utah could lead to demands for change from Congress. It is changes, rather than stoppage, critics say they seek. The project, they say, is too far along to be annihilated. Gene Riordan, a volunteer attorney for the National Wildlife Federation in Boulder, Colorado, says the hope is to set up a negotiating process like the Garrison Commission in North Dakota or Colorado's Metropolitan Water Roundtable.

In NWF's view, the Bonneville Unit has grown almost at random, without regard to physical need, economic feasibility, or environmental impacts. The critics say negotiations could lead to a more rational, smaller, cheaper project. Fred Reimherr of Salt Lake City, a member of the Stonefly Society, a Utah chapter of Trout Unlimited, is one of the few nonprofessionals with an on-the-ground feel for the Bonneville Unit. He believes that even with $600 million spent, the uses of the project's water are not yet cast in stone. He says there are relatively inexpensive ways to make it useful to Utah without further harming the environment.

Negotiations will not be easy. First at the table will be the Bureau, which is in charge of construction and which has the largest stake in an expensive, long-running construction project. In theory, the

Bureau works for the Central Utah Water Conservancy District, which represents the farmers and cities that will eventually use the water. CUWCD is a twelve-county public body, run by a board of directors, with taxing and bonding power. It is responsible for seeing that residents of the twelve-county area repay the local share of the project. CUWCD must keep its twelve counties happy by doling out raw water, water treatment plants, irrigation ditches and drains, research grants, and bowling alleys. CUWCD distributes at the local level the pork Utah's congressional delegation obtains at the national level.

CUWCD will sit next to the Bureau at the negotiations, but their relationship is not an easy one. While CUWCD blames Congress and environmentalists for costly delays, it has also been critical of Bureau management. It has even threatened to sue the Bureau for $300 million. It believes the agency has wasted that money, and Utah residents should not have to repay it to the federal government.

The negotiating table will be crowded because CUWCD cannot speak for all twelve counties. The city of Provo, for example, says the Bonneville Unit will result in the theft of its water rights if the Jordanelle Reservoir on Provo River is built. The city's water manager, Wayne Hillier, says the city is in court contesting the Bureau's water rights application and is also campaigning against CUP in the November 19 vote. So Provo will certainly want its own seat at the table, as may farmers concerned about the possible loss of their CUP water to the Salt Lake area, and Salt Lake residents concerned about the taxes and high water rates they will pay as a result of CUP.

The third group at the table will be national environmental and Utah public interest groups. Environmentalists will have many concerns. In the Colorado River basin, they worry about streams that are dried up in the Uinta and Wasatch mountains so that the water can be diverted to the Wasatch Front. They will also want to negotiate the diking and shrinking of Utah Lake, and the effect of further growth on the already polluted Salt Lake City area.

The negotiators will have to deal with a system which is already one-third built. In place is the Strawberry Collection System—a pipe and tunnel network which hugs the southern and eastern slopes of the Uinta and Wasatch mountains. The purpose of the 37-mile-long collector is to intercept nine mountain streams at about the 8,000-foot elevation and convey their water into the 1.1 million acre-foot

Enlarged Strawberry Reservoir. (An early Strawberry Reservoir and Tunnel already sends about 60,000 acre-feet of water to the Wasatch Front.)

The Enlarged Strawberry Reservoir is complete but not filled. Were it filled, it wouldn't be of much use because the pipes and tunnels to carry water west through the Wasatch Range are not started. As a result, the main environmental impacts of the Strawberry Collection System—the drying up of streams and the destruction of wetlands and fish habitat—have not yet occurred. Project proponents say that when the system is operating, its harm will be lessened by minimum stream flows. But Reimherr says the CUWCD is backing away from that commitment.

It makes sense that the collection system was built first. It is the key to Utah dipping its straw into the Colorado River. So Utah is like its Upper Colorado River Basin neighbor, Colorado. Both states are guaranteed a share of the Colorado River water by an interstate compact. But neither has been able to put its full allotment to use, and both fear permanent loss of the water to California and Arizona. Colorado and Utah are geographic and demographic mirror images of each other. Western Colorado is sparsely populated but rich in minerals, energy, and water flowing off its mountains into the Colorado River. The Denver Front Range, to the east, which has the people, has been progressively dewatering western Colorado through transbasin diversions of Colorado River water.

In Utah, it is the eastern part of the state which is underpopulated and rich in coal, tar sands, oil shale, and Colorado River water. The Wasatch Front, in the western half of the state, has the people. The Bonneville Unit of CUP enables the Wasatch Front to siphon 140,000 acre-feet of Colorado River water into the Great Salt Lake basin. However, unlike in Colorado, there appears little opposition to the transbasin diversion. That may be because, as members of the Central Utah Water Conservancy District, eastern Utah has been promised or has already received several relatively small projects which put Colorado River water to agricultural and municipal use. But Dorothy Harvey of the Intermountain Water Alliance says it's because "They're timid, like everyone else in Utah."

Although the Strawberry Collection System can intercept streams and prevent them from flowing down off the mountains into the Green River and then the Colorado River, there is no precise picture yet of what the extra 140,000 acre-feet of water (60,000 acre-feet is already diverted through the existing Strawberry Tunnel) will be used for on the western side of the mountains. There is even uncertainty about how to get the water through the Wasatch Mountains to the Wasatch Front.

Until 1984, the proposed Diamond Fork Power System was to take advantage of the 2,100-foot fall from the Enlarged Strawberry Reservoir, and generate 1,100 megawatts of pumped storage hydropower on its way to the Wasatch Front. But in this day of electric energy conservation and unused coal-fired plants, there was no demand for this power. So the plan was dropped, along with a hoped-for $300 million in revenue. Now the Bureau still intends to build the Diamond Fork tunnel system and a much smaller amount of hydropower, although it is also studying the existing seventy-five-year-old Strawberry Tunnel for possible rebuilding.

How will the Colorado River water be used on the Wasatch Front? It will flow south to help irrigate about 240,000 acres of farmland. Some of that farmland is in the Sevier River Valley. Critics particularly object to that part of the system, because farmers there sold 40,000 acre-feet of existing irrigation water to the Intermountain Power Project for $80 million. The Stonefly Society's Reimherr says the taxpayers are replacing the sold water with subsidized CUP water. (The cities and water districts will pay the full cost of municipal and industry water. But the irrigation water will be subsidized to almost $1 billion by power revenues out of Hoover Dam, Glen Canyon, etc.) CUWCD attorney Edward Clyde says the Sevier area farmers have been paying taxes into CUP for many years, and are entitled to the water. He also says safeguards will prevent them from selling off the water for another profit.

If the Bonneville Unit were only a transfer of 140,000 acre-feet of Colorado River water to irrigate farms along the Wasatch Front, it would be relatively easy to understand. But the project also involves the damming of the Provo River to form the 300,000-acre-foot Jordanelle Reservoir. If the city of Provo succeeds in its lawsuit against water rights the Bureau claims on behalf of the project, the project is dead. Otherwise, the reservoir will feed 70,000 acre-feet a year into aqueducts which will carry it to the Salt Lake City area, and another 48,000 acre-feet to nearby cities.

Normally, the water diverted out of the Provo River would flow into Utah Lake. The diversion of the water out of the Provo River to Salt Lake City will cause the lake level to drop. Irrigators who use

Utah Lake as a reservoir would then be unable to get water into their ditches. According to Bureau spokesman Jay Franson of Provo, if all else fails, the Colorado River water from Strawberry can be fed into Utah Lake to allow the top-priority municipal and industrial water to flow to Salt Lake City. But since such an exchange would kill the irrigation project, the Bureau is looking at alternatives.

In one, a five-mile-long dike would be built across Utah Lake's Goshen Bay, thus drying up one-third of the lake, or 27,000 acres. Shrinking the lake will decrease evaporation, Franson says, by 100,000 acre-feet, making up for the diverted Provo River water. Aside from the $200 million cost, there are problems with the diking. It would further jeopardize the June sucker, a fish left over from the days when Lake Bonneville covered the entire region, and so could bring the Endangered Species Act into play. A safer option is a buy-out of unused or marginally used irrigation rights around Utah Lake to replace the diverted Provo River water.

Critics, led by the Intermountain Water Alliance, argue that these gyrations are not necessary. They say that on the Wasatch Front, the subdividing and abandonment of farms has led to surplus irrigation water which now flows, unused, into the Great Salt Lake. Fred Reimherr says studies show 200,000 acre-feet of unused irrigation water available. In addition, he says, with the shutdown of the Kennecott copper operation, its 100,000 acre-feet of water a year is also unused. If the firm reopens, Reimherr says, it will probably be smaller and more efficient, with some of its water available for other uses.

Dorothy Harvey says Utah may be the second driest state in the nation, but the Wasatch Front is literally awash in water. Harvey says the CUP proponents are captivated by Utah's 1.4 million acre-foot entitlement to the Colorado River. But, she says, the U.S. Geological Survey reports there is 60 million acre-feet of groundwater in the region, with at least 125,000 acre-feet per year available for drinking. She also says the Bear and Weber rivers have about 1.6 million acre-feet, much of which flows into the Great Salt Lake. Another 278,000 acre-feet of unused irrigation water is available. Finally, she charges, at 250 gallons per day, Salt Lake City residents are profligate users of water.

University of Utah economist Jon Miller, who has emerged as a major spokesman for the opposition, says CUP develops Utah's most expensive water first. Instead of tapping CUP water at a very high

$200 per acre-foot, Miller says it should first develop the cheaper water cited by the critics. Then if, in the twenty-first century, it needs additional water, it can drill through to the Enlarged Strawberry Reservoir and bring that water west.

Proponents say Utah will eventually need all of its water. They point to Salt Lake County's spectacular growth—from 274,000 people in 1950 to 655,000 in 1984—and say there is no sign the growth will stop. Given that certainty, they continue, Utah should complete CUP while federal money is available. They also argue that unless Utah uses all of its Colorado River water, it will someday be unable to wrest it away from Arizona and California.

It is unlikely that even the small percentage of the people expected to go to the polls next Tuesday will understand the project in broad outline, let alone its subtleties. The decision will be made on the basis of gut feelings: A distaste for bureaucratic waste and gargantuan projects will war with a fear that an eventual water shortage will shut off Utah's prized objective—constant growth.

*November 11, 1985*

# Why Utah Wants "the Bureau Out"

## Steve Hinchman

Utah, the second driest state in the nation after Nevada, was settled as much by the Bureau of Reclamation as by the Mormons. It was the bureau that fulfilled Brigham Young's vow to "make the desert bloom like a rose." But by 1991, that era seemed over. After constructing fourteen large water projects and eleven smaller ones, the Bureau is about to go out of business in Utah. A major reason is the Central Utah Project, an engineer's dream that—over three decades—turned into an unworkable nightmare.

This story is about how the Bureau of Reclamation created a mammoth water project that nevertheless ended up betraying even those it was supposed to serve. It also tells how the Bureau cut its own throat in the process, and how some of the CUP may yet be salvaged. Beyond that, this is a tale of unchecked bureaucratic ambition that flourished within a Utahn culture that was totally wedded to traditional water development.

As late as 1985, the twelve Utah counties that supposedly were to benefit from the CUP voted by a majority of 70 percent to increase their indebtedness threefold just to keep the project alive. It was an incredible measure of support few other western water projects have ever garnered. Yet, as Congress considers a vastly scaled-back version of the CUP this summer, public support for the original CUP in Utah still remains high. This is despite the now obvious fact that few Utahns really understood that project's immense complexities and staggering costs.

Over the years since 1956, when Congress first authorized the CUP, its proponents developed a self-serving mythology that became virtually unchallengeable. The first myth was that the rapidly growing Salt Lake City-Wasatch Front region would run out of water without a dramatic infusion from outside the basin. The second was that tapping into the Colorado River watershed offered the only route to a secure water supply. The third was that the $2.2 billion CUP would generate an economic bonanza for Utah.

One of the few critics to challenge these beliefs was Jay M. Bagley, a professor of civil and environmental engineering at Utah State University's Water Research Laboratory. Bagley, who is now retired, contended that the CUP met almost none of Utah's real water needs. Salt Lake County, Bagley, argued, sits in an extremely water-rich region, unlike most other Western metropolitan areas. Using the local water agencies' own data, Bagley noted that the county's estimated groundwater recharge (natural flow to underground aquifers) exceeded annual withdrawals by 241,000 acre-feet. If the county installed a dual potable and non-potable water supply system, he said, it could serve three times its present population.

The Salt Lake area has one of the highest per-capita water consumption rates in the region. Half of all the water delivered to the metropolitan area is used for "outside purposes," such as lawns and gardens.

Bagley also noted that traditional dam projects in the Bonneville (Great Salt Lake) Basin closer to Salt Lake City would be more cost-effective than the CUP. In short, making use of Utah's share of Colorado River Basin water would not necessarily be the best use of that water. "Opting for the big federal water project has foreclosed on the next generation's freedom to implement cost-effective options adapted to their own situation," he concluded in a 1987 review of Salt Lake City's water supply options.

Such criticisms of the CUP, however, never were debated in Utah. Bagley was vilified and threatened with loss of funding for his Water Research Laboratory. His reports were either suppressed or ignored. Utah's pro-CUP political atmosphere was described this way by Lee Swensen, an award-winning reporter for the *Deseret News*: "Anytime I wrote a negative story about the CUP, the Central Utah Water Conservancy District and their allies would attack. But they wouldn't attack the story; they would attack me." Now his newspaper's bureau chief in Washington, D.C., Swensen says all of Utah's newspapers and reporters still treat CUP stories cautiously because of the project's powerful backers. "For decades no politician has ever criticized the CUP," he recalls. "Anyone who questions any aspect of it is almost viewed as a commie, or an Easterner who just doesn't understand water in Utah."

In 1956, when the Central Utah Project was first authorized, Congress set its cost at $330 million. Since then, the Bureau of Reclamation has spent more than $1 billion to complete about half of the blueprint. This work includes eight dams and reservoirs; more than 200 miles of aqueducts and tunnels; several giant pumping stations; and various siphons, drains, and power stations.

After thirty-five years of work, however, the Bureau has yet to move one drop of water from the Uintah Basin in the Green River drainage to the Wasatch Front. Moreover, the Bureau says it will take another $1 billion to finish constructing the CUP—or at least those parts it says it can finish! Small wonder, then, that Congress refused to pass another blank-check reauthorization bill. The Bureau's lengthening history of CUP mismanagement and mistakes alienated even its two biggest Utah allies—Republican Senator Jake Garn, who sits on the all-important Appropriations Committee, and the Central Utah Water Conservancy District, CUP's local sponsor. Both have asked Congress to remove the Bureau from further involvement with the project.

Instead, the Utah congressional delegation and the district have done the unthinkable—negotiated with the environmentalists to redesign the CUP. Those negotiations, all-night sessions held a year ago April in Representative Wayne Owens' Capitol Hill office, wrought a fundamental transformation of the CUP. The new proposal, now before Congress, is called the Central Utah Project Completion Act. "We just totally rewrote the CUP," says Owens, the Utah delegation's maverick Democrat and key liaison with the environmental community. "We killed $300 million in new construction starts and substituted $138 million of Fish and Wildlife rehabilitation projects."

The new bill mandates instream flows, taking project water and putting it back in five of eight streams that were being dried up. It creates two new wetland preserves, buys increased big game winter range and hatcheries for endangered fish, and establishes a fund for future rehabilitation projects. In addition to the unprecedented environmental mitigation package, the measure requires a thorough water conservation program in the twelve Utah counties that will receive CUP water, and provides a $200 million water settlement for the Northern Ute Indian Tribe.

The remaining construction—mostly for irrigation and drainage—is scaled back dramatically. However, before any dirt is moved Utah must first come up with the money for 35 percent of the remaining costs (about $150 million) and find buyers for at least 90 percent of the water. It has five years to meet these requirements, or it loses the project. These conditions are firsts for a federal water project. The bill's most stunning provision, however, is that it fires the Bureau of Reclamation. The Central Utah Water Conservancy District will receive the bill's $895 million to finish the new CUP, and a special presidentially appointed commission will oversee the environmental work. This would virtually shut down the Bureau of Reclamation's Utah office and end the agency's role in Utah.

Senator Garn, who has spent most of his political life pushing the CUP and fighting environmentalists, says the bill "reflects the realities of the 1990s, while honoring the commitments made by the government to the people of Utah in the 1950s." Many environmentalists, on the other hand, would have liked to kill the CUP outright. But they eventually agreed that the project was too far along. Instead, as Kenley Brunsdale, former staff assistant to Rep. Owens, put it, the bill "took the Cadillac of Cadillac Desert and turned it into a Volkswagen with environmental running gear."

The original CUP was a behemoth federal water project, born in the Bureau's heady dam-building days. For Utah, however, the CUP embodied a century-old dream of prosperity in the desert and security for future generations. In 1847, two years before the California Gold Rush gave birth to the Prior Appropriation Doctrine, the Mormon pioneers became the first Anglo settlers in the West to divert water for irrigation and domestic use. Ever since, growth in Utah—originally named Deseret by Brigham Young—has been predicated on water development. The reason is that most of the state's people and some of its best farmland are in the Bonneville Basin. The people are clustered in Salt Lake City and along the Wasatch Front; the farms are on the bottomland around Utah Lake. Much of Utah's water, however, is in the Green and Colorado watersheds hundreds of miles away at the bottom of deep canyons.

As the Salt Lake City area grew, Utah and the Bureau built several water projects on the Bonneville Basin's few big rivers. While there was never a shortage of water, the Colorado River basin always was considered the last watering hole. Its flush snowmelt streams drain the southern slopes of the Uinta Mountains, about 100 miles east of Salt Lake City. Those Uintah Basin streams—tributaries of the Green River and thence the Colorado—are close enough to make a transbasin diversion possible. In 1913 the Bureau completed the Strawberry Valley Project, which did just that. However, it only harnessed the Strawberry River. There were nearly a dozen more untouched rivers and streams, all ripe for development.

In the 1940s Utah leaders began a concerted campaign to win congressional approval for a massive federal water project. First the state negotiated the Upper Colorado River Basin Compact with Colorado, Wyoming, and New Mexico. The 1948 treaty allotted Utah 23 percent of the river, or about 3.25 million acre-feet of water a year. (The three lower basin states, California, Nevada, and Arizona, secured their water rights in the 1922 Colorado River Compact.) The four upper basin states spent the next eight years writing and lobbying for the Colorado River Storage Project. CRSP is one of the most extensive federal water projects ever. Four main dams—Glen Canyon on the Colorado River, Flaming Gorge on the Green, Navajo on the San Juan, and Blue Mesa on the Gunnison— would store water to protect the upper basin from a call on the river by the lower basin. Once built, the dams would serve as cash registers, generating hydropower dollars that would pay for thirteen more "participating projects." Those would develop irrigation, municipal and industrial water systems for the upper basin. The CUP was Utah's only project of these thirteen, but it was the largest and most complex. After a long fight, Congress passed the $1.6 billion CRSP in April 1956, including $330 million for the CUP. This was a critical victory for tiny Utah—one of the more sparsely populated and politically weak states in the West of the 1950s. It meant that the state could finally tap into the two greatest sources of wealth available to the West: the Colorado River and the federal treasury.

The CUP was organized into five independent units. Four of them, the Vernal, Jensen, Uintah, and Upalco units, are located entirely within the Uintah Basin and serve local agricultural and municipal needs. They are relatively small dams and reservoirs. The fifth unit, the Bonneville, is the key to the whole project. It brings Uintah Basin water westward across the divide to urban areas and farms in the Bonneville Basin; it also supplies irrigation water to five counties in the Sevier River basin to the south. The Bonneville Unit is what makes the CUP huge. It is several times larger and more expensive than the other four units combined.

All this required very complex engineering. The Bureau's designs called for sixteen new reservoirs, more than 200 miles of tunnels and aqueducts, six power plants with a combined capacity of 166 megawatts, twelve pumping stations, hundreds of miles of irrigation canals and drains, and two massive dikes in Utah Lake. The Bureau also designed a sixth unit called the Ute, or Ultimate Phase, for later construction. This would tunnel under the Uinta Mountains from Flaming Gorge Reservoir in the northeast corner of the state to link up with the Bonneville Unit in the Uintah Basin.

The first set of plans for the Bonneville Unit was released in 1964. Bureau and Central Utah Water Conservancy District officials expected the project to be finished within a decade. Today, only one of the four Uintah Basin projects, the Vernal Unit, is completed (1962), and it is the smallest. A second, the Jensen Unit, was declared done in 1986 when it was 80 percent complete and nearly 700 percent over budget. The other two units, Uintah and Upalco, were never even started. Bonneville, the fifth unit, is about 66 percent complete at a cost of $1 billion. Even if it gets more money from Congress, it could take another five years before it makes its first delivery of water.

The CUP may have been doomed from the start. It was just too big. The engineering was too difficult and the costs—both environmental and economic—were too high. Blame for the failure of the project has landed squarely on the Bureau of Reclamation from all sides. The water users became upset because the Bureau couldn't pour concrete fast enough. The environmentalists were angry over all the rivers the project would dry up. But the problem really was the way the Bureau designed the project.

Despite its massive construction, the CUP would not have delivered a lot of water. The entire project, if completed, would have only diverted 270,000 acre-feet of water a year from the Colorado River, which was less than one-tenth of Utah's legal share. The Bonneville Unit—which accounts for $1.9 billion of the CUP's $2.2 billion price tag—would have diverted only 140,000 acre-feet a year from the Uintah Basin. It would have developed an additional 22,000 acre-feet for the Uintah Basin, and an additional 100,000 acre-feet in the Bonneville Basin.

The Bonneville Unit captures so little water because more is simply not available. In fact, the project produces so little water that only one-ninth of the 225,000 acres of land irrigated by the Bonneville Unit would have been new lands—lands never farmed before. The rest is already in production. The CUP would provide supplemental irrigation water, such as to help the farmers get a third cutting of hay. In Salt Lake City, the CUP would supply less water than numerous other alternatives, such as tapping the Bear River, revising groundwater management, transferring water from agricultural uses, and conservation.

The CUP also did not make sense economically. For example, the benefit-cost ratio for the Bonneville Unit's irrigation and drainage facilities is 0.3 to 1. According to the Bureau's numbers, it would have spent $3,948 an acre to irrigate land whose crops generally don't justify that level of investment. Because the farmers couldn't afford it, the irrigation facilities would have had to be subsidized by public power—to the tune of almost $1 billion. Similarly, in Salt Lake City rates are already going up in anticipation of the more expensive CUP water. Professor Bagley, of the Utah State University's Water Research Laboratory in Logan, said the CUP water, at $250 to $300 an acre-foot, would be the most expensive water the city could buy, with the exception of treating sewage.

Michael Clinton, a former Bureau engineer, criticizes the agency for designing the showcase dams and power generation facilities first. Only at the very end of the process did the Bureau ever get around to talking to the farmers who were going to use the water. Clinton believes it was the Bureau's attitude that killed the CUP. "The seeds were there long ago, when Teddy Roosevelt and Gifford Pinchot created the Bureau of Reclamation with the philosophy that a centralized technocratic bureaucracy could make better decisions than the public at large," Clinton explains. "That is the way the Bureau's culture was established, and that culture is still alive and well." The Bureau designed the basic system for the CUP and then went out and told the water users what the answer was, he says. "They never did sit down and define the project's purpose, what facilities were necessary to do that, and then get political agreement on it."

Thus many of the original plans didn't work and had to be constantly revised or scrapped—at tremendous cost. Whole portions of the project were overbuilt and now sit unused. In other cases, million-dollar engineering studies sit on the shelf, never to be used. Estimated costs and even bid prices were chronically low, causing constant overruns. And everything took too long to finish.

Key units of the project also failed to work right. Soldier Creek Dam—whose 1 million acre-foot reservoir was the CUP's biggest in the Bonneville Unit—leaked upon completion. Consultants determined that because of faulty design and construction procedures, the dam was at significant risk of failure. The Bureau was forced to open the gates and partially drain the reservoir to fix it. Likewise, controversy is still raging over the geologic integrity of the half-built Jordanelle Dam on the Provo River. The U.S. Geological Survey will begin an investigation of the dam site this summer. More studies will determine if there is enough water in the Provo River to fill the 320,000 acre-foot reservoir when the dam is safely built. In the meantime, the Bureau is proceeding full steam ahead with construction.

Some parts of the CUP are simply white elephants. Red Fleet Dam in the Jensen Unit was built right after the Teton Dam broke, sending a deadly wall of water down the Snake River in Idaho. New federal dam safety standards then raised Red Fleet's total cost from $12 million to $80 million. However, the dam sits almost entirely unused, with no population base to support it. The new CUP bill would have the federal government buy back 16,000 of the Jensen Unit's 18,000 acre-feet of municipal and industrial water, and dedicate it to the U.S. Fish and Wildlife Service.

There also were lots of expensive little disasters. Bob Weidner, a thirteen-year staff assistant to Senator Jake Garn and the person responsible for uncovering most of the Bureau's mistakes, says that aqueduct contractors twice demolished large lengths of freshly buried cement pipe while doing other work. They were forced to dig them up and start over again. At the start of the Carter administration the Bureau got a mole (an underground tunnel-mining machine) stuck while constructing the Stillwater Tunnel. Four years later, when Reagan took office, it was still stuck. "They actually stopped construction of that part of the project for four years," says Weidner. "They had to go renegotiate the contract, and then some guy just walked in and blithely started up the mole and backed it out, so who knows what happened there. That cost us millions."

Every mistake or problem set the project back a little further. And every delay raised the cost a little higher. Ultimately, the Bureau of Reclamation alienated just about every constituency concerned with water in Utah.

The most alienated, of course, were the environmentalists, anglers, duck hunters, biologists, and outdoor enthusiasts. "Utah's environment has suffered greatly at the hands of the Bureau of Reclamation and its thoughtless, irresponsible, poorly planned water developments," says Dr. Fred Reimherr, president of the Stonefly Society, the Salt Lake chapter of Trout Unlimited. The CUP wrought extensive damage in the Uintah Basin—the source of most of the water. The project dewaters nine rivers in the basin, destroying over a hundred miles of Utah's best native trout streams and flooding thousands of acres of riparian habitat and winter range. But it was the Bureau's heavy- handedness as much as the actual damage that incited the conservation community, Reimherr says. Representative Wayne Owens says the Bureau has been "terribly inept and insensitive. They've spent $1.2 billion and only $10 million of that has gone into direct mitigation.... In essence they left it knowing that if they got all their construction in first the federal government would be more disposed to mitigate what's damaged."

Jeff Appel, attorney for a coalition of seventy Utah sportsmen and conservation groups that have protested the CUP, says the agency constantly violated the National Environmental Policy Act. In a number of cases, he says, the Bureau didn't write environmental impact statements at all. Those that it did write segmented the project into small units, completely ignoring the cumulative impacts, he argues. The Bonneville Unit, for instance, was divided into three separate EISes, but only one was ever finished. What most angered Appel and other conservationists was the Bureau's practice of making major revisions in the project after an EIS was completed, without allowing public comment on the new plans.

Over time, the fight against the CUP built strong ties among a small cadre of activists who worked in both the local and national arenas. These people laid the foundation arguments against the CUP and ultimately played a lead role in its overthrow. No one seemed to listen, however, until the Bureau started running out of money. First, because project costs had increased so much, the twelve counties in the Central Utah Water Conservancy District had to approve a new repayment contract. They approved the contract by a 70 percent majority in a 1985 election, which increased the district's debt on the CUP from $150 million to $550 million. In the process, however, the district got a new management that lost much of its faith in the Bureau. "We have changed our focus and our way of doing business 180 degrees at least," says Don Christiansen, the new general manager.

Second, the Bureau had spent all of the money Congress originally authorized for the CRSP, plus most of two additional re-authorizations. So in 1987 the Bureau was forced to go back to Congress for a third. But because the Central Utah Project is the last remaining CRSP project, it had to stand alone for the first time in its history. The Bureau could no longer hide the CUP in large appropriation bills. Nor could the Utah delegation trade votes with other states that needed approval of their project. That's when the project began to come under real scrutiny.

Ironically, most of the problems were uncovered by the Bureau's own supporters. Don Christiansen, concerned that the project was not keeping up with inflation, asked Senator Garn's office for an accounting of the Bureau's expenditures. "The first thing we learned," says Garn's aide, Bob Weidner, "was that in 1985 the Bureau spent 56 percent of its Bonneville construction budget on administrative overhead. On average it was about 30 percent for most of the 1980s." Most of the money went to the Denver and Utah offices.

The agency also stretched its accounting practices. Under federal law the Bureau can shift up to 15 percent of a project's yearly budget to another job without asking permission from Congress. This became routine on the CUP, and money was funnelled to several smaller projects, including the Dallas Creek project and McPhee Dam in Colorado, and the Yakima project in Washington state. "Because the smaller projects don't have the legislative clout to get the money, they sort of bleed off the larger projects," explains Weidner. "We found out it was our project, to the tune of about $80 million over at least the first six years of the 1980s. That's just what we found—we have no idea what the total amount is." When those numbers were revealed in 1987, they outraged the CUP's supporters in Utah, but no one more than Jake Garn. From his seat on the Senate Appropriations Committee, Garn waged fierce battles every year to get the CUP appropriations. That year, instead of pushing the CUP reauthorization bill, Garn attached amendments to the Bureau's CUP appropriation limiting the agency's overhead and banning transfers.

Bureau officials, on the other hand, contend that Congress was to blame for CUP's financial problems and, therefore, most of the rest of its problems. "I think we probably could have built the project in less than ten years had we been able to get sufficient funding from

Congress," says Larry Fluharty, chief of planning in the Bureau's Utah projects office. The rich-poor funding cycles from Congress wreaked havoc on the administration and planning of the CUP, Fluharty says. The Bureau's work capability in a given year depended on that year's appropriation from Congress, and the CUP's annual funds were unpredictable, ranging from more than $100 million to almost nothing, he recalls. In years with no money, the Bureau had to either lay off its workforce and hire a new crew the next year, or spend all its money to keep them on. In rich years there was often more money than the office could spend effectively, especially if the previous year's appropriation was low, says Donald Dean, a Bureau CUP accountant in Salt Lake City. Rather than hold it over, the money was usually transferred to projects that needed it. The cycles were particularly bad during the Vietnam War, when very little money was available for domestic projects. In 1973 it got so bad that the entire construction office and 80 percent of the project office were laid off, Fluharty remembers. Those were years of high inflation, and every delay raised costs.

Finally, Utah's tiny five-person congressional delegation couldn't produce the money. Compared with California's fifty-seven-member delegation and Arizona's powerful Representative Morris Udall and Senator Barry Goldwater, Utah never had a chance. "I guess we [Utah] just did not have the political power to get what we needed to finish the project," Fluharty says.

Many people in Utah, however, feel that the only mistake their congressional delegation made was in not watching the Bureau more closely. "They tended to use us as a funding conduit in order to preserve their overall mission in the West," says Weidner. "That was unfortunate, because now that everyone is onto their game, it has really soiled their reputation."

Ultimately, the Bureau's mismanagement of the CUP set the stage for a revolution. Between 1987 and 1990, the Bureau's reauthorization bill failed in Congress three times, never even making it out of committee. Eventually, the Utah delegation realized it could never get the Bureau's bill through. So it developed a new strategy: Owens, the Democrat, would get the environmentalists on board, and Garn, the senior Republican, would line up the administration.

The environmentalists were well organized. Ed Osann and David Conrad of the National Wildlife Federation in Washington, D.C., had spent years working on the CUP. Meanwhile, in Utah, a coalition of some seventy fishing, hunting, environmental, and conservation groups began meeting in 1989 at Robert Redford's Sundance Resort. They put together a thirty-page report for Congress with a litany of the CUP's problems and their recommendations. The report called for major revisions: drop the Bonneville Unit's entire irrigation and drainage system (still unbuilt); require 35 percent cost-sharing by Utah for all the remaining work; put some water back in the damaged streams; initiate a water conservation program; and carry out more environmental mitigation. Most of the environmentalists also supported a new water settlement for the Northern Ute Tribe, whose water rights had been integral to the project. The environmentalists wielded a big club. Appel, who became the Utah coalition's spokesperson, says it threatened to sue the Bureau over violations of the National Environmental Policy Act. The coalition had such a good case it probably could have stopped construction for years. The Northern Ute Tribe also had threatened to withdraw their water rights from the project if the tribe's concerns weren't met.

The water users, who were desperate to get the CUP reauthorized, had no choice but to negotiate with the environmentalists, their historic enemies. "We forced our way to the table," recalls Appel. "There were times when it was really quite ugly." But once the talks began there was a sort of magical meeting of the minds. The water users discovered they had many of the same concerns the environmentalists had, especially about the Bureau of Reclamation. Don Christiansen, the new manager of the Central Utah Water Conservancy District, says the district and its board finally realized that the project would probably never get finished while the Bureau was in control.

The district accepted the need for a conservation program and brought in the local water users to hammer out an acceptable plan with the National Wildlife Federation. It agreed to the environmental mitigation and enhancement package, giving up 39,000 acre-feet of the Bonneville's 140,000 acre-feet of transbasin diversion to use for instream flows. The district also accepted cost-sharing—paying 35 percent of the costs up front. The district insisted, however, on construction of the Bonneville irrigation system—the aqueduct that connects to the Sevier River Basin. "We tried as hard as we could to eliminate it, but it became clear to us that no bill was going through that didn't have some sort of potential for an irrigation and drainage system in it," says Appel.

The system was scaled back because of the cost-sharing requirements. The original $300-million irrigation system was capped at $150 million. That's when the district also insisted on kicking the Bureau out in order to control the design and construction. "We would have spent the $150 million on overhead and never have a project," says Christiansen. No one wanted the Bureau to touch the $138 million environmental settlement, either. "It's just a terrible bureaucracy," Owens said. "We could do it faster, better, cleaner and cheaper without them. That's why we wrote them out of the bill." Instead, the parties agreed to create a special commission appointed by the President to design and oversee the mitigation. The bill also requires that mitigation be done concurrently with construction. In addition, the delegation worked out a $200-million settlement with the Northern Ute Tribe.

On April 26, 1990, both sides signed off on the compromise. Since then the environmentalists and the district have honored the agreement, jointly lobbying Congress to pass the measure. And both give all the credit to Owens and Garn. "In those negotiations, which went on to five in the morning, Owens was sitting there typing language at his word processor for us," says Appel. "That's how involved he was." Garn took care of the Bureau. From the beginning, Christiansen says, the agency was intransigent: "We negotiated this piece of legislation without their involvement because they weren't playing a constructive part. They always wanted to pull us back into the old type of water project."

During the hearings before the Senate Energy and Natural Resources Committee in September 1990, Reclamation Commissioner Dennis Underwood tried to sabotage the compromise. He opposed the environmental mitigation and Indian water settlement, and demanded that the Bureau retain oversight and final approval on all remaining work on the CUP. His testimony set Garn on fire. Appel, who was waiting to testify, says Garn lit into Underwood, promising to go to John Sununu and even President Bush if necessary to reverse the agency's position. A month later the Bureau announced it had changed its mind and withdrew its opposition. While many in the Bureau privately opposed the legislation, insiders say the entire agency was under orders to keep quiet.

Will passage of the CUP Completion Act save the CUP? Don Christiansen and the Central Utah Water Conservancy District say yes. Because the district is in charge and because it will be spending its own money, they say the Bureau's inefficiencies will be eliminated. Christiansen points to two recent jobs that the Bureau turned over to the district—a canal rehabilitation and a tunnel. Both were completed early and for far less money than the Bureau had budgeted.

Christiansen also says the district can solve the Bureau's design problems. Instead of hiring a huge in-house staff to do the work and create another self-serving bureaucracy, the district plans to hire outside engineering companies. The California firm of Bookman-Edmunston Engineering Inc. already has been asked to redesign and build the Bonneville's irrigation and drainage system. Perhaps it is no coincidence that Bookman-Edmunston's head man on the project is Michael Clinton, the former Bureau official who seems to have come full circle. "The district has retained our firm to start not at the top like the Bureau traditionally does, but from the bottom up with the water users, to start rebuilding those relationships." The farmers' needs, says Clinton, will ultimately determine what physical structures he will recommend to the district.

But in the end, it will all depend on money. Under the bill, 35 percent of all future construction costs and 50 percent of all future feasibility and environmental studies must be paid up-front by Utah. Christiansen says that comes to about $150 million, but he is not sure how he will raise the money. His potential sources are the state legislature, the twelve counties in the Central Utah Water Conservancy District and the water users themselves. If the district can't raise the money within five years of the bill's final passage, it loses the project.

The revised CUP would give Utah's cities about the same amount of water as the original project would have. In addition, however, the cities would be able to save money by gaining credits for water saved through conservation measures. Sevier River Basin farmers would lose about 40,000 acre-feet of irrigation water a year—water that would be left in the Uintah Basin. But the Uintah Basin will still end up drier because of the CUP. To help compensate that region, the bill would provide $40 million to build small-scale water replacement projects, rehabilitate canals and reduce salinity.

The revision's major significance, however, is in its environmental benefits. Representative Wayne Owens calls the bill the "finest piece of environmental legislation Utah has ever seen." Its $138-million mitigation and enhancement package is safely in the hands of a separate commission. And the bill's long-range mitigation fund will help compensate for unforeseen impacts. Similarly, the water conservation package may ultimately end the need for any future water developments of this size. "Over the long haul the water conservation program will be as much value to the state as the physical features of the CUP itself," says Ed Osann of the National Wildlife Federation. No one, however, argues that the conservation package does anything more than make the best of a bad situation. The CUP Completion Act will help repair the damage wrought by the CUP, but nothing will ever put things back the way they were before or get back all the money that was wasted.

*July 15, 1991*

# The Northern Utes' Long Water Ordeal

## Daniel McCool

Curtis Cesspooch, vice chairman of the Northern Ute Tribe, leaned back in his chair and gazed out his office window at the broad expanse of the Uintah and Ouray Reservation. His desk was littered with numerous books and articles on water in the West. "I was an electrician before I was elected to the Tribal Council in 1988," he explained. "Suddenly I had to know everything about water law. The other side brought in these experts who'd try to tell us what to do. Luke and I had to learn quick."

Cesspooch and Luke Duncan, the tribal chairman, were elected to the Tribal Council of the Northern Ute Tribe at a critical time. The tribe, the U.S. government, the state of Utah, and the sponsors of the $2.2 billion Central Utah Project were immersed in a long series of negotiations concerning the tribe's water. Funding for the massive CUP water project was stalled in Congress, in part because the claims of the tribe had never been settled. But after twenty-five years of delays and broken promises, tribal leaders were leery of any new settlement. "People have to understand that since 1965 we've been a part of the CUP, but we really haven't been included in the benefits," Duncan said firmly. "Now we're asking for compensation."

Particularly galling to the Utes is the fact that their participation in the CUP helped get it authorized. Years ago Anglo water developers discovered that they could generate more political support for a proposed project if they cloaked it with a veneer of Indian benefits. This strategy, often called the "Indian blanket," has helped water developers obtain authorization and funding for many projects that primarily serve Anglo water users.

In 1965 CUP supporters signed an agreement with the Northern Ute Tribe that promised the Indians a large water project if they would defer using water on their irrigable lands until 2005 (the 1965 Deferral Agreement). The Indian project was to be one of six units in the Central Utah Project. Another part of the CUP, the Bonneville Unit, was designed to transport water out of the Uintah Basin, where the Utes' reservation is located, and over the mountains to the heavily populated Wasatch Front. In the ensuing decades the CUP has received millions in federal funds for construction, but the Indian unit was never built. Cesspooch is a soft-spoken man, but the anger in his voice was evident as he gestured toward the office window. "See that? That's all we got." Bottle Hollow Reservoir, a small impoundment just north of tribal headquarters, was barely visible. There was virtually no water in it. "And now, even that's no good. It was built on a trash dump and the water became contaminated."

The Ute leaders are well aware that their water settlement will affect their tribe for many years. It could also affect many other people in the West. In recent years many tribes have begun to negotiate their water rights, which are based on the Winters Doctrine of reserved water. Three major settlements were signed in 1988, and four more in 1990. According to Interior Department officials, approximately two dozen more are "in the pipeline." Indian water claims are currently being litigated in fifty different court cases involving every major watershed in the West.

Negotiated settlements are supposed to offer two distinct advantages. First, they may save time and money, compared to litigation. Court cases can drag on for years and cost unbelievable sums in attorneys' fees. For example, it is estimated that the state of Wyoming spent $14 million, and the U.S. government spent $10 million, to litigate the water rights of the Wind River Reservation. Second, settlements can provide funding to tribes to develop water resources; they get "wet water" rather than an avalanche of legal paperwork, the so-called "paper water." But the negotiations and re-negotiations with the Northern Utes constitute an important exception to this. The process has been time-consuming and expensive, and the tribe has yet to receive any appreciable benefits. Other tribes are watching the Northern Utes. If the promised benefits never accrue, it could scare tribes away from the bargaining table.

Cesspooch drove us over to Ute Indian Manufacturing, where tribal members make casings for the Defense Department. On the way we crossed a barren mesa dotted with sage. In the valley below we could see the green bottomlands along the Duchesne River—lands that were once part of the reservation, but were sold to Anglos as "surplus lands" the Indians didn't need. Across the valley to the north rose the Uinta Mountains. "The bill they're working on now will give us money to develop the reservation and the basin-wide economy," Cesspooch said as we toured the plant. "We need money to improve our industry, education and vocational training. A lot of Anglos think we live in teepees and don't have electricity," he added. "They think we don't need any money."

Often, during the years of negotiations and disappointments, the relationship between the Ute Tribe and state and local interests has been strained. The Utes complain that the state has sometimes tried to minimize the tribe's benefits in the negotiations. Dee Hansen, executive director of the Utah Department of Natural Resources, and the state's chief negotiator, disagrees. He notes that at the beginning of the latest round of talks, the state argued that the Utes could get money or water, but not both. Eventually the state abandoned that position. "In the spirit of getting things resolved," Hansen said, "we've agreed to a settlement that provides both water rights and development funds for the tribe. We are trying to mend fences." The money for the settlement is from the federal government; the state of Utah, which did not sign the 1965 Agreement, has no direct payment obligations in the proposed settlement.

Although the Ute Tribe has repeatedly threatened to initiate a lawsuit for its reserved water rights, it has never done so. This makes the Ute settlement the only major negotiation that has not been preceded by years of court battles. Yet just the mention of a lawsuit over reserved Indian water rights strikes fear into the hearts of supporters of the Central Utah Project. They are well aware that a settlement of the Utes' water rights is critical to continued funding for the project; that the Utes could scuttle the entire CUP by refusing to accept their terms.

Project supporters must convince the Utes that they can be trusted to keep their promises, but their track record is not good. The ink was barely dry on the 1965 Deferral Agreement when the federal government began hinting that the Ute Indian portion of the project would probably not be built. In 1967 the Bureau of Reclamation project manager for the CUP stated in a press conference that there was probably not enough water in the Colorado River system for the Ute Indian Unit. By the early 1970s, political support for big water projects was beginning to wane, and the Ute's unit was one of the first to go.

In 1980 many of the unresolved issues created by the Deferral Agreement were dealt with in a compact between the state of Utah and the Northern Ute Tribe. Proponents of the compact argued in

the Utah Senate that "if we don't ratify this compact and this water
has to go to litigation … it could slow down the Central Utah Project
by ten or fifteen years." Both houses of the Utah Legislature
unanimously endorsed the Ute Indian Compact. The compact had
to be approved by the tribe, however, before it could become law.
But by this time the Ute Tribe had begun to lose faith in the process.
Opposition to the compact began to build, and ultimately a majority
of tribal voters opposed its ratification.

In 1984 the tribe requested that negotiations be re-opened. The
following year the Interior Deparment's negotiating team made an
offer that tribal leaders found insulting, and again negotiations
broke off. In 1988 a new effort to resolve differences was initiated.
By that time the CUP had exhausted its authorized funding and an
increase was required. Proponents of the project knew the re-
authorization bill probably would not pass without a settlement of
the Utes' claims. A settlement bill was introduced in Congress, but
the Reagan administration opposed it because of its $430 million
price tag.

In the meantime the Ute Tribe was going through convulsive
tribal elections. Despite a tribal referendum in 1988 that approved
the Ute Water Compact, many tribal leaders spoke out against the
settlement bill. A dissident faction that included Luke Duncan and
Curtis Cesspooch labeled the bill a "sellout." In April 1989 the
dissidents won control of the Tribal Council and quickly withdrew
tribal support for the settlement, which then died in Congress. Later
that year the Tribal Council declared the 1965 Deferral Agreement
void. It looked as if the Utes might sink the massive project.

But large water projects, once begun, have a life of their own.
Abandoning the CUP was unthinkable to most Utah politicians and
water developers. Negotiators eventually worked out an entirely new
settlement that became part of the 1990 CUP re-authorization bill
and was reintroduced in January of this year as Title IV of the 1991
CUP bill. Unlike the previous bills, the current settlement is
designed as direct compensation for the broken promises made in
the 1965 Deferral Agreement, in order to "put the tribe in the same
economic position it would have enjoyed had the project … been
constructed." According to one estimate, the benefits promised in
the 1965 Agreement would have totaled about $17 million annually.
The settlement in its current version awards the tribe both water and
money. It ratifies a revised compact between the state of Utah and
the tribe that grants the tribe a right of 480,000 acre-feet of water for

diversion (250,000 acre-feet of actual depletion). The act authorizes $125 million for a tribal development fund, $45 million for a farming and feed lot operation, and nearly $27 million for a variety of small projects on the reservation, including the repair of Bottle Hollow Reservoir. In addition, the bill allows the tribe to keep a percentage of the repayment funds for the Bonneville Unit, which is estimated to be worth over $100 million.

For a tribe of about 3,200 Indians, many of them destitute, this sounds like the deal of the century. But there is a catch. In return for a guaranteed reserved water right and a packet of money, the tribe must relinquish all other claims to water and submit to a high degree of state and federal control over its water resources. In essence, the tribe is compromising its sovereignty for a price.

In the long run, the most significant limitation imposed on the Utes by the settlement agreement concerns their ability to market their water. The marketing of Indian water has been the most contentious issue in most of the recent water settlements, because the economic and environmental implications are enormous. The Ute bill, like most of the other settlements, permits off-reservation sale or lease within the state. But the real market for Indian water is out-of-state. Following the example of other western states, Utah has made it extremely difficult for the Utes to sell the water to anyone other than Utahns. If the Utes could lease their water downstream, they would not need any water project at all. They would simply leave the water in the watercourse, where it would flow naturally to the intake pipes of cities such as Los Angeles, Phoenix, Tucson, and Las Vegas. These cities, strapped for water, would pay many times the amount that the CUP contract can offer. It could mean a bonanza for the Northern Utes and every other tribe that is situated upstream from large urban areas. It would also help cities avoid building more water projects. The cost to the government would be minimal because no big projects would need to be built. It sounds too good to be true.

It is. There are three reasons tribes such as the Northern Utes are willing to give away their right to market water in any manner they choose. First, state and local governments are usually opposed to out-of-state sales or leases. They view all water within the state as theirs and they want to keep it in-state so that some day they can develop it and use it locally. Many upper basin politicians are willing to go to great lengths to "keep California from getting our water." Second, lower basin states also oppose the marketing of Indian water, because they now get that water for free. As long as tribes cannot consumptively use their water, it ends up in downstream cities without an accompanying water bill. And last, tribes are unsure that the Supreme Court will support their right to market water out-of-state. The current court has not been particularly friendly toward the Indians; in a 1989 case (*Wyoming v. U.S. et. al.*), several justices questioned the very existence of the Winters Doctrine. The questionable stance of the High Court, and the apparent intransigence of state water officials, both upstream and down, have convinced many tribes that a negotiated payoff, accompanied by a guaranteed water right, is their best option. Most observers agree that economic necessity will eventually force acceptance of interstate water marketing, but impoverished Indian tribes cannot afford to wait.

Some Utes express doubts about the extent of outside control that the settlement imposes on them. Some local non-Indian interests also oppose the new re-authorization bill because two Uintah Basin dams—Taskeech and Whiterocks—were stripped from the bill in 1990. These projects were eliminated because the Bureau of Reclamation was unable to find suitable dam sites, and because the bill's sponsors feared that Congress would not fund more dam-building activities. The elimination of the local dam projects has provoked cries of betrayal. The Anglos who live on or near the reservation are in a difficult position because many of them oppose the CUP re-authorization as it is now formulated, but support the section of the bill that settles the Ute water claims.

Jim Reidhead, Uintah County commissioner, has been a vocal opponent of the re-authorization. "I'll be the first to say that the Indians haven't received what they were promised, but neither has the rest of the Uintah Basin," he said. "The majority of concessions in the bill were made on behalf of environmentalists. None were made for the water users in the Uintah Basin. We'd like to see the dams added to the bill. We need the storage." The Uintah County Commission recently voted to officially oppose the new re-authorization bill.

Brad Hancock, the city administrator for Roosevelt, an Anglo enclave on the Reservation, said many local people support the Ute settlement "because it will improve the water situation and pump some money into the local economy." The local economy could use a shot in the arm. The Uintah Basin was hit hard by the oil bust in the 1980s. In the town of Duchesne abandoned buildings and rusted cars are commonplace. The high mesa country is dotted with motionless oil rigs. The bottomland along the Duchesne River supports a good crop, but most of this high desert country offers marginal agriculture at best.

Despite the opposition, the bill's sponsors remain confident, especially in regard to the Ute settlement portion of the bill. They say there is a widespread perception in Congress that the Utes were cheated by the 1965 Deferral Agreement, and that the current settlement is well-deserved compensation. "I don't think they'll try to cut the money and benefits for the Utes; everyone knows this is a good deal compared to what was promised the Indians in the past," noted a staff member for one of the bill's House sponsors. Thus the Utes' portion of the bill may help carry the entire package of legislation to victory.

If the CUP bill again dies in Congress, the Northern Ute Tribe will have to decide if it wants to introduce its settlement as a separate bill. That strategy is risky because it would expose the settlement to critics in the Interior Department and the Office of Management and Budget who think the settlement is too costly, regardless of how badly the tribe has been treated in the past. There would probably be an effort to significantly reduce the amount of money awarded to the Utes. This in turn would make the settlement much less palatable to the tribe.

Passage of the bill in Congress would not be the end of the story; the settlement, and the revised Ute Water Compact, will have to be approved by both the tribe and the Utah Legislature. Approval by the state will probably be pro forma, but the tribal referendum could go either way.

If the settlement becomes law, it may solve some of the tribe's problems, perhaps reducing the 67 percent unemployment rate on the reservation. But tribal leaders still wonder if this is the best deal they can get. Are settlements the fulfillment of promises made, or just the consolation prize for a people with few real choices? Are they simply modern versions of the nineteenth-century treaties that relinquished millions of acres of Indian lands? It is difficult to tell. "The bottom line," says Vice Chairman Cesspooch, "is we are trying to save and protect our homes, our land, and our culture."

*July 15, 1991*

# The CUP: A Project in Search of a Purpose

## Dan McCool

**T**he Interior Department official was angry with his Utah visitors. "You wanted the dog off the leash, so we let him off. Now you want us to go catch the dog."

The "dog" in this case was the Central Utah Water Conservancy District. In 1992, at the behest of Utah politicians, Congress passed a law that took the Central Utah Project away from the U. S. Bureau of Reclamation and gave it to the district. It was an unprecedented act of trust, giving a local water district total control over the construction and management of a massive water project that was costing the taxpayers billions of dollars. It has been eight years since the district took over—eight years of poor management, wasted money, and canceled projects. The Utahns who were visiting the Interior Department official went through a litany of problems with the district, and suggested that the federal government needed to resume control over the CUP—and put the dog back on the leash.

The district seems to have a knack for planning bad projects that go nowhere. It spent millions planning for a dam in Monk's Hollow. Following a fierce protest led by the Utah Rivers Council, the district canceled the dam. Not to be deterred, the district continued with plans to build a massive irrigation project (SFN) at a time when such projects were considered wasteful boondoggles; in 1997, ABC Nightly News featured the SFN in their "It's Your Money" series, which profiles examples of government waste. Environmental groups, taxpayers, and officials from the Salt Lake area roundly criticized the project. Eventually the Interior Department forced the district to cancel SFN. In the meantime, the district continued planning for two dams in the Uintah Basin in northeastern Utah, even though both dams were mired in disagreements between the Northern Utes and local water users. In April of 1999, the tribe sent a terse, two-sentence letter to the district announcing they would no longer participate in the dam projects; this effectively killed both dams.

The latest problem for the district is a state audit that found numerous examples of poor cash and fund management, egregious conflicts of interest, and a $55 million fund consisting of "cash or liquid assets." The audit also discovered the district had spent $270,000 in lobbying expenses in the past three years; in other words, the district was spending tax dollars to get ... more tax dollars. The district buried its lobbying expenses in an innocuous-sounding budget item labeled "direct expenses." The district's general manager, Don Christiansen, was given a $75,000 bonus for "work not yet performed" and a $37,000 car—all at taxpayers' expense. The word "corruption" never appears in the carefully worded state audit, but it oozes from between the lines.

With this track record, what's left for the district? More money, it seems. It just received $50 million from the federal government to complete the Diamond Fork water delivery system, which will pipe water from the Uintah Basin over the mountains to the Bonneville Basin. But at present it's a pipeline to nowhere; with the demise of SFN, there is no agreement on what to do with the water. The district still wants to send the water south to a handful of farmers so they can grow an extra cutting or two of alfalfa. But there is tremendous pressure to divert the water north to the Provo/Salt Lake urban region. The governor has created a task force to consider what to do with the water once the Diamond Fork pipeline is completed. In the meantime, the district continues laying pipe, despite the lack of a destination.

The only element of the CUP that seems to have an identifiable objective is the Utah Reclamation, Mitigation, and Conservation Commission set up in 1992 to repair some of the environmental damage done by the CUP and other water projects in the region. This commission issued a plan in June 1999, detailing dozens of projects that range from acquiring riparian lands for "angler access," to a program to reduce the number of deer killed on the new highways built by the district. One of the commission's highest priorities is to acquire and preserve wetlands on the east side of the Great Salt Lake—the same area where the state of Utah wants to build the "Legacy" superhighway.

The commission's plans are ambitious, but may be thwarted by the perverse politics of the CUP. For example, Leonard Blackham, a state senator from Juab County, is threatening to withdraw the state's cost-share for the commission's budget if the district is not allowed to build an irrigation project in Juab County.

The CUP was conceived when Dwight Eisenhower was president and irrigation was thought to be the keystone to Utah's future. But by late-1999, agriculture employs less than 2 percent of the state's work force, and the Salt Lake area is burgeoning. The Central Utah Water Conservancy District appears incapable of adjusting to this new reality; twelve of the district's eighteen board members represent rural irrigation interests. It may well be time to put the dog back on the leash.

*Written for this volume*

# 5

## Urban Water Projects

### Denver's Two Forks Dam

# Two Forks Proposal Has Roused Western Colorado

## Steve Hinchman

By 1988, Two Forks Dam had rural Coloradans up in arms. Denver's existing water diversions already had taken a good share of the flow of western Colorado rivers to the Front Range, and hundreds of angry residents showed up at public hearings to tell Denver "no more." "The supporters of Two Forks are putting the profits of Eastern Slope and developers before the health and economic viability of the people of western Colorado," Grand Junction resident Rollin Bitting told a cheering full house in Grand Junction that April at the first of three West Slope hearings. More than sixty people testified against the dam proposal before the Army Corps of Engineers and other officials at the four-hour hearing. Some had traveled 150 miles or more to be there.

"I've never seen the unity on the West Slope regarding any issue like I've seen today. We have unity that is unprecedented in West Slope politics," said Joe Skinner of the Mesa County Water Association. Actually, the unity was not total. The Colorado River Water Conservation District—an entity supported by taxes levied on fifteen West Slope counties—has cut its own deal with the Front Range. The arrangement essentially provides the river district with Denver money to build a reservoir on the West Slope. A big part of the agreement requires river district neutrality, even though the district is the legal entity charged with protecting West Slope water.

Speakers at the meeting included ranchers, farmers, environmentalists, loggers, rafters, retirees, and business and political leaders, all unified on one point: wasting water is sacrilege in the arid West, and Denver is guilty of that waste. John Baldus, vice president of the Western Colorado Congress, said, "It is an outrage to ask western Coloradans to sacrifice present and future benefits of abundant clean water ... simply to help metro Denver citizens waste more water." Groundwater hydrologist Lorrie Cahn

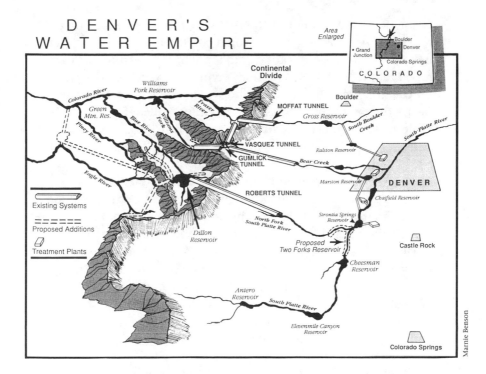

## DENVER'S WATER EMPIRE

said, "I am appalled by the amount of water used by the people of Denver." The environmental impact study estimates current water use is 187 gallons per person per day. Silver-haired residents far outnumbered young people at the meeting, and they let the corps know what western water is worth. "Having grown up on a ranch without running water, I can assure you I know the value of water," said one rancher. Other native western Coloradans told of hauling water by hand or truck and raising a family of eight on less than 100 gallons a day. The group demanded water meters and conservation measures in Denver before building more water projects.

Others protested that while Denver secured water for its future, the West Slope would be left with pollution and a salty river. A Grand Junction resident said building Two Forks to capture excess spring runoff at the headwaters was analogous to "skimming cream off the top of the barrel and leaving the dregs for the rest of us." Tim Carlson, a water engineer, noted that Two Forks would increase the salt load in the Colorado River by 101,000 tons per year. He said the corps study spent only ten pages on salinity and dismissed the issue as insignificant. Based on the Bureau of Reclamation's ongoing

Colorado River Salinity Control Project, Carlson estimated that removing Two Forks' salt load would cost over $56 million. "That," he said, "is not insignificant." Fruita rancher Ruth Hutchins then raised that figure to $256 million, saying that was the price the Bureau of Reclamation estimated it would have to pay to remove nearly the same amount of salt from Grand Valley irrigation projects. William Ela, a board member of the Clifton Water District, said if Two Forks is built, the district's already low-quality water will become unusable: "This will totally destroy our water supply. We'll lose our entire investment." Joining the complaints on salinity were the cities of Grand Junction and Fruita, the Mesa County and Rio Blanco county commissioners, the Mesa County Water Association, the city councils of Silt and Glenwood Springs, among others.

Henry Tiegan, a staff attorney for the Denver Water Board, was the sole speaker for the project. He said he came to Grand Junction because dam sponsors knew salinity would come under fire on the West Slope. Tiegan said the project was designed only to take water in the spring and early summer, when salt levels were at their lowest, and that the Corps had addressed salinity and found it insignificant. The crowd responded with laughter and disbelief.

Other speakers criticized the project for not only taking the region's water but also harming the West Slope's chances for survival in a hard-hit economy. "Pressure on water over here is getting extreme," said Paonia blacksmith Bill Brunner. "All the growth in the state doesn't have to be in Denver." Randy Corey, representing Silt and Glenwood Springs, also warned against Denver's plans for future growth. "Unlimited growth must not be allowed to destroy the beauty of this state." Carol Grahm of Fruita brought down the house with her comment: "People do not come to visit Colorado to see big cities covered by clouds of brown smog and carpeted by acres of lush lawns and aqua blue swimming pools. They can see that at home in Detroit, Chicago or Pittsburgh."

Representatives of commercial rafting companies said without water the rivers and the state's rafting economy would dry up, and so would many small mountain towns.

Rebecca Frank, a member of the Colorado Wildlife Commission who said she was speaking for only herself, said the corps did not address cumulative impacts from the project on several species of endangered fish in the Colorado River.

Two members of the radical environmental group Earth First!, saying they represented endangered species and wild rivers that could not be present at the meeting, pledged to commit civil disobedience if the dam were built.

Toward the end of the meeting, Mesa County Democratic Party members who had just finished their party caucus drifted in to tell the corps that all 329 delegates had voted unanimously to oppose the Two Forks project.

The beating the Denver Water Board and the Metropolitan Water Providers took in Grand Junction was repeated at later hearings in Grand and Summit counties, located at the headwaters of the Colorado River where Denver wants to build new collection systems. Water would then flow through a tunnel under the Continental Divide to fill the Two Forks Reservoir. Grand County, which would host the Williams Fork collection system, lies at the top of the watershed, but has more water rationing than Denver, with some of the county's streams reduced to mud puddles every summer when the Denver Water Department's canals divert water to city residents.

More than 280 people packed an April 18 hearing at the Silver Creek Resort near Granby. Fifty spoke, all against the project. Speakers criticized the Two Forks project from several angles, with many saying that the area depends on fishing, rafting, and hunting, which would dry up along with its rivers. Outside the meeting hung a banner reading, "Damn the DWB [Denver Water Board] Instead." When the supervisor of a nearby national forest asked for a show of hands of people opposed to Two Forks, the entire crowd jumped to its feet with whistles and catcalls.

There was a repeat performance the next day in Summit County, when 250 people jammed the Holiday Inn in Frisco. However, much of the comment there was directed not only at the Denver Water Board, but also at the four speakers who supported the Two Forks Dam. Summit County Commissioner Don Peterson, Dillon Mayor Flo Raitano, and Frisco Administrator Carl Stephanie all supported the project based on a 1985 agreement with the Denver Water Board. In that agreement, Denver promised to keep levels in Dillon Reservoir stable and pay mitigation costs. In return, Summit County would allow Denver access to water upstream of the reservoir and support Two Forks.

Critics said the three government entities had sold out the rest of the county and Western Slope. Trout Unlimited President and Frisco resident Nick Doperalski said, "If Dillon and Summit County put one more layer of pink on their rose-colored glasses they are going to go blind," reported the *Summit County Journal*. Doperalski said the agreement protects the lake but not snow-making needs or flows and water quality in the Blue River. Others said no agreement could ever replace the Blue River once it was lost, and that they hoped Denver would choke on the water it was stealing.

*May 9, 1988*

# EPA to Denver: Wake up and Smell the Coffee!

## Steve Hinchman

enver's giant Two Forks Dam received a crippling blow on March 24, 1989, when Environmental Protection Agency national administrator William Reilly ordered his Denver office to begin a veto of the project. Reilly's decision—made against the recommendation of Denver regional administrator Jim Scherer—stunned environmentalists and water developers alike, and sent Denver politicians into an uproar. Under the Clean Water Act's rules, the EPA veto process will take several months, and if confirmed will overturn the Army Corps of Engineers' permit approval and kill the $500 million to $1 billion dam.

In announcing the Two Forks decision at a Denver press conference, Scherer said Reilly's greatest concern was that less damaging alternatives, such as conservation, had not been fully developed, and that the Denver metropolitan area had not demonstrated a compelling need for the dam. "The proposed project contemplates the destruction of an outstanding natural resource, Cheesman Canyon, to provide new water supplies for the Front Range of Colorado," Reilly said in a prepared statement. "I am not convinced that the project as proposed will avoid environmental harm to the extent practicable or that the proposed permit conditions will minimize or compensate for damage to fisheries, wildlife habitat and recreational areas ... In sum, I do not believe this project meets the guidelines ... of the Clean Water Act."

The EPA's decision came as a surprise, but the agency's concerns matched those of environmental and outdoor groups, which have argued for years that Two Forks is destructive, expensive, and unnecessary. Those concerns were listed in a January 30 letter to Reilly signed by leaders of the nation's nine largest environmental organizations. They asked Reilly, the former executive director of the Conservation Foundation, to intervene and reject the 615-foot-high dam.

Reilly was also under heavy pressure from project supporters, and, as one of his first acts in office, suspended the permit process until he could review the project. That kicked off an intensive lobbying effort by both sides, including a daily barrage of meetings, telephone interviews, and political string-pulling that lasted right down to the day the final decision was announced.

"We think Reilly has shown an incredible amount of integrity and leadership ... Everybody else in the decision-making process has passed the buck," says Carse Pustmueller, director of the National Audubon Society's Platte River Campaign. "The facts and the truth about Two Forks are finally outweighing the political muscle of the Denver Water Board."

"This is a message from the Bush administration," says Dan Luecke, a scientist with the Environmental Defense Fund's Boulder, Colorado, office and one of the founders of the Environmental Caucus, a coalition of Colorado environmental groups that has fought Two Forks since its modern inception in 1981. "What this means from Bush is 'I really meant it when I said I was an environmentalist.'"

Colorado Senator Bill Armstrong, R, has pressured Bush to change Reilly's decision; however, Bush said on March 31 that he would not intervene in the battle.

If the EPA veto is upheld (the agency has never dropped a veto once the process was started), it will mean a major victory for the Colorado and national environmental groups, as well as lovers of the South Platte River. "I can hear the funeral march from here," Luecke told the *Rocky Mountain News*. "We have at this point seen the end of the big dam era."

While seen as primarily a Denver battle, a Two Forks veto is also a big victory for downstream communities, rivers, and wildlife in western Colorado and Nebraska. "Hopefully it signals the end of the almost arrogant power of the Denver Water Board, that they don't have to consider anyone or anything but themselves," says Marv Ballantyne, former president of the Western Colorado Congress. "It's been a nasty situation on the Western Slope in the past. Whenever Denver wanted water they would just come and get it ... Now it's a new era for Colorado."

Nebraskans also celebrated. The state has already lost 70 to 80 percent of the historic flow of the Platte River to upstream consumption, and the Two Forks dam would have dried up 116 miles of the Platte in drought years. Critics say the dam would have destroyed habitat for the endangered whooping crane, sandhill cranes, and other migrating waterfowl, as well as the endangered least tern and threatened piping plover. Senator James Exon, D-Neb., who fought strenuously against Two Forks and last winter released internal EPA documents that said the dam would violate the Clean Water Act, says he was "especially pleased" by the EPA's action. "I would hope the Denver water zealots and the Army Corps of Engineers would be more careful in the future before they rush into decisions where there is no environmental justification," Exon adds.

Two Forks backers, however, have refused to concede the battle. The day of the decision, Denver Water Board chairman Monte Pascoe and Denver Mayor Federico Peña held a joint press conference to denounce the EPA decision and encourage other public officials to join them in an effort to overturn it. Pascoe told the *Rocky Mountain News* the decision should not have been made by a newly appointed federal official "who is not at all familiar with the record and the process that has gone on for these past eight years at a cost to local water entities in excess of $40 million." Colorado Governor Roy Romer said he hoped the giant project could be salvaged and told the *News*, "I'm concerned about the consequences of this decision ... I simply do not believe the federal government understands the conditions here."

Project backers and local politicians have little time to change the EPA's mind. Under the Clean Water Act, Two Forks proponents and the Corps of Engineers have fifteen days—until April 7—to consult with the EPA's Denver office and propose changes in the project or increase the mitigation.

Because Denver EPA administrator Scherer has said he would not be able to "in good conscience" reverse himself and recommend a veto, Reilly has brought in an outside arbitrator, Lee DeHihns, who is currently the agency's deputy regional administrator in Atlanta, Georgia. If the negotiations don't satisfy DeHihns, he will publish a notice of intent to veto the dam in the Federal Register. He must then allow thirty to sixty days for public comment and may hold a public hearing. Then DeHihns will either withdraw the veto, or send the project record to Reilly at EPA headquarters in Washington, D.C. There Reilly will meet with the assistant secretary of the Army in charge of the Corps of Engineers. Reilly then has sixty working days to affirm, deny, or modify the veto.

Robert McWhinnie, executive director of the Metropolitan Water Providers—the coalition of forty-two suburban governments that would have paid 80 percent of Two Forks' cost and used 80 percent of its water—says, "We think what happened to us was a purely political decision, not based on the facts and not based on EPA regulations. We think we're being denied due process," McWhinnie told *The Denver Post*. McWhinnie also questioned the legitimacy of Reilly's intervention in the process, noting that according to EPA procedures, a veto begins at the regional level, not at the top. Denver Water Board lawyers have accused the EPA of changing the rules in midstream and are currently poring over the agency's documents to determine whether the agency has violated its regulations.

The Two Forks veto will toss a monkey wrench into some Denver leaders' and developers' plans for future growth, and they have predicted dire consequences as a result. "Rejection of Two Forks will have a devastating impact on the Denver metropolitan area," Pascoe said at the press conference. "The effects from something like this aren't felt in a day or a month, but we are now in a terrible dilemma." Pascoe added that Denver may have to sacrifice its green image and resort to rate increases, tougher lawn-watering restrictions, and limits on water taps for new homes, reports AP. Pascoe also said the veto may start a new round of water wars in Colorado that could lead to smaller but more damaging projects on other rivers in the state, including the Gunnison, Arkansas, Cache La Poudre, St. Vrain, and Rio Grande.

McWhinnie argues the veto will also destroy any opportunity for cooperation among local governments in the Denver metropolitan area. "Cooperation on water in the metro area is tied to Two Forks and continued cooperation in the metro area is tied to us having an adequate water supply." He says the veto will start cutthroat competition among suburbs for growth, and public perceptions of the $1 billion water project will soon change. "If we get a drought from this continued warm weather, there will be a water crisis. There will be such a shortage that there will be a public demand that we build Two Forks."

Senator Bill Armstrong warns that the veto may start a rush on agricultural water, turning rural Colorado counties into deserts and causing the collapse of small communities and the state's agricultural economy. "The portrait painted by the other side is not very flattering to them," Luecke told the *Post*. "They are the people they say will be doing all these horrible things."

Senator Tim Wirth argues that the effects of the veto will be healthy for Colorado. "There are going to be some greater efficiencies in usage. It puts a premium on conservation and efficiency," he told the *Post*.

While the Denver Water Board says there is not enough water to share, environmentalists argue there is plenty of water, both in existing diversion projects and in aquifers, if it is shared and used efficiently. However, they say that getting the Denver Water Department to cooperate may prove difficult. Rocky Smith, an organizer with the Colorado Environmental Coalition who put together much of the grass-roots opposition to the dam during last spring's public hearings, says, "The Denver Water Department, being the power mongering institution that it is, is likely to make good on their threats until everybody gets nervous again and there is a big clamoring for Two Forks."

So far the threat has moderated, from Pascoe's threat before the EPA decision that Denver wouldn't share a drop, to his recent statement that the agency would agree only to share on a year-by-year basis. Walter Jessel, chair of the Environmental Caucus, says the water board's water and water rights are too plentiful and valuable for the agency to hold out for ever. Jessel says the water board's threats may be hurting it. The threats, he says, will force the suburbs to band together, and they won't need Denver anymore. That may already be happening. The city of Aurora and Arapahoe County, which have been battling in court over rights to water in the upper Gunnison basin, have announced they may try to settle their differences out of court.

Jessel says Pascoe's anger is now damaging the image of Denver. "While Romer is trying everything he can to attract business to Denver, he is being undercut by this petulance." Jessel notes now that Two Forks won't be built, the Denver Water Department has an enormous kitty in its bank accounts that won't be spent on the dam and could be spent on education, mass transit, or other public works. "The people of Denver will now have to re-assess what this water board's function should be," says Jessel. "With the defeat of Two Forks it's going to be an extremely complicated game," he adds. "It will change everything."

*April 10, 1989*

# Water Development Turns a Corner

## Dyan Zaslowsky

**W**hen the fountain in the lobby of the Denver Water Department is operating, people must talk above the sound of falling water. Sheets of water spill over the sides of a square platform and land with a loud slap in a shallow pool below. The water is pumped, unseen, back up the platform to drop again into the pool. Mechanically impressive, undeviating, and capable of drowning the words of those nearby, this handsome monument to the marvels of engineered water illustrates some institutional traits of the 1,100-employee Denver Water Department and the five-member Board of Water Commissioners that directs it. Together, they have won both praise and condemnation for their determination to make water flow where it would not naturally go.

Two Forks Dam is the latest, largest expression of that determination. One of the most controversial projects ever proposed in the state, Two Forks would capture water flowing down Colorado's Western Slope and pipe it under the Continental Divide to be stored in a giant 1 million-acre-foot reservoir on the South Platte River just upstream of Denver. To satisfy federal requirements, the board spent eight years and $40 million studying the dam's feasibility and environmental impacts. But the board always expressed the conviction, despite growing public opposition, that Two Forks would be built. This is the way Colorado water projects had always worked, and none had made them work this way as successfully as the Denver Water Board had.

Then, in spring 1989, the head of the U.S. Environmental Protection Agency, William K. Reilly, did the unthinkable. He set in motion the process to veto the proposed $1 billion, 600-foot-high dam. In the wake of the resulting storm, Reilly appointed Lee A. DeHihns to study Two Forks. On August 29, DeHihns reached the same conclusion, and announced that he was recommending that EPA veto the dam because of unacceptable environmental impacts.

Months later, it became clear that Reilly and DeHihns did more than doom a dam. They also undermined the Denver Water Board and other water authorities by using federal environmental laws to supersede the Prior Appropriation Doctrine. The Prior Appropriation Doctrine is the region's unique water law which, until now, has been the single most powerful determinant of the order and pace of western development. It has also been the water board's most powerful legal tool in its endless drive to acquire water for Denver.

Malcolm M. Murray, first vice president of the Denver Water Board, bemoaned the failure of the Prior Appropriation Doctrine at the Gunnison Water Conference in Colorado last summer. Board members, he said, "no longer have a reasonable atmosphere in which to plan for future water supplies." Denver Water Board President Hubert A. Farbes Jr. concurs. "What we have here is a conflict between two systems, one based on a federal mandate, the other on a vested property right under the Prior Appropriation Doctrine. The Prior Appropriation Doctrine is truly in jeopardy. Our own system is destabilized."

Implicit in the board members' claims is the threat that if the Prior Appropriation Doctrine is no longer working for Denver, then it is also in jeopardy throughout the West. It is a call to arms reminiscent of western water developers' outrage at President Jimmy Carter's 1977 dam hit list. That time the West responded in unison and rescued most of the dams. But this time it seems no one is listening. It may be that the Denver Water Board and the water development community's monopoly on the Prior Appropriation Doctrine is in trouble, and not the doctrine itself.

The Denver Water Department was created by Denver voters in 1918. The vote turned a private water company into a public agency and gave it a charter to acquire water for the city's future as cheaply as possible. To insulate it from the politics of the day, the charter authorized the department to keep its own accounts and gave the board great autonomy in setting metropolitan water policy. Unlike other public utilities and all other major metropolitan water authorities in the West, the Denver Water Board is not subject to a regulatory agency, nor must it seek approval from the mayor or city council for its decisions.

The water board's charter, together with its shrewd deployment of the Prior Appropriation Doctrine, has created an uncommon and formidable agency. By executing only a fraction of some 250 water rights the board holds or claims, the agency's ambitious plumbing system draws water from both sides of the Continental Divide—from the South Platte on the east and the Colorado River on the west. In 1988, the Denver Water Department delivered more than 78 billion gallons of treated water to about 1 million customers, almost half of whom live or run businesses outside Denver city limits. Including the area annexed for the new Denver airport, the water department serves 450 square miles. With the construction of projects such as Two Forks, various master plans have projected that the department could deliver water to about five times the metropolitan area's current population.

The Denver water system grew not only by supplying water for drinking and washing, but by making the resource available year-round for lawns and gardens. Early settlers brought their passion for the color green with them to the semi-desert. Back in 1942, the water department boasted that "the fact that Denver meters only where necessary and permits sprinkling on flat rate affords the double advantage of civic attractiveness and economy."

Such was the state of conservation when Glenn Saunders was growing up in Denver. Saunders, now eighty-five, is the daunting water lawyer who, at the behest of his friend Mayor Ben Stapleton, directed the board's efforts to secure its earliest water rights and forge new ones. Saunders worked as the water board's top attorney for fifty years, instilling the agency with his conviction that the Denver area had an absolute need for and right to West Slope water. "People forget that this a raw, harsh environment we live in, and that the elements imposed on us were not designed to help human life but to impair it," Saunders told me, when I visited him in his warm living room last summer. This sort of rhetoric still brings a room of applauding water developers to their feet in affirmation.

Early in his career Saunders rescued the board's faltered claim to water in the Fraser River, more than 100 miles west on the other side of the Continental Divide. His courtroom-save led to Denver's first diversion of water from the West Slope to the East Slope. It reached Denver through the 6-mile-long Moffat Tunnel in 1936. Saunders won, then and since, by arguing that there is only one Colorado, not two as implied by the geographical division of the state into West Slope and East Slope. Saunders asserted that West Slope water did not "belong" there, it belonged to whoever claimed it first and could put it to use. In Saunders' mind, Denver would always be the only entity capable of doing that.

The Fraser River decision and others in Saunders' favor enabled him to transform the modest Denver Water Board into "a kind of understudy of the Metropolitan Water District of Los Angeles," wrote Marc Reisner in *Cadillac Desert*. Under Saunders, the water board became a "well-oiled, well-funded suprapolitical machine trying to purloin water from every corner of the state, all in the interest of turning Denver into the Los Angeles of the Rockies ..."

Saunders says the water board's "constancy of purpose" has forged its successes. He maintains that the agency's mission is still to build a water system "for thousands of years in the future." I asked Saunders about the seeming arrogance of this undertaking, since it ignores what those outside Denver may want or need. "Arrogance?" he shot back. Rail-thin and mentally acute, Saunders is composed of edges. "Arrogance you say? Why, it's the kind of arrogance that runs the nation's space program, and that builds great water systems, that separates the human mind from the mind of a rabbit."

If Two Forks marks the end of an era, it will not be due to internal rot. Saunders' vision and arrogance still guide the Denver Water Board, with Two Forks serving as a perfect example of meticulous foresight under the Prior Appropriation Doctrine. The Two Forks filing for 132,415 acre-feet of water from the South Platte River dates to 1905, and was the largest single filing in the state up to that point. The claim was made for the city of Denver, then served by the private Denver Union Water Company, forerunner to the Denver Water Department. The filing was transferred to the water board in the 1920s, and has been inching toward perfection ever since.

Confidence in the stability of the appropriation doctrine and the board's Two Forks claim was voiced only a few years earlier, when Denver Water Board President Monte Pascoe told the audience at a conference on water planning that Colorado already had a water plan, and that it was called the Prior Appropriation Doctrine. By logical extension the planning accorded by the doctrine was in the hands of the Denver Water Board, which knew best what was needed.

Although the Denver Water Board has pushed the Prior Appropriation Doctrine to its limits, the doctrine is not unique to Colorado. It is well-established throughout the arid West. But it remains purest in Colorado, where it is embedded in the Colorado constitution. Since the late 1960s, sixteen western states have diluted the pure Colorado doctrine with public interest criteria. The Colorado doctrine is also softened in some states by the need for water appropriators to acquire a permit from a state engineer, who considers broader issues than those facing the most senior developer. In Colorado, water rights are decided in water court.

The water court system is more costly than the permit system, which explains why about half the nation's water lawyers are in Colorado. The state fathers had hoped water courts would keep the issue from political influence. But the strategy not only insulated water from political corruption, but also from broader public pressure. In the end, critics say, the Colorado version of Prior Appropriation turned a doctrine for governing a public resource into a private club for settling disputes among water developers.

In Colorado, water rights are only granted for consumptive uses. Instream flows can only be held by the state. For example, leaving water in a river for fish, native vegetation, scenic beauty, and recreation is to waste it, and thereby lose the right to it. But diverting water to the lawns of the plains is a duly recognized beneficial use. It is a plain "use it or lose it" philosophy, enabling present waste to assure future waste and barring the environmental community from playing the game.

"If you don't own a water right, and none of us in the environmental community do, you are automatically without standing in water court," says Dan Luecke, a senior scientist with the Environmental Defense Fund in Boulder. Luecke—who is also a founding member of the Environmental Caucus, the coalition of environmentalists that fought the Two Forks proposal—says attempts by environmental groups to obtain water rights for instream flows by using the public trust doctrine in court are rigorously opposed by the water development community. Moreover, the state water agency—the Colorado Water Conservation Board—which is supposed to protect instream flows, has entered those cases on the side of the water developers.

Colorado water court judges, even those inclined toward reform, are aware of how narrow their venue is. They still hand down water decrees based on seniority and the conventional definition of beneficial use. Montrose Water Court Judge Robert Brown expressed the need for a change last year in a case in which he granted the city of Aurora water rights in the pristine Upper Gunnison Basin. In his opinion, Judge Brown warned: "A day of reckoning is coming when the 'public interests' raised by the opposers herein will have to be addressed in proceedings adjudicating water rights."

With the Two Forks veto, that day may have dawned for the Denver Water Board and the other members of its club. "People have shown they will be heard," says David Getches, a University of Colorado law professor and former director of Colorado's Natural Resources Department. "If there are no regular channels for them to use, they'll be forced to go outside them," he says, explaining the extraordinary EPA veto.

At a recent conference titled "Colorado in the Wake of the Two Forks Decision," Colorado Governor Roy Romer told an audience of water developers, "The federal government is in here because they represent some of the values that were not represented in this state. Our system for planning and developing water was developed a century ago. The public values in Colorado have changed dramatically since the system was established," reports *The Denver Post.*

But environmental spokesmen say this does not mean, as Murray and Farbes asserted, an end to the Prior Appropriation Doctrine. Indeed, few environmental leaders say they find fault with the doctrine in its current form. They believe the existing constitutional language already addresses their concerns; it is the court administration of the language that does not. "The federal decision on Two Forks doesn't threaten a word of the Prior Appropriation statute as it appears in the state constitution," says Jo Evans, an environmental lobbyist. Chris Meyer of the National Wildlife Federation in Denver says: "We don't want to change the game, we just want to be permitted to play it." They refer to the opening paragraph of the Colorado constitution's irrigation statute. It declares that the water of every natural stream is public property. "This language is so broad that it does not take magic or any leap of faith to maintain that the protection of the public interest is what was intended all along," says Larry MacDonnell, a University of Colorado law professor. According to MacDonnell, "addressing environmental concerns is not at odds with the Prior Appropriation Doctrine, but in line with it." He also points out that all vested property rights are restrained in some fashion by the concommitant duty to protect the general good.

In a way, the water board's warning that an era is ending may be correct. But the era that's ending isn't that of the Prior Appropriation Doctrine; it is the era under which the doctrine was the sole property of water developers. In the coming era, it may be that the doctrine will accommodate a much broader spectrum of interests.

*December 4, 1989*

# Ripples Grow When a Dam Dies

## Ed Marston

After the final defeat of Denver's proposed Two Forks Dam in 1990, water development in Colorado has changed drastically. No longer is Denver the imperialistic leader of Front Range urban development. No longer are environmentalists a fringe influence, forever fighting the good fight against dams and forever losing.

The change has been visible at three major water powers: the Denver Water Department, the Northern Colorado Water Conservancy District and the Colorado River Water Conservation District.

• The Denver Water Department has a new board, a new manager, new middle management, and a new, clearly articulated policy;

• Northern has a new manager and an evolving board, and is slowly developing a new policy; while

• the River District, with the same manager and no new water policy, has lost its position as the West Slope's leader in water matters. Some in western Colorado see the outfit, which is charged by charter with protecting Colorado River water, as a traitor.

These changes would have occurred eventually. But they came about sooner because Colorado's environmental community, organized as the Environmental Caucus, chose to work within the Two Forks permitting process during the 1980s. Rather than stand firm against any water development, the caucus accepted the inevitability of some development but chose to seek the least damaging, least expensive path. After years of participation, the caucus built a case that the ecologically and environmentally expensive Two Forks wasn't needed if conservation and water transfers were implemented and a few small projects were built. In the end, the caucus convinced the head of the Environmental Protection Agency, Bill Reilly, and he convinced President George

Bush. The dam was rejected in 1990, and Denver's build-build-build policies were swept away when the advantages of a soft-path approach to water development became apparent.

The change in the Denver Water Department was on display in late August when its new leader, Chips Barry, came to the rural West Slope to tell a group of farmers and utility managers: "Beliefs that belonged to the environmental fringe in the 1960s have become mainstream values today." So the Denver Water Department has shed "its earlier adolescent personality. We're now a more mature organization. We have a different board, a different manager, and very different conditions and financial constraints. The opportunities for future water development in the entire state, and especially on the Front Range, are very difficult."

It is unlikely that Barry's predecessor, Bill Miller, would have met with a bunch of ditch company board members and heads of small utilities. There would have been no point, since the old Denver Water Department saw the West Slope as a collection of rivers waiting to be diverted to the growing Front Range. That diversion was always done unilaterally, without consulting the water's former users. But nothing fails like failure, and Denver's attitude began to change as the agency, under Miller and former attorney Glenn Saunders, suffered reversals in its search for additional water out of the Colorado River Basin.

Small defeats were followed by an immense defeat in 1990, when Denver and forty or so suburban allies, having spent $40 million to obtain permits for the $1 billion Two Forks Dam, were turned back at the eleventh hour by President Bush. The crushing setback reworked the department and sent Denver on a search for peace and new allies that brought Barry to Grand Junction to talk about his organization's changing policy.

Denver has done more than talk. It has acted to get its water consumption under control. It has adopted universal metering, changed rates to encourage conservation, and promoted use of water-thrifty appliances and desert-type landscaping. Barry said the results were visible this year. In the hot, dry summer of 1986, Denver had peak uses of 586 million gallons per day. During this year's hotter, drier summer and with more customers, Denver never topped 500 million gallons per day. In addition, per capita use has dropped steadily from about 900 gallons per household per day in 1970, to about 750 gallons today. Much of that drop came in the last six years.

Looking ahead, Denver is limiting its responsibility for Front Range growth. In the past, Denver used its water system, its expertise, and its political muscle to help surrounding suburbs grow. Denver's desire for growth may not have changed (it now builds airports instead of dams), but it no longer exerts itself to supply the water for new development. Barry told the Grand Junction group, "We won't solve the water supply problem for the Front Range. North Douglas County (Castle Rock, Parker, et al.) doesn't have a water supply, and we're not going to provide one."

Denver has supply contracts with eighty towns and water districts around it. Many contracts, Barry said, are "open-ended. They say, 'We'll serve you, Littleton, no matter how big you're going to get.' " Now, Barry said, Denver has gone to all eighty entities "with new contracts that limit our obligation by limiting" the area Denver is committed to serve. Barry said Denver has renegotiated about one-third of the contracts. He estimates that Denver's present water supply of 215,000 acre-feet needs another 40,000 to 80,000 acre-feet to meet present and future commitments. Some additional water would come from new dams and reservoirs; some would come from reuse of waste water, conservation and the like.

Denver has also changed its approach to water politics. Until recently, urban and rural water developers might fight over a particular right but were united on general policy. However, in 1992, Barry said, the Western Urban Water Coalition, a relatively new organization made up of Denver, Las Vegas, Los Angeles and other Western cities, testified in Washington for Representative George Miller's water reform bill. That bill, enacted over fierce opposition from California irrigators, will send water from California's Central Valley farms to cities and back into streams and river deltas to aid fish and wildlife. Barry said, "The driving force is that the old alliance of urban entities and irrigation is not as useful in the 1990s as it was in the old days." He added that irrigation interests cannot afford economically to meet the nation's new environmental standards. He foresees alliances with environmentalists because "urban interests have the money to accommodate environmental interests. I see environmentalists and cities lining up in ways they didn't before. And irrigation interests and cities won't line up as they did before."

If what Barry says is true, the Northern Colorado Water Conservancy District is in double trouble. Denver is the best-known

diverter of water out of the Colorado River, but it siphons only
110,000 acre-feet under the Continental Divide to the Front Range.
By comparison, Northern, through its Colorado-Big Thompson
project, takes 220,000 acre-feet of water out of the Colorado River to
water the farms of northern Colorado. It also takes substantial
amounts of water out of the South Platte River, which flows off the
east slope of the Rockies onto the Colorado Plains. Diversions of this
scale inevitably involve environmental problems, but thus far
Northern's diversions have not attracted the attention that the
California Central Valley Project's did. Northern's new head, Eric
Wilkinson, says there is no comparison with the Central Valley
because Northern diverts its water in a responsible way.

In any case, environmental reform is not Northern's immediate
challenge. Right now, Northern is up against geography. It presides
over an irrigated agricultural empire just to the north of the thirsty
Front Range. Northern distributes water to about three thousand
farmers, who irrigate land that added about $340 million to
Colorado's economy in 1993. If any of that land is to be dried up for
urban development, Northern wants the water to go to cities within
its boundaries, such as Loveland, Fort Collins, and Greeley.

Some suburbs around Denver, now blocked from West Slope
water, covet Northern's water. Even before Two Forks collapsed,
Thornton, a city north of Denver and near Denver International
Airport, bought up half a ditch company in Northern's district. In
1994, almost a decade after the purchase, Colorado water judge
Robert G. Behrman ruled that Thornton could divert 33,000 acre-
feet of irrigation water. Of the 21,000 acres of farmland that
Thornton bought, 18,000 will be dried up. It will be expensive water.
Two Forks would have been costly, and Thornton's water is expected
to cost perhaps four times as much. In part that is because Northern
opposed Thornton's diversion in court, and the court granted
Thornton less water than the city had expected.

Although Northern says that it will fight all water raiders,
Wilkinson also says the district has agreed to the Southern Pipeline,
which will send some of Northern's Windy Gap municipal water
south to several Denver-area towns. Northern is also part of a larger
cooperative venture. It and the cities within its boundaries are
members, with Denver and its suburbs and environmentalists, of the
Metropolitan Water Supply Investigation, which is attempting to
solve Front Range water needs into the next century.

On the surface, the Colorado River Water Conservation District has been least affected by the Two Forks debacle. The River District is still led by its long-time Secretary-Engineer, Rolly "H2O" Fischer. The board is largely the same, and if the River District has changed policy, that change has not been articulated.

Nevertheless, Two Forks hit the River District hard. From its formation in 1937 until 1986, the River District fought all diversions of water out of the Colorado River Basin. In addition to fighting defensively, the River District filed on streams and reservoir sites with the hope that the West Slope's economy would eventually allow it to build dams for use within its territory. Perhaps despairing that that day would ever come, and perhaps because its culture required that it finally build a dam, in 1986 the district signed a peace treaty with Denver. That treaty, which included Northern, gave the River District the money to build a dam. The money came from Northern, as compensation for its latest project, the Windy Gap municipal diversion out of the Colorado River basin, and from Denver.

In return for the money from Denver, the River District agreed to lease water out of its reservoir to Denver until Two Forks came on line. At that point, the River District would own the entire reservoir. In addition, the River District agreed that it would not oppose Two Forks. To Denver's traditional leaders, the treaty must have seemed to seal their quest for a federal permit because they had neutralized Denver's long-time enemy. But the River District's neutrality was barely noticed as the West Slope's new players—led by ski towns such as Vail—lined up with the Environmental Caucus to beat Two Forks. The allies beat Two Forks using weapons the River District would have been uncomfortable with: environmental protection, endangered species, and low-cost solutions to water needs.

Before the defeat of Two Forks, the River District's Fischer was a very public representative of traditional rural water policy, alternately railing at Front Range cities seeking Colorado River water and attacking environmentalists for attempting to keep water in streams. In the wake of Two Forks, Fischer has vanished from public view.

In the past, the River District was run by and for traditional West Slope interests led by irrigated agriculture. But in recent years the River District has been most effective working with the high-elevation counties to provide ski towns and recreation areas with relatively small amounts of water for snow-making and high-altitude city dwellers. In addition, the district has all but abandoned its Juniper-Cross Project, which would have put a major dam on the undammed Yampa River. Finally, it is possible that River District water rights must go to protect endangered Colorado River fish—unthinkable in the past.

At the moment, the River District is putting the finishing touches on the Wolford Mountain Reservoir. But Denver no longer has a lease on the water in Wolford. It now permanently owns 40 percent of the reservoir's capacity, with the River District owning the other 60 percent. The 40 percent ownership will yield Denver 10,000 acre-feet per year through an exchange process. Denver will draw 10,000 acre-feet of additional water out of the Blue River, near the Continental Divide, while Wolford Mountain will release the same amount of water lower down on the Colorado River to meet the long-term water rights of irrigators in the Grand Junction area.

The West Slope irrigators, who met with Chips Barry in Grand Junction in late August, said they would like to sue the River District and Denver to stop the diversion, but they couldn't afford the legal fees. They object to the saltier water they will get out of the Wolford Mountain Reservoir, as compared with the high-quality water that now flows down to them out of the Blue River. The irrigators were somewhat placated by Denver, which worked out a compromise on water-quality monitoring and the timing of releases from Wolford Mountain that the irrigators felt they could live with. Although there will be no lawsuit, there are strained feelings. Greg Trainor, head of utilities for Grand Junction and an organizer of the meeting between Barry and the irrigators, said, "On the Colorado River, the River District has compromised its ability to adequately defend us." Trainor said the River District levies a tax on $4 billion of West Slope property to defend West Slope water, and then "builds a dam to supply Denver with water."

The irrigators and utility managers at the Grand Junction meeting with Barry left suspicious. Denver has several additional projects on the drawing boards, and its peace treaty with the River District provides for cooperation on future West Slope reservoirs. As a result, the West Slope fears that Denver intends to take additional water out of the Colorado River. Recent history, however, indicates that it is harder than ever for cities to raid rural areas for water. After Two Forks was defeated, American Water Development Inc. tried to divert water out of Colorado's San Luis Valley to urban areas. A coalition of that valley's farmers and environmentalists, financed by a special property tax, beat back the attempt even though the valley is one of Colorado's poorest areas. An attempt by Aurora, a Denver suburb, to divert water from the Gunnison River was turned back by a coalition of ranchers, recreation interests, vacation homeowners, and environmentalists. Farther afield, the West's most dynamic city, Las Vegas, was beaten when it tried to drain groundwater out of rural areas of northern Nevada.

The near-completion of Wolford Mountain Reservoir indicates that diversions of modest size aren't impossible. But Dan Luecke, a key member of the Environmental Caucus in the 1980s and a staff member of the Environmental Defense Fund in Boulder, doesn't think the West Slope has more water-diversion projects to worry about. Luecke said Front Range environmentalists didn't oppose Wolford Mountain because they had agreed to it as one of the replacement parts for Two Forks. Without help from environmentalists, Western irrigators and towns couldn't block the 60,000-acre-foot reservoir. Luecke said Wolford Mountain isn't likely to be repeated. "There aren't any more deals like that out there."

*October 3, 1994*

Las Vegas Mirage

# Water Forces Las Vegas to Choose: Gaming Town or Suburb of Los Angeles

## Jon Christensen

*T*he boom had appeared to have gone bust in the city that never sleeps. Until the early 1990s, Las Vegas seemed to thrive on its unique brand of illusion, while the rest of the country wallowed in a deepening recession. But hard times came to Glitter Gulch and the Strip, too, once thought immune to economic doldrums. The question is whether the slowdown will slacken this city's seemingly insatiable thirst for water. In 1990, the Las Vegas Valley Water District staked claims to nearly all the unappropriated groundwater in a 20,000-square-mile area of southern and central Nevada. The city also sought any unclaimed water in the Virgin River. Without new water, district officials warned, growth in Las Vegas would halt. To back up the threat, the water district imposed a moratorium on providing water to new developments.

Then the bad economic news hit home. In late 1991, gambling revenues tumbled by up to 12 percent in Las Vegas and 6 percent statewide. Casinos in downtown Las Vegas, Reno, and Carson City sought protection from creditors. The number of new jobs created in Clark County fell to a dismal one hundred last year compared to more than thirty-six thousand the year before. Along the fabled Strip, worries about "over-capacity" are now heard, even as ground is broken for what will be the world's largest hotel when it opens next year. Billionaire Kirk Kerkorian's MGM Grand Hotel and Theme Park—a populist "Wizard of Oz" fantasy, yellow brick road and all—will be followed shortly by two more billion-dollar-plus projects, a "Treasure Island" theme park by Mirage Resorts and a thirty-story pyramid from Circus Circus, which kicked off the latest theme-park trend only two years ago with the Excalibur, a Disney-style medieval concoction with jousting, banquets, and arcades. The quest for the next great attraction—casino theme parks to which baby boomers and high rollers can bring the whole family—has driven casino capital costs sky high. And the shakeout of smaller, debt-ridden properties has just begun.

Meanwhile, the city of Las Vegas and Clark County struggled to catch up with the population explosion that brought up to six thousand new residents a month to Las Vegas in 1989. Roads, water mains, sewers, and schools have lagged far behind the housing developments that bloomed like wildflowers after a downpour in the surrounding desert.

Because the economic engine of Las Vegas drives the state, its problems become the problems of Nevada as a whole. Faced with shortfalls in meeting revenue estimates that were figured during the flush days of the boom, the state government has had to cut $120 million in programs, services, and personnel to make ends meet. "Less is best" has become the new catch phrase in Nevada government.

Second thoughts about growth are surfacing even in Las Vegas, where doubting the wildest dreams of speculators has previously been a risky bet. Their real estate developments helped Las Vegas and the surrounding metropolitan area nearly double in population during the 1980s. But most of the new residents came from California. Fleeing gridlock and other urban problems, many of them do not wish to see Las Vegas become Los Angeles. Their attitudes are beginning to show up in opinion polls and at the ballot box. The majority of Nevadans have swung from a "laissez-faire, let the good times roll" attitude to one strongly favoring controlled growth, says Mike Sloan, a vice president of Circus Circus who frequently polls the populace. The election of Don Schlesinger, a vocal advocate of growth controls, to the Clark County board of commissioners in 1990 signaled a shift in the politics of growth in Las Vegas.

California will continue to influence Nevada by sheer size. The Golden State added 6.1 million people to its population in the 1980s and is now home to more than 30 million residents. During the same period, Nevada grew from 800,000 to 1.2 million residents. Many Nevada newcomers are "equity exiles" who cashed out of high-priced homes in California to buy dream homes for half the price in a state with a constitutional ban on income tax. Home builders, who are relentlessly optimistic, count on these Californians to provide steady growth for the future. This is one assumption that inspired and keeps alive the Las Vegas quest for water.

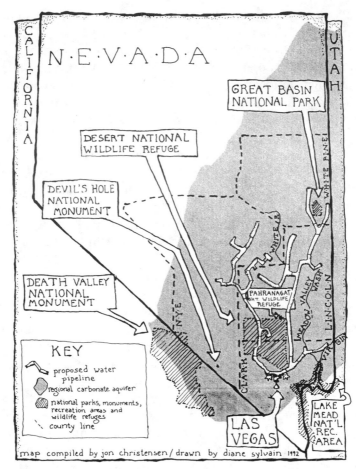

KEY

proposed water pipeline

regional carbonate aquifer

national parks, monuments, recreation areas and wildlife refuges

county line

map compiled by jon christensen / drawn by diane sylvain 1992

In October 1989, with lightning speed and no warning, Las Vegas launched what has been dubbed "the biggest water grab in the history of the West." The Las Vegas Valley Water District, run by the Clark County commissioners, filed applications with the Nevada state engineer for 865,000 acre-feet of water in the rural areas north of the city, more than double the county's current Colorado River supply. The stage had been set earlier in the year, when the Nevada Legislature, controlled by a southern urban majority, passed changes in state water laws. The changes allow municipal suppliers to hold on to water rights indefinitely, for future growth. Having nearly exhausted its Colorado River allotment, the district went after an underground aquifer in central Nevada and the Virgin River.

Rural opponents of the "water grab" have complained that the water rights application process is ruled by the politics of chummy consensus bred by southern Nevada's control of state government. The Las Vegas Valley Water District has attempted to stifle debate within Clark County and has kept rural representatives from being invited to take part in public debates and discussions, says Steve Bradhurst, the Nye County planner who is coordinating rural opposition to Las Vegas's plans. Bradhurst says the water district has operated in a closed, secretive style. Its model for projecting growth rates and water demand in Las Vegas into the next century, for example, has been unavailable for public scrutiny. "Nobody can take a look at the assumptions behind it," Bradhurst says.

Shortly after the Las Vegas filings, the state engineer was inundated with a record 3,612 protests by nine hundred parties, including individuals, ranchers, environmental groups, Indian tribes, and state and federal agencies. Many were concerned about wetlands and wildlife fed by the underground aquifer, which flows through a deep layer of carbonate rocks underlying central Nevada to discharge in the springs at Ash Meadows and Death Valley National Monument. The aquifer has been studied extensively because it flows under the Nevada Test Site. But claims about its potential yield still vary wildly.

The rural counties, however, have been most concerned about Las Vegas "foreclosing" on their future. "This will ensure Clark County's control of the state forever," warns planner Bradhurst. "It's nothing more than de facto annexation to insure the demographic landscape of Clark County and Nevada for years to come." Bradhurst cites the example of the Delamar gold mine, which recently had to negotiate with Clark County to secure water rights to begin operations in Lincoln County. "Can you imagine?" he asks. "Clark County now has control of the mining industry, too."

Rural residents worry that Nevada is putting "all of its eggs in one basket—Las Vegas," says Bradhurst. With the help of former Arizona Governor Bruce Babbitt, rural representatives are forming a nonprofit organization, the Coalition to Protect Rural Water (CPR Water), that will channel funds to rural areas fighting to control their water. Defeating the Las Vegas "water grab" is its first test. Bradhurst says the rural opposition has a two-pronged strategy: to get the federal agencies and Congress concerned about the environmental costs and to get people in Clark County concerned about the economic costs of the project.

Since the 1930s, according to historian Eugene Moehring, Las Vegas has been shaped by the federal government, water purveyors, and gambling. The federal government built Hoover Dam and the highways that brought people to the sunbelt resort. While gambling largely underwrote the local and state economy and government, the federal government also contributed to growth, with the Basic Magnesium Industries ammunition plant, Nellis Air Force Base, and the Nevada Test Site. With land for development provided by the Bureau of Land Management—which slated all of its holdings in the Las Vegas Valley for "disposal"—developers worked with the county water purveyor to channel growth along its ever-extending waterworks. Then in the 1980s, California became the driving force, changing southern Nevada. While the last decade boosted Las Vegas's fortunes as never before, its go-go philosophy is giving way to a new mood that has crept across the border with the newcomers from California.

The rapid residential growth has also led to the possibility of a clash between gaming and future growth. "Las Vegas will never grow again like it has in the past," says Circus Circus executive Mike Sloan, "because the people who live here will not let it happen. Hey, I've lived here since the 1950s. I don't want it to look like L.A."

"We need to step back and determine what kind of valley we want to live in twenty years from now," says Don Schlesinger, who represents the emerging politics of Las Vegas. "We need to find out what are the outer limits of growth in this valley and plan for that to occur in some kind of sensible, reasonable manner." Lately, Schlesinger's approach has been supported by Commissioner Karen Hayes. And as election time approaches for three of the seven other county commissioners, even the pro-growth commissioners have begun to change their tunes. Clark County has finally begun comprehensive planning, a concept that was once alien to Las Vegas. "Two years ago," says Schlesinger, "we didn't have any kind of master plans for towns and unincorporated areas. We have had hodgepodge growth with little rhyme or reason. Now we finally have a road map."

The road map includes a mass transit system funded by a tax residents voted last year to impose on new construction. Letting "growth pay for growth" is a philosophy with more and more adherents in Las Vegas. The new casinos rising along the Strip will pick up a large part of the mass transit tab. But the gaming industry seems increasingly reluctant to shoulder more of the burden to pay for residential growth. With gambling spreading like wildfire around the country, casino executives worry about ruining the attraction of Las Vegas. "Things that make you look less attractive hurt your business," says Mike Sloan, who is a key mover in the Nevada Resort Association, the casino industry lobby. "There's a growing recognition that if we're going to let the home-building industry just build whatever they want to build without identifying the consequences, it may come to roost on the gaming industry's head," he says. "We can't stand by and let that happen."

"The lifeblood of this community is the gaming industry," says Don Schlesinger. "We have to preserve an environment that maintains our community as a tourist destination. If tripling the population introduces crime, pollution, and traffic that diminishes our appeal, we may be biting the hand that feeds us."

Although casinos use only 8 percent of the Las Vegas municipal water supply—compared to the 60 percent used by people to water lawns—resort executives also worry about the perception that their waterfalls, pools, and golf courses waste a lot of water. "We need to be careful we don't get stuck with a disproportionate cost of some grandiose scheme because of that perception," says Sloan. Las Vegans could be stuck with dramatically higher water bills.

The cost of the Las Vegas water importation project is now estimated at around $2 billion. But the price tag could escalate. For comparison, Steve Bradhurst cites the Central Arizona Project, which cost $4 billion for a 355-mile delivery system. The Las Vegas project calls for more than 1,000 miles of pipeline, Bradhurst says, and costs could go to $12 billion, he estimates.

Chris Brown, the southern Nevada coordinator of the statewide environmental group, Citizen Alert, predicts that "when people find out about the cost, and who will have to pay, the polls which now show a slim majority opposed to the project will swing even farther apart."

In early March, 1992 Las Vegas signed a contract to get the last of Nevada's Colorado River allotment. The additional 58,000 acre-feet of water come from return-flow credits for treated effluent. Ironically, the environmental assessment of the contract, prepared by the Las Vegas Water District, said the district's rural water applications were too "speculative" to analyze as an alternative source. Although rural representatives and environmentalists questioned the environmental impact of the new water supply, they refrained from delaying the contract by demanding a complete environmental impact statement or appealing the decision. "This water isn't that important to us," admits Chris Brown.

In fact, the new contract for Colorado River water may set the stage for defeat of the much grander importation plan. Although most of the water is already committed, the contract lifts the moratorium on "will serve" letters, which had been imposed because the water district was over-committed and threatened with lawsuits by developers who had been promised water. The district now has breathing room.

According to the environmental assessment of the contract, the new water from Lake Mead will allow Clark County to grow from the current population of 800,000 to 1.4 million residents, with minimal conservation measures. More important, the contract allows the three huge new casino projects by Circus Circus, Mirage Resorts, and MGM to move forward. And that means casino executives can now take a critical look at the water importation plan without putting their projects on the line. "The gaming industry wants to take an objective look at the costs and consequences of any plan," says Mike Sloan. "To the extent that (the water plan) is harmful to our interests, we will speak up. There will be wide public dialogue on this issue before it's decided," Sloan promises.

There is already talk of scaling back the Cooperative Water Project, as the importation project was dubbed by the Las Vegas Valley Water District. The state engineer's hearings on the project are scheduled to begin in November. The engineer has not demanded an environmental impact statement. But there are signs that an EIS, which is being prepared in anticipation of federal requirements for the well sites and rights-of-way, is being used to pare down the project by identifying environmentally sensitive or controversial aspects.

The water district has offered to share some twenty-five claims with the rural counties. Steve Bradhurst calls that a "P.R. ploy" announced the night a CBS News crew came to a hearing. Now the water district says it will simply drop the claims. But it has yet to do so.

Ironically, just as Clark County may be pulling back, a willingness to negotiate seems to be spreading in the rural counties. Jo Anne Garrett, a resident of the small town of Baker near Great Basin National Park, who has been involved in the protests, says some rural residents and county commissioners fear an opportunity may be slipping by. "The poverty of Lincoln and White Pine counties makes them vulnerable to the constant pressure to negotiate and get a good deal," says Garrett. "You can't tell a guy he can't sell out if he wants to," she recalls a rancher insisting at one of the recent meetings.

But flush with tax revenues from four "world class" gold mines and federal payments in lieu of taxes from the Nevada Test Site, Nye County has been able to keep the rural opposition afloat. The county has hired Bruce Babbitt as well as experts in hydrology and conservation to help with the coming battles. Their reports are expected to provide the technical and financial details to "blow Las Vegas out of the water," says Steve Bradhurst.

Arguments against its costs are expected to turn on its costs and the opportunities for more efficient use and reuse of existing water. Las Vegas now consumes more water per capita—350 gallons per day—than any other city in the West and roughly twice that of comparable cities such as Phoenix and Tucson.

Bradhurst is also compiling a complete paper trail in preparation for the battle over the EIS, which may be years down the line. Eventually, he suspects, the southern Nevada water war will end in federal court. But it could be over before that. Las Vegans have the power to decide the fate of the project, perhaps as early as the November election, when the majority of the county commission could be swung against the project.

Citizen Alert's Chris Brown worries that there is not yet "a political vehicle to carry forward the slow-growth sentiment. There are some indications that the water grab may be falling apart," he says. "But there is so much institutional momentum and money behind it that I wouldn't count on it disappearing of its own accord." In any case, County Commissioner Don Schlesinger vows to put the project to a vote of the people. "We can't ask the people to tax themselves without a vote," he says. And Circus Circus executive Mike Sloan predicts that the importation project eventually could be limited to the outlying areas of Clark County on the grounds of cost alone.

Steve Bradhurst says that would be a great victory for rural Nevada. Bradhurst is confident that "given the environmental disaster that would occur, I don't think the water grab will ever happen." Nonetheless, he worries that, under state law, Las Vegas could sit on the water rights applications for thirty years or more without building a pipeline. Bradhurst suggests that Las Vegas turn the applications over to the counties of origin. "In twenty or thirty years, we could have some great communities in rural Nevada, if they are allowed to develop their own water," says Bradhurst. "Our only hope now is the people of Las Vegas."

*April 6, 1992*

# Las Vegas Seeks Watery Jackpot in Northern Nevada

## Jon Christensen

Created by a vote of city residents in 1948 to take over a chaotic system of private wells and water companies and to tap Lake Mead to supply future growth, the Las Vegas Valley Water District has a history of securing new water sources just as existing supplies are about to run out. The district supplies 600,000 residents, plus more than 20 million visitors each year in Las Vegas and the unincorporated areas of Searchlight, Jean, and Kyle Canyon. Eighty percent of the customers are residential and they use roughly 80 percent of the water—60 percent is used for landscaping, mostly lawns. The other 20 percent of the customers are businesses, industries, and hotels and casinos.

The water district earned $69 million last year, according to finance director Cary Casey, while expenses totaled $79 million, reflecting spending of capital accumulated during the boom years of the late 1980s. The district has four potential sources of revenues to fund expansion: connection charges, water rates, voter-approved tax assessments, and bonds.

Florence Jiu of the public services department says about half the district's 450 employees work on the water system, constructing, installing, and repairing water mains, branch lines, and meters. Others work at district headquarters, where customer service, billing, finance, and public relations take place, along with research, design, engineering, and planning. The research and resources departments are charged with finding more water for Las Vegas.

The Las Vegas Valley Water District dubbed its controversial water-importation project the "Cooperative Water Project" long after opponents labeled it a "water grab." The project was conceived in secrecy and launched without fanfare on October 17, 1989, when the water district filed 146 applications with the Nevada State Engineer. The applications were for 805,000 acre-feet of groundwater from twenty-six valleys north of Las Vegas. At the same time, the district filed on 60,000 acre-feet of Virgin River water. An acre-foot of water can supply one family for a year.

The district estimated the perennial yield of the groundwater basins at around 250,000 acre-feet, but it claimed much more, so as to be first in line for any unappropriated water found in the area. Since then, the district has offered to drop twenty-five applications in environmentally sensitive locations, such as Meadow Valley Wash, White River, and Pahranagat Valley. Although its applications still total 752,000 acre-feet, the district now expects to get only 180,000 acre-feet annually from the project. "More applications could be dropped," says Jiu, "but we don't know anything yet."

The price tag for the Cooperative Water Project is now estimated at $2 billion. The official timeline shows federal environmental studies, state water hearings, and the federal environmental analysis process running through the year 2005. Construction will begin then and water will flow in the pipeline by 2007. By 2035 all phases of the project are expected to be completed.

Engineers are studying the feasibility of purifying the Virgin River, which enters Nevada after flowing through Arizona from Utah, to get at the 60,000 acre-feet of river water that the district has claimed. A desalination plant estimated to cost $336 million would be needed to make the water drinkable.

The water district hopes that at least some of these new sources of water will be available before Las Vegas is forced to move beyond the mainly voluntary "level 1" conservation measures now in place. Current supplies are expected to last only until 2006 with minimal conservation. But the district has no plans to implement more stringent measures. "We hope we don't get to that point," says Jiu. "We don't want to change the lifestyle of people in southern Nevada. That's why we're pursuing all these sources of water."

*April 6, 1992*

# Las Vegas Wheels and Deals for Colorado River Water

## Jon Christensen

L as Vegas in 1994 was prepared to give up its controversial quest to pipe underground water from rural Nevada, but only if the booming metropolis could get more water from the Colorado River. That was a big if, requiring changes in how the Colorado River has been run for most of this century. But Las Vegas, one of the fastest growing cities in the nation, and Patricia Mulroy, the hard-driving general manager of the Southern Nevada Water Authority, bet everything on it. As Las Vegas's growth boomed anew, so has the power of Mulroy's agency. It merged over the past few years with several competing water districts, and now serves 900,000 people, 65 percent of the state's population. Mulroy is throwing that power into changing how the Colorado River is managed. If she can get access to Colorado River water for Las Vegas, Mulroy is offering to abandon one of the biggest urban water grabs in western history. The move puts Las Vegas at the center of reforms that are changing the way water is managed throughout the West. And it may unite her urban constituency and environmentalists against traditional water interests.

It's a startling about-face. In 1990, when Mulroy unveiled a plan to pump all the available groundwater from twenty-six valleys stretching as far as 200 miles north of Las Vegas, she asserted that rural Nevada could not stand in the way of the state's economic engine. The plan seemed a bold blast from the past. Its scale—over 1,000 miles of pipeline—would dwarf the Owens Valley pipeline to Los Angeles, to which it was often compared.

Mulroy now acknowledges that the groundwater importation plan has been proclaimed "the singularly most stupid idea anyone's ever had." But, she says, "I don't think we would have gotten attention to southern Nevada's needs without the outpouring of concerns on those applications." David Donnelly, chief engineer for the water authority, is also openly disdainful of the importation project that he defended until recently. "Frankly, it doesn't make any sense. We don't want to build any more dams, reservoirs, or construction projects. We want to do things that cost less and that are more politically, socially and environmentally acceptable."

With the groundwater project—a traditional approach to a city's need for water—out of the way for the moment, Mulroy and her colleagues now see Las Vegas as a major player on the Colorado River. Last year, she took her message to Washington, D.C., as the first chair of the Western Urban Water Coalition, a new lobbying group for cities seeking a greater share of water in the West.

Western water attracts visionaries. Some pursue mirages; others prove to be ahead of their time. And there are a few who figure out how to get what they want from the changes they see coming. Patricia Mulroy may be one of the practical visionaries of the post-reclamation era. She appears to understand where reform of western water is headed: away from new construction projects and toward better management of rivers and ecosystems. She watched Denver's Two Forks Dam proposal go down to defeat. Closer to home, she saw southern California fail to get its peripheral canal. From those lessons, she has come up with an alternative to a massive construction and dewatering project.

Mulroy says that if Nevada can add 200,000 to 250,000 acre-feet of Colorado River water to the state's current annual allocation of 300,000 acre-feet from the Colorado River, then she will recommend dropping the agency's claims on rural Nevada water. Those claims are for about 200,000 acre-feet. Mulroy says the water needed to supply the next century of growth in southern Nevada is not a major amount, given the allocations to other states on the Colorado River. But to get there, she acknowledges, will require "major rethinking" up and down the river.

The 1922 Colorado River Compact—a major strand in the web of interstate compacts, legislation, regulations, court decisions, and rules collectively known as the "law of the river"—allots 7.5 million acre-feet of water annually to the upper-basin states of Colorado, Wyoming, Utah, and New Mexico, and 7.5 million to the lower basin states of Nevada, Arizona, and California. Of that, California gets 4.4 million acre-feet, Arizona gets 2.85 million acre-feet, and Nevada gets 300,000 acre-feet. Most of California's and Arizona's Colorado River water goes to agriculture, as does the upper basin's water.

Those allocations made sense when the 1922 compact was signed, and when the West was seen as a potential agricultural powerhouse if it only had water. But today irrigated agriculture is on the defensive. In California, for example, Representative George Miller helped put together a coalition of urban interests and environmentalists that pushed a major water reform bill through the Congress in 1992, despite intense opposition from California agricultural interests. That reform will make it easier for cities to buy up agricultural water.

Southern Nevada, an overwhelmingly urban area, has essentially no irrigated agriculture for Las Vegas to buy and dry up. Unlike California and Arizona, where huge chunks of those states' Colorado River water goes to farms, the Southern Nevada Water Authority already controls nearly all of Nevada's Colorado River water. Nor will conservation help much. Even with the most optimistic projections for conservation, Mulroy says, the Las Vegas area will need more water soon after the turn of the century. To get that extra water, Mulroy wants to change the "law of the river" to allow southern Nevada to buy, borrow, or otherwise bargain for water from other states' farmers and ranchers and deliver it through the agency's existing "straw" in Lake Mead.

The "law of the river" presents a formidable obstacle to her quest—an obstacle rooted in the traditional West, much like the laws and traditions governing mining, logging, and grazing. But in an era when irrigation districts across the West are having trouble paying for their water, Las Vegas has what they need: cash. Mulroy has also found new allies in high federal positions, and in cities across the West, who share her vision of a changing region that needs some new rules.

Before he became secretary of Interior, Bruce Babbitt advised the rural Nevada counties fighting the Las Vegas groundwater importation plan. Now, Babbitt says, he is an "advocate" for southern Nevada. "I'm trying to find a way for Nevada to get an increased share of Colorado River water," he announced last summer. "Las Vegas needs an expanded water supply from the Colorado River."

Around the same time, Betsy Reike, the assistant secretary of Interior who oversees the Bureau of Reclamation, was explaining her plans for reform to an annual gathering of high-powered water managers and attorneys at the University of Colorado's Natural

Resources Law Center. "The Colorado River has been locked up in the chains created by the law of the river," Reike said. "It is time to figuratively melt those chains." Reike said the Department of Interior, which manages most of the river, would "patiently leverage change" on the Colorado River, starting in the lower basin. That was just what Patricia Mulroy, sitting in the audience, hoped to hear.

The Bureau of Reclamation is drafting rules and regulations to "provide some new flexibility by allowing and facilitating voluntary transfers of water" on the lower Colorado, says Ed Osann, an assistant to bureau director Dan Beard. The proposal will be the subject of public workshops and hearings after it is released in March. "This is something that does not require fundamental changes in the law of the river" or "tampering with the basic apportionments among and between states," says Osann. But it will be "a big step forward in encouraging the marketing of water in the lower Colorado."

The Southern Nevada Water Authority has already opened a small crack in the Colorado River arrangement with a three-way deal Mulroy put together last year with the powerful Metropolitan Water District of Southern California and the Central Arizona Water Conservation District. The California and Nevada urban water districts agreed to pay the financially troubled irrigation district, which operates the Central Arizona Project, to store 100,000 acre-feet of Colorado River water in groundwater aquifers under farms served by the aqueduct. During droughts, the cities could draw on that stored water. The deal, which was approved as a demonstration project by the Bureau of Reclamation, is simple conceptually but complicated in the details. Basically, some of Arizona's share of the Colorado River is moved through the Central Arizona Project canals—at Nevada's and Southern California's expense—to Arizona farmers who normally irrigate with groundwater. These farmers use the Colorado River water, leaving the groundwater in the aquifers. In a drought, the farmers would draw on the stored groundwater, and California and Nevada would take additional water out of Lake Mead. Other conditions apply, of course. But in outline, some of Arizona's share of Colorado River water is being transferred to Nevada and Southern California. "It's a chip away at water marketing" on the Colorado River, says David Donnelly, chief engineer of the Las Vegas water agency. "It required people to bend the rules a little bit. It's significant and precedent-setting that both California and Nevada now have water stored in Arizona."

Eventually, Las Vegas hopes to use its growing muscle to enlarge that crack and nearly double its supply from the Colorado River. Las Vegas is eagerly awaiting a proposal from the Arizona Department of Water Resources and the Central Arizona Water Conservation District that might expand the program to "several million acre-feet," says Donnelly. But, he says, the water-banking program and the Bureau of Reclamation's new rules for the lower Colorado River are not likely to provide all the water Las Vegas needs. That will require negotiations with other Colorado River states.

Those states are watching how the bureau's efforts "to leverage change" will help Mulroy's crusade. The 1922 Colorado River Compact was designed to protect the other six compact states from the economic power of California. The protection was needed because, if money and population had been the only measure, all the Colorado River water would have quickly flowed to southern California, rather than remaining in Wyoming and Utah and Arizona to raise low-value crops like alfalfa and cotton. Not much has changed from 1922 to today. From the perspective of Utah or New Mexico or Wyoming, still awaiting further urbanization and industrialization, watching their compact water flow off marginal farms and toward buyers in Las Vegas is no different from watching it flow to Los Angeles.

Mulroy has not yet directly taken on the upper-basin states of Colorado, Wyoming, Utah, and New Mexico. She says her immediate goal is to change how the lower-basin states (California, Nevada, and Arizona) apportion water among themselves. She says that until Arizona, Nevada, and California have their house in order, it doesn't make sense to talk to the upper basin states about water transfers. Arizona is her most obvious target, given the financial trouble of the Central Arizona Project. But California also uses an enormous amount of Colorado River water for agriculture. And even high-value crops in California can't compete with urban uses when it comes to water.

Mulroy laid out her strategy for negotiating with other lower basin states at recent hearings before the Nevada state engineer on the Southern Nevada Water Authority's applications for water in the Virgin River. This river originates in southwestern Utah, and flows through the northwestern corner of Arizona and into Nevada, where it joins the Colorado River in Lake Mead. The Virgin River is not part of the Colorado River Compact or any other interstate agreement. Nevada, therefore, claims that the Virgin's water is up for grabs by whoever can first develop it.

On paper, the agency's development plans call for building a dam and reservoir near Mesquite, Nevada, and a pipeline to Las Vegas. Under the current law of the Colorado River, Mulroy says, Las Vegas must take the water before it enters Lake Mead and becomes part of the Colorado River. But the Southern Nevada Water Authority doesn't really want to build the dam and pipeline just to fulfill that technicality. She says the agency would rather let the river flow into Lake Mead and take the water from there. Environmentalists, who oppose the damage that dam, reservoir, and pipeline would cause, also favor letting the water flow into Lake Mead. That, however, would require loosening the "law of the river" to allow "wheeling" water through Lake Mead. And that is the prize that Las Vegas is really playing for, says Mulroy. "The Virgin is the linchpin to the rest of the Colorado River." Getting more water through Lake Mead, including water from the Virgin River, will require negotiations with Utah and Arizona, says Mulroy, and agreement from other states, especially California, which holds priority rights on the lower Colorado by virtue of a 1963 Supreme Court ruling. So far, officials in those states have been reluctant to let Las Vegas push too far too fast.

Mulroy says approval of the Virgin River applications for a dam and pipeline, expected from the Nevada state engineer later this year, is a necessary step to strengthen Nevada when it comes time to negotiate with the other states. Having united her southern Nevada power base, having placated most of her opponents in state, and having found a common agenda with other urban centers and the Bureau of Reclamation, Mulroy is confident it can be done. "The preparatory pieces are in place," she says. "Now we'll push hard to move forward." She predicts that changes on the lower Colorado will move quickly this year and negotiations with other states will get under way. Las Vegas will be a "driver" of change, she vows. But, she adds, the new water regime must be ready by the year 2000. "You can't take a community as thriving as this one and put a stop sign out there," Mulroy warns. "The train will run right over you."

Opponents of southern Nevada's plan to import water from rural Nevada remain skeptical of Las Vegas's intentions. "We're all for more water from the Colorado River," says Don de la Cruz, an organizer with the Nevada environmental group Citizen Alert. Keeping water in the Virgin River is the best way to protect it, he agrees. But as for Mulroy's offer to drop the rural groundwater applications, so far, he says, "that's just talk."

The talk, however, has won over many other opponents. Mulroy convinced towns along the Virgin River in Nevada to drop their protests of the Las Vegas applications by cutting them in on the water and offering them a seat on the Southern Nevada Water Authority. She got the Interior Department to drop protests by the U.S. Fish and Wildlife Service, Bureau of Land Management, and National Park Service by promising that the agency would comply with all required federal studies and permits. And the remaining opponents of the Las Vegas groundwater importation plan—the rural counties and environmentalists—support what the district wants: more water from the Colorado River so that the city doesn't drain 20,000 square miles of rural land in southeastern Nevada.

*February 21, 1994*

# Water and the Future of Las Vegas

## Hal Rothman

I n Nevada, as in every western state, one fact underpins all discussion about the future: agriculture and ranching consume upwards of 80 percent of the water and produce minuscule percentages of jobs, revenue, taxes, and other income. Nowhere does this tidbit mean more than in Las Vegas, where water is the key to the continued growth of a city that has been the fastest growing metropolitan area in the nation for each of the past thirteen years. In Las Vegas, the "Last Detroit," the last place where unskilled workers can make a middle-class wage and thus earn middle-class status, access to water is crucial to the continued growth of the city and to its ability to propel upward the children of unskilled service workers.

Las Vegas's problem? It is limited by compact to 300,000 acre-feet out of the Colorado River. Never mind that 30 million acre-feet of water are stored in nearby Lake Mead; Nevada can withdraw only 1 percent of the lake each year. Nevertheless, by the millennium's end, Las Vegas had solved the short-term problems of water. In a series of complicated maneuvers, Southern Nevada Water Authority head Patricia Mulroy snared more water for Las Vegas by capitalizing on the transformation of how the West gets its water from the building of new dams, reservoirs and canals to more efficient management.

Water still flows uphill to money in the American West, and, thanks to a revolution that took the city from gambling to gaming and on to tourism and then entertainment, Las Vegas has had plenty of cash. The key was to figuring out how to use its financial clout to turn enemies within the state into friends and allies. Las Vegas had enough to provide rural Nevada with money and the autonomy to manage it water as its communities saw fit.

Mulroy accomplished this by laying claim in the mid-1990s to the unadjudicated and unappropriated Virgin River, which flows from Zion National Park in Utah through the northeast corner of Arizona and into Nevada on its way to Lake Mead. The fact that the Virgin

River is unadjudicated means it is not part of Colorado River basin water that has been allocated among the seven basin states. Its water was up for grabs. Traditionally, the water would be grabbed by creating a reservoir somewhere along the river's course. But not this time. Rather than dam the river, and create an environmental fight, Mulroy proposed letting the river continue to flow where it has flowed since Hoover Dam was built: into Lake Mead. From there, it would be pumped along two pipelines to the Las Vegas Valley. Environmentalists were thrilled because Mulroy did not want to build a dam. Communities along the Virgin River were equally excited. Not only did they get water from the deal, they also received seats on the Southern Nevada Water Authority board.

That takes care of Las Vegas's short-term needs. Its long term is tied to another trend in the West, the reallocation of water from rural to urban uses. In California, where reallocation was well underway as 1999 ended, water transfers happen within that huge state. In southern Nevada, which is limited to 300,000 acre-feet out of the Colorado River, the source had to be reallocation of the river itself. Again, Las Vegas' cash greased the wheels. Irrigation districts have rarely been able to pay their bills in the West, and a shot of outside money is almost always welcome, if not a necessity. The cash came thanks to the creation of a water banking system that let Nevada and California store excess irrigation water in underground aquifers in Arizona. The irrigation districts were paid to put their water underground, instead of spreading it above ground to grow crops.

With computer models showing that even without an increase in the state's Colorado River allocation, southern Nevada could thrive with a system of water banking and leasing, Las Vegas had not only the rationale but the means to insure water well into the next century. The estimates suggest that Arizona farmers could provide the difference that Las Vegas needs to sustain its growth.

No American city has ever ceased to grow because of a lack of water and it's unlikely that Las Vegas will be the first. Los Angeles, Phoenix, Tucson, and the rest all found sources for their expansion and, at least for now, so has Las Vegas. It's easy to see that Las Vegas is confident about its access to plentiful amounts of water. Air quality provides a perfect example. The city has had problems complying with Environmental Protection Agency air-quality standards. The result is that construction sites are required by law to limit the amount of dust particles they produce, a difficult task in an arid, desert environment. But they have been successful by following this profligate regimen: every morning, and often twice a day, water trucks roll onto the many sites and spray water on the dirt to keep down the dust....

*Written for this volume*

# 6

## Native American Water Issues

# West Faces a Time Bomb

## Steve Hinchman

For the West, Wyoming's Wind River dispute may be just the beginning. The Shoshone and Arapaho tribes' settled water-rights case is one of more than fifty major water settlements currently being litigated or negotiated in 1990 between Native American tribes and western states. Another hundred or more Indian reservations have water rights that exist on paper, but have yet to be quantified. When considered together, those rights add up to a huge amount of water and a veritable time bomb for the water-scarce West. While some problems can be solved through negotiations, many observers predict that Indian water will be among the major natural-resource and civil-rights questions facing this region at the turn of the century.

The tribes have an almost ironclad legal right to the water. According to the Winters Doctrine, all federal preserves in the West—whether Indian reservations, parks, national forests, or wilderness—are entitled to enough water to meet the purposes Congress had in mind when it set the land aside. For most Indian reservations, that purpose was to domesticate nomadic peoples and provide them with an agricultural homeland, says Chris Kenney, a Bureau of Indian Affairs (BIA) expert on Indian water-rights settlements. In 1963, the Supreme Court ruled that an Indian reservation is entitled to enough water to irrigate all the acreage that is practical to farm on that reservation. As in the Wind River case, that can be a lot of water.

Moreover, under the Prior Appropriations Doctrine—the West's unique first-come, first-served water law—a tribe's federal reserved water right dates to when the reservation was created. Since most reservations were established before white settlers arrived, that makes the tribes owners of large senior water rights throughout the West. But in the intervening hundred years, most water in the West has been claimed and used by non-Indians, a fact that is now coming back to haunt the region. "The U.S. government allowed a lot of reclamation projects and development on river systems where they knew they had a legal obligation to protect water for Indians," says Kenney. The Department of the Interior's trust responsibility to protect Native American land and resources means that it must now go back and fix the mess.

The conflicts are usually triggered when a state decides to adjudicate a river basin, a process that legally encodes each user's water right and priority. The BIA and the Department of Justice have about fifty-five Indian water cases in litigation, says Kenney. There are thirteen negotiating teams currently in the field.

A few of the major cases:

**The Yakima River Adjudication:** Washington state is suing the United States over the BIA's claim to an unspecified amount of water from the Yakima River for the Yakima Indian Reservation. Much of that water is currently being used by the Bureau of Reclamation's 500,000-acre Yakima Irrigation Project.

**The Gila River Adjudication:** The cities of Phoenix and Tucson and the Salt River Project are negotiating with six reservations over their substantial rights to the Gila River in southern Arizona. Those reservations are the Tohono O'odham, the Salt River Pima-Maricopa Community, Fort McDowell, San Carlos, Gila River, and the White Mountain Apache.

**Milk River Adjudication:** Users of the Bureau of Reclamation's Milk River Irrigation Project in Montana are negotiating with the Fort Belknap, Blackfoot, and Rocky Boy reservations over rights to the Milk River, which now runs an average shortfall of 121,000 acre-feet a year.

With all the West watching the state of Wyoming's ongoing imbroglio, Kenney says more states may prefer to negotiate Indian water rights. The advantages are that it takes about one-fourth as much time (litigation typically takes twenty years), the expenses go to structural improvements in the water system instead of lawyers, and social tensions are eased.

The best example is the Fort Hall agreement in Idaho. "At Fort Hall we got everyone talking to each other and considering that they are good neighbors," says Kenney. "At Wind River we have people carrying guns and talking about killing each other." Either way, settling Indian water rights exacts about the same costs. Both the Fort Hall and the Wind River cases will end up costing taxpayers around $25 million, says Kenney. "These water rights cases are pretty expensive," he admits, "but not when you consider that you've been using somebody else's water for fifty or sixty years."

*August 27, 1990*

# Wyoming Tribes Lose Again in Court

## Katharine Collins and Debra Thunder

*If water is a property right that belongs to us, how can (the Wyoming Supreme Court justices) go on to say, "You have a property right that belongs to the state (of Wyoming)?"*

— John Washakie, co-chairman, Joint Business Council of the Northern Arapaho and Eastern Shoshone tribes of the Wind River Indian Reservation

The Wyoming Supreme Court in 1992 rejected a plea to reconsider its earlier 3-2 ruling that restricts the Northern Arapaho and Eastern Shoshone tribes' use of "future" water and makes the state the administrator of federal reserved-water rights. The tribes asked the court to reconsider its June 5, 1992, decision, which gave the state of Wyoming control over the two key water issues. Shoshone Tribe attorney Susan Williams said the splintered nature of the five separate opinions issued by the five justices was a factor in the tribes' decision to ask the court to reconsider its ruling; they may appeal the decision directly to the U.S. Supreme Court.

The ruling, which overturns a lower state court decision, is the latest in a complex and bitter water rights dispute between the state and the tribes. The state initiated the legal battle in 1977, when it sued the tribes and federal government. The landmark case is the first in which Indian water rights have been adjudicated by state courts. The case returned to court in 1990, when the tribes sued the state for refusing to curtail state permittees from taking water the tribes had dedicated for instream flow on the Wind River. For years, permittees in the reservation's U.S. Bureau of Reclamation irrigation districts have de-watered the same stretch of the Wind River, considered an important tribal fishery. The tribes argued before the state's high court during a November 1991 hearing that their federal reserved rights are different from state water rights and subject to the tribes' sovereign control, not to state administration. The Wyoming Supreme Court disagreed.

In 1989, the U.S. Supreme Court affirmed that the tribes had the best and earliest water rights on the Wind River. But the Wyoming Supreme Court's most recent decision effectively says that special status belongs only to water the tribes are already using, not to "future" water the courts quantified for the tribes' future use. The Wyoming ruling essentially restricts the tribes' future water to agriculture. The court ruled the tribes cannot leave water in the river to maintain instream flow for fisheries, but can only divert it to meet the state's definition of "beneficial use." The court also upheld the state's claim that only it can own an instream flow and therefore it outlawed the tribal instream flow permit.

*[handwritten margin note: beneficial = ags, not fisheries]*

Retired Justice C. Stuart Brown, who sat on the case instead of Chief Justice Walter Urbigkit, who declared a conflict of interest, disagreed with the court's restrictions on how the tribes can use their future water. The majority decision improperly treats the tribes' "reserved water right substantially as an appropriation under Wyoming statutes. The effect of the majority determination is to make marginal farmers out of the tribes forever," he wrote in his opinion.

On June 10, tribal leaders expressed publicly for the first time their disappointment with the decision, which Williams said is based on "blatant legal errors." Tribal leaders said the decision effectively takes the tribes' federal reserved rights to more than 500,000 acre-feet of water—about one-third of the water that flows through the reservation in an average year—and places it under the yoke of state water law. "Despite the court's decision, the tribes will not go away," Arapaho Business Council Chairman Burton Hutchinson Sr., stated. "We will continue to make every effort to obtain maximum benefit for our membership from our water resources."

Explaining the Wyoming court's reasoning behind the June 5 decision, Justice Richard Macy wrote: "Our decision today recognizes only that which has been the traditional wisdom relating to Wyoming water: water is simply too precious to the well-being of society to permit water-right holders unfettered control over its use."

Wyoming Supreme Court Justice Michael Golden, who was the only justice to dissent on both issues, criticized his fellow justices. "If one may mark the turn of the twentieth century by the massive expropriation of Indian lands, then the turn of the twenty-first century is the era which the Indian tribes risk the same fate for their water resources. Today some members of the court sound a warning to the tribes that they are determined to complete the agenda initiated over a hundred years ago and are willing to pervert prior decisions to advance that aim. I cannot be a party to deliberate and transparent efforts to eliminate the political and economic base of Indian peoples under the distorted guise of state water-law superiority."

Wyoming Attorney General Joe Meyer has said he will make no public comment about the court's decision because "we're still in negotiations with the tribes, and the last thing I want to do is polarize anything."

Wyoming Gov. Mike Sullivan, who in 1991 denied he was using economic aid to leverage a settlement from the poverty-stricken tribes over water rights, said he was "pleased" with the decision. The ruling is consistent with the state constitution and state water law and "in keeping with the court's earlier decision affirming the tribes' reserved water rights," he stated. In its constitution, the state of Wyoming claims ownership of and authority over all water within the state's boundaries. The state was established in 1890, twenty-two years after the Fort Bridger Treaty of 1868 established the reservation. The Wyoming governor also said the state and the tribes should move ahead on working cooperatively to resolve water shortages this summer, in response to a proposal offered by the tribes prior to the June 5 ruling. In a June 1 letter, the governor announced that he had accepted a recent tribal offer to reduce instream flow requirements and other measures to prevent economic injury to non-Indian irrigators on the reservation faced with a water shortage this summer.

The tribes, in a June 10 release, however, suggested that if a mutually satisfactory long-term state-tribal agreement on water management cannot be reached, the tribes will embark on extensive agricultural projects. Such projects, the tribes' release suggested, will leave state-permitted irrigators within the reservation in worse shape than the use of water for protection of instream flows on the Wind River. Tribal leaders did not specify how they would fund such projects or their cost.

*July 13, 1992*

# Water: Fear of Supreme Court Leads Tribes to Accept an Adverse Decision

## Katharine Collins

A decision by the Wind River Indian Reservation tribes not to appeal an adverse Wyoming Supreme Court water decision in June, 1992 signals—at least for the moment—an end to litigation launched nearly sixteen years ago by the state of Wyoming. Tribes have always clashed with states over tribal sovereignty issues. But the Wind River tribes' reluctance to appeal this water decision indicates that Indians may no longer be able to seek protection from the states in the federal judiciary.

The deadline for the appeal was September 3, ninety days after the Wyoming Supreme Court issued its June 5 ruling. In five separate opinions, the five justices ruled that at least a portion of the tribes' federally reserved water right is subject to state law, and the tribes therefore cannot decide on their own to use it for instream flow protection. The panel also ruled that the Wyoming state engineer, and not the tribal water authority, is the "administrator" of all water rights within the Wind River Indian Reservation—whether they are federally reserved water rights held by the tribes or state-permitted rights held by individuals.

When the high court issued its decision, dissenting voices on the court itself, followed by comments from tribal leaders and lawyers, suggested that the decision imposed burdensome limits on the tribes' sovereign right to deal with tribal resources as they see fit. John Washakie, chairman of the Shoshone Business Council, said he disagreed "profoundly with the decision that was made. But our attorneys and other attorneys very knowledgeable in this area … advised we shouldn't appeal the decision."

Washakie and two law professors, Charles Wilkinson, a prominent water law professor at the University of Colorado Law School, and Pete Maxfield, a University of Wyoming law professor specializing in

Indian law, agreed that the Northern Arapahoe and Eastern
Shoshone tribes, which share the reservation, would have little
chance before the current U.S. Supreme Court. Wilkinson called the
tribes' case "very compelling ... (and) supported by a century of
Western water law. But this U.S. Supreme Court, with the recent
appointments, is, in its own way, probably the most radical court
we've had since the late nineteenth century—in terms of
overturning and moving away from existing, settled principles,"
Wilkinson added.

Washakie agreed the current makeup of the nation's highest court
is "a big deterrent right now" for tribes considering appealing to the
panel. "I don't think the U.S. Supreme Court is friendly to any of
these issues," he said. "There's not much consideration being given
to our positions, our standing with the United States government, to
our treaties, to our sovereignty."

Maxfield has studied the impact of a 1978 U.S. Supreme Court
case—dubbed "Oliphant"—on subsequent cases involving tribal
sovereignty issues. Those cases convinced Maxfield that the current
prospects for "even-handed decisions" when tribes litigate against
states are nil. "The court is not neutral on the issues," he said.

The tribes' decision not to further appeal the June decision by the
Wyoming high court brings at least a temporary halt to litigation
that has cost $20 million. The fight began in early 1977, when
Wyoming, in a surprise move, asked the court to adjudicate state
and tribal water rights within the historic boundaries of the Wind
River Reservation. The state acted after the tribes began to use their
legal muscle to oppose plans by the city of Riverton to develop
groundwater resources. As it turned out, Wyoming lost the fight it
had started. The tribes won affirmation from the Wyoming Supreme
Court in 1988 of a federal reserved, or Winters Doctrine, water right,
based on an 1868 treaty, to 500,017 acre-feet annually in the Wind
River. The U.S. Supreme Court upheld that award in 1989.

Many Indian tribes have been awarded water rights by the courts,
but more often than not, the tribes lack the money to develop and
put the water to use. In general, non-Indian communities have been
much more successful than tribes in gaining federal dollars through
the U.S. Bureau of Reclamation to build dams and irrigation projects
The tribes end up with so-called paper water rather than wet water.
That has led some tribes to make deals with non-Indian water
developers to get funds to develop some of their water. The Central

Utah Project in Utah and the Dolores and Animas-LaPlata projects in Colorado are two examples of this "Indian blanket" approach, in which projects that Congress would otherwise balk at are approved because they provide some water for Indians.

Initially, it appeared that the Wind River tribes had found a way around the lack of development money. In late April of 1990, the tribes decided to dedicate a portion of their award—about 80,000 acre-feet—to protection of instream flow and restoration of a fishery in a historically dewatered section of the Big Wind River. But the instream flow, combined with a dry year, required that certain non-Indian irrigators be deprived of water. And the Wyoming state engineer refused to cut off the irrigators to protect the tribally asserted instream flow. So in August 1990 the tribes asked the courts to require Wyoming State Engineer Jeff Fassett to enforce the instream flow provision.

The tribes won the first round. Fifth District Judge Gary Hartman in a March 1991 ruling recognized their right to use their water to protect instream flow. But on appeal, a divided Wyoming Supreme Court in its ruling last June overruled Hartman's decision. The state's high court said that "no person other than the state of Wyoming shall own any instream flow water right."

In place of an appeal to the U.S. Supreme Court, the tribes may attempt to achieve an instream flow by building two irrigation projects at key points along the Big Wind River. According to Washakie, water flowing to these two "futures" projects would remain in the water-short segment of the stream, effectively assuring an adequate instream flow. The federal reserved water right awarded to the tribes was based on a calculation of the needs of agricultural projects already in operation and others—called futures projects— that theoretically could be developed. "Those projects would take care of the legal questions on instream flow," Washakie said. "There would be water left in the river … there would no longer be an instream flow issue."

Wilkinson agreed with Washakie that even in the wake of the recent Wyoming Supreme Court decision, the tribes have "enough leverage that they can apply some pressure" to negotiate a final agreement on water management with the state. But the possibility that the tribe could work around the high court ruling did not make the decision unimportant, Wilkinson said. He described it as a "step backward" in interpretation of water law. "The opinion really cuts against every single modern trend," Wilkinson said. "We as a region are determined we're going to have water in our rivers—for beauty, for fish, for recreation and just for the dignity of having running streams … Westerners are determined to make that shift, I think."

And although the Wyoming Supreme Court ruling may be "one step backward for protecting instream values," in Wyoming and elsewhere there will be "two steps forward just because the public will is so strong for getting some protection for our rivers," Wilkinson added. He said the legal question of administration of water rights in basins where there is a mix of federal reserved rights and state rights is far from settled. The Wyoming high court ruling on that element is "so splintered" that it is not likely to "be strongly persuasive" in the courts of other states, Wilkinson said, and the U.S. Supreme Court has not yet ruled on that question.

*October 19, 1992*

# Sometimes the Feds Do Pinch Pennies

## Judith Jacobsen

The West's irrigation projects are known as boondoggles—as places where the federal government spends money like water. But in the case of the Navajo Indian Irrigation Project, the government shows that it can also squeeze a project dry.

In the midst of the dry, brown northwest corner of New Mexico lie thousands of acres of enormous green circles and part-circles. Neither an out-of-scale Pac Man computer game nor an AstroTurf sales gimmick, the circles are crops—onions, hay, beans and potatoes—irrigated by miles of high-tech pipes, canals, siphons, and pumping stations. The water comes from the San Juan River's Navajo Reservoir, more than 30 miles away, via open canals and underground pipes. The San Juan River is New Mexico's only tributary to the Colorado River.

These green circles in the desert south of Farmington, N.M., on the eastern edge of the Navajo Reservation, startle the casual visitor. They would have the same effect on the Navajo officials who began negotiations with the Bureau of Indian Affairs and Bureau of Reclamation over thirty years ago for an irrigation project on the reservation. Tribal Council Chairman Sam Akheah told Congress in 1954, "At first, the land should be planted to pasture grasses and forage for raising livestock and a small area used to grow garden produce and row crops." In early plans, several thousand Navajo family farmers were to settle on the project to pursue their subsistence pastoral livelihood.

In 1989 the Navajo Indian Irrigation Project, or NIIP, was half finished, and that half was late twentieth-century American. The water flowing onto the reservation cannot be used by a Navajo with a hoe, or even with a tractor. Its use requires access to capital, to the expertise of modern farming, and to national and international markets. Like other Indian irrigation projects, NIIP exists because it was paired with an Anglo project. Just as the Navajos were talking of a down-home irrigation project in the San Juan basin, the state of

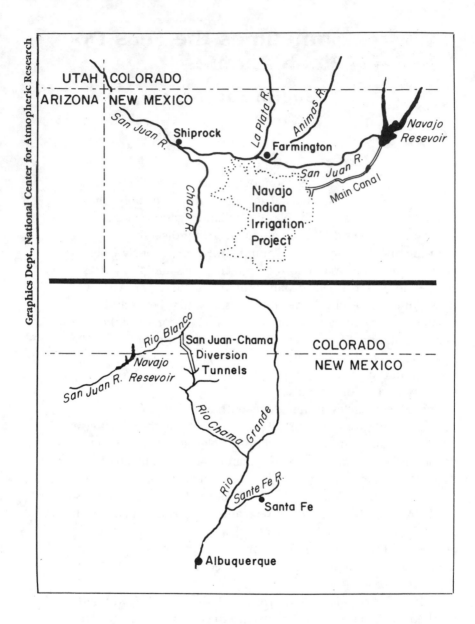

New Mexico was interested in diverting San Juan water to the water-short but heavily populated Rio Grande Valley. Interests in both basins wanted to cash in on ambitious Bureau of Reclamation plans to develop the Colorado River Basin in the post-World War II era.

The Navajos held a very high card in the poker game over the San Juan. Legally, the tribe has a claim to a good deal, if not all, of the waters of the San Juan. Under the Winters Doctrine, named for a 1908 Supreme Court case, Indians have rights to sufficient water to accomplish the purposes of their reservation, which are usually agriculture. Claims can be enormous, and they date from the reservation's inception—in the Navajos' case, 1868. But the Winters Doctrine does not have a mechanism that allows a tribe to raise the money to develop the water. For that, the tribe must go to Congress.

Navajo and Anglo interests in the San Juan basin at first opposed diversion into the Rio Grande. In Tribal Council debate in 1951, Sam Gorman said, "We will never see this water again if it does over the mountain." New Mexico State Engineer Steve Reynolds recalls that he asked a San Juan basin irrigation district official, "Wouldn't you rather see some of the San Juan's water go to the Rio Grande than all run down to California and Arizona?' The official replied, "No, and if someone is going to bed with my wife, I'd rather it wasn't my brother."

Nevertheless, San Juan basin Anglos and Indians eventually supported a diversion to the Rio Grande, and Rio Grande interests supported NIIP. In 1962, NIIP and a project called the San Juan–Chama diversion received joint congressional authorization. To Claudeen Arthur, Navajo Tribal Attorney General during the Peterson Zah administration of 1982-86, linking NIIP and the Chama diversion "was a political maneuver." In her view, "They said to the Navajos, 'you're not going to get a project politically by yourself,' so we had to tag along on the Chama project."

NIIP was to irrigate 110,630 acres of land with 508,000 acre-feet of San Juan River water; Chama was to divert another 110,000 acre-feet out of the San Juan and into the Rio Grande. Both projects were to be completed in the late 1970s. The different courses these companion projects followed are telling: in 1976 Chama was finished, right on schedule. But in that same year, less than one-tenth of NIIP's acreage received water for the first time. Indeed, before beginning construction of NIIP, the Bureau of Reclamation first asked that the whole thing be reconsidered. Since construction began, NIIP's annual appropriations, contained in the budget of the BIA, which then passed the money through to the Bureau of Reclamation, have averaged half the amount requested by the BIA. Totaling about $425 million, the cost is still more than three times the original estimate for the entire project. In addition to underfunding and delays, NIIP has been reduced in size, in a step-by-step way, over the years.

The Bureau of Reclamation recommended in the 1960s that the peak capacity of the initial 30 miles of project tunnels and canals—called the Main Canal—be downsized by about 25 percent to save money. This reduction included both the elimination of capacity for municipal and industrial water, which the NIIP legislation authorized under certain circumstances, and reliance on a reservoir not in the original plan. The new reservoir would allow the smaller tunnels and canals to do the job. Then in the early 1970s, the Bureau recommended a switch from gravity flow of water over the field, to sprinkler irrigation to save water. The shift further reduced the capacity required, eliminating the need for the reservoir.

Several commentators have said that these decisions cheated the Navajos out of their water rights. And a BIA official remarks privately, "The tribe could easily say that there are just too many coincidences." Reclamation officials defend the decisions on engineering and cost-saving grounds. Of the decision to eliminate the capacity to carry municipal and industrial water, NIIP's first reclamation project director, Bert Levine, points out that no municipal and industrial contracts had been negotiated when the system was made smaller. "You can't spend government money on speculation," he says, and a smaller capacity in the initial reach of tunnels and canals, which went through rough badlands, saved millions of dollars. Furthermore, Levine says, NIIP canals could still carry municipal and industrial water, but would have to do so outside the irrigation season.

Reclamation project engineer Dale Jackson, admitting that "in a sense, we are undersizing the system," points out that the smaller size does not mean that crops won't get enough water. Sprinkler irrigation means canals and tunnels need to carry less water to provide the same amount to crops, so the system can be smaller. But that sensitivity to cost didn't seem to apply to NIIP's sister project, the Chama diversion. Its works under the 1962 act were authorized to be twice the size needed to carry its 110,000 acre-feet. State

Engineer Reynolds says that building an oversized tunnel initially would save money if it ever needed to be expanded. "The tunnel is the most expensive thing," says Reynolds.

The key to the dispute is what the Navajos are entitled to. Reynolds and Interior say the tribe has a right to enough water to irrigate the land. Because sprinklers use less water than the original irrigation method, the Navajos are entitled to less water, they say. According to Reynolds, "508,000 (acre-feet) is not the binding number. The binding number is the acreage" to be irrigated.

But the law says that NIIP will "have an annual diversion of 508,000 acre-feet of water." The Navajos' Claudeen Arthur says, "It's just word games to say the Navajos' allocation is anything other than 508,000 acre-feet."

It is perhaps not surprising that much has happened either to keep NIIP from being built or to diminish its size. The NIIP allocation—508,000 acre-feet—is a sizeable portion of the much-coveted San Juan and a large bite out of New Mexico's claim under the Colorado Compacts. In fact, New Mexico is concerned enough about allocation of San Juan water that it brought suit in 1975 to settle the competing claims. That adjudication has not progressed beyond procedural issues to date.

Efforts to keep NIIP from using the full 508,000 acre-feet are alive today. In spring 1988, the Interior Department's inspector general recommended in an audit that NIIP be "terminated" at roughly 60,000 acres, the amount now developed, chiefly because of cost. Admitting that the Navajos would be cheated out of promised water if its advice were followed, he suggested "reasonable compensation" to the tribe for all losses. The Interior Department responded—it need not take the advice of an audit—by opposing termination because of investments already made. But it set in motion plans for deciding a "termination point of the project" in the future, clearly implying that NIIP will not reach full size. In reaction, the tribe and congressional supporters secured $11 million in NIIP funding for 1989, the first appropriation ever to equal the requested amount, and enough to bring the project to 70,000 acres, inching closer to the legislated goal of 110,630 acres.

Despite the pressures, the Navajos are making a success of the project by the standard of a competitive, business-as-usual market. The tribe runs an enterprise called the Navajo Agricultural Products Industry, or NAPI, on the project lands, and NAPI showed a profit for the first time in 1986. With around $20 million in gross receipts, it has retired about $2 million of a roughly $20 million debt in the past two years, according to General Manager Albert Keller. Potatoes, onions and dry beans (pinto, navy, and pink) are its highest-value crops. NAPI also runs two feedlots—one for cattle, one for lambs— and packing sheds for both potatoes and onions. In the past year, NAPI has, through joint ventures, begun preparations to grow watermelons, ornamental squashes, and gourds, apples, and shitake mushrooms. In fact, the 1988 harvest was NAPI's largest ever, and profits for the year are expected to be high. For the future, plants for producing frozen vegetables and french fries are planned to increase profits and employment. All but four NAPI managers are Navajo, and while deadlines for turning affairs over to Navajos exclusively are extended repeatedly, all current employment contracts call for NAPI to do so by 1990. There have been many bleak years since water first irrigated the land in 1976, including several complete shake-ups in management and a debt that was once $44 million. But in the last few years, the irrigation project has begun to work, in economic turns.

To be economic in the United States today means to be Anglo in culture. NAPI's french fry factory is not what one might think of as "Navajo." Disapproving of a french fry factory on the Navajo reservation may reflect legitimate concern for Navajo cultural integrity, but it also may be nostalgia. Until he was ousted, Navajo chairman Peter MacDonald was squarely behind Anglo-style economic development. According to NAPI attorney Albert Hale, MacDonald supported capitalizing on NIIP's ability to provide infrastructure—roads, water and sewer, primarily—to enable industries to locate on project lands. General Dynamics, for example, broke ground for a plant on NAPI lands in August of last year. Whatever happens to MacDonald, these policies are likely to continue. Delays, underfunding, undersizing, and the eagerness of the Navajo leadership for infrastructure and industry have all produced a project far different from Sam Akheah's vision of irrigated pasture and family farms.

In all of this, Reclamation officials tend to blame the BIA; BIA officials tend to blame Reclamation; the Navajos blame both; and outside critics throw in the state of New Mexico for good measure. But no single bureau or bureaucrat can fairly receive responsibility for NIIP's complicated history.

Despite plans and dreams, NIIP could not be irrigated pasture or even family farms without massive subsidy. Congress, according to plan, funded construction only (and it inadequately) and did not finance training programs or loans needed to create a NIIP of family farms. Navajo family farms could not compete in the marketplace, so a high-tech, low-employment, Anglo-style corporate farm resulted. If any one entity bears responsibility, it is Congress. Starvation ration fundings threw NIIP into the market, where cost-effectiveness, and not culture, is the criterion for success. Navajo culture, like other Native American cultures, grafts onto the dominant U.S. economy as easily as enormous green circles cover the desert scrub landscape of northwestern New Mexico. The result is not a Navajo vision of prosperity but french-fry factories and defense industries.

*August 28, 1989*

# The Pick-Sloan Plan's "Shameful Legacy"

## Peter Carrels

Indian tribes in the Missouri River basin could one day lay claim to up to 8 million acre-feet of water a year. But even if the tribes along the upper Missouri River are awarded all water rights due them, they would still remain undercompensated for the productive farmland they lost to the dams and reservoirs built on the mainstem of the river.

The federal government's treatment of Missouri River Indians during and after the development of its Pick-Sloan Plan to control the river is a shameful legacy. The Army Corps of Engineers trampled on Indian rights to secure the bottomlands it needed to build its series of dams. Condemnation proceedings were used liberally, despite a 1920 Supreme Court ruling that mandated congressional approval before such action could be taken. The Corps never received authorization to oust the Indians. All told, over 350,000 acres, or about 550 square miles, were taken from the tribes for the six mainstem dams in Montana and the Dakotas. Clearly, no other public works project in our nation's history caused more damage to Indian land. Many whites still have no idea how much the tribes sacrificed to the Pick-Sloan Plan.

Three of the four Pick-Sloan mainstem dams in South Dakota flooded over 202,000 acres of Sioux land. North Dakota's Three Affiliated Tribes (Mandan, Hidatsa, and Arikara) lost 155,000 acres to the Garrison Dam's Lake Sacajawea. But more than the best tribal land disappeared. The Three Affiliated Tribes' prosperous Fort Berthold Reservation slipped into poverty. Successful ranching operations and a viable way of life disappeared, and three hundred and fifty families were forced to abandon their homes. Before there was a Garrison Dam, unemployment had been near zero on the reservation. After the dam, up to 70 percent had no work. The social ills of joblessness followed.

The Three Tribes were paid $33 an acre for their sacrifice to Pick-Sloan. Tribal members reluctantly accepted the meager settlement as

Garrison backed water up to their ankles. The dam was closed before negotiations had concluded, so confident was the Corps that the Indians would be evicted. The Corps was just as confident from the outset of Pick-Sloan that the Sioux could be uprooted, as the Fort Berthold tribes had been. Construction of Fort Randall, Big Bend, and Oahe dams, which all posed threats to Sioux holdings, were started before Sioux leaders had been formally approached about compensation. Indian families on the Crow Creek Reservation were relocated upriver from Fort Randall's proposed reservoir. When the Corps later announced plans to build Big Bend Dam, above Fort Randall, these same Indian people were forced to move again, since they had been resettled in what would soon be another reservoir.

Settlement negotiations between the Sioux and the Corps were a rocky process. The Indians eventually received $34 million, half of what they wanted.

The tribes also were humiliated by the Corps in other ways. The displaced Indians were denied cheap hydropower. Grazing opportunities along the reservoirs were severely limited. Access in general was difficult. The tribes were not allowed to cut standing timber in the future reservoirs; the Corps preferred, it seemed, to waste the trees.

Years after the reservoirs filled, when it was apparent that the Corps had taken more land than the reservoirs required, conflicts ensued about returning these lands to the reservations. When asked about his reservation's relationship with the Corps regarding a 6,000-acre excess-land dispute along Lake Sacajawea, Edward Lone Fight, tribal chairman of the Three Affiliated Tribes, replied: "The Corps thinks this is a war. That's their mentality."

*March 11, 1991*

# Tribe Wins Back Stolen Water

## James Bishop Jr.

*"There has never been a single concession by the executive branch of the U.S. government in dealing with the water claims of the Salt River Pima-Maricopa Indian Community that wasn't absolutely forced upon them first."*

— Dick Wilks, attorney for the Salt River Pima-Maricopa Indian Community

On November 7, 1991, a century-long battle for water rights waged by the Salt River Pima-Maricopa Indian Community in Arizona against the United States ended as Western films rarely do: The Indians won. With a single whack of Arizona Superior Court Judge Stanley Goodfarb's gavel, water purloined from the combined tribes ninety years ago was legally returned. With the 85,000 acre-feet of water annually came some $50 million in damages.

Tribal president Ivan Makil, forty, a rodeo-riding, trumpet-playing Northern Arizona University graduate, says of the settlement:

> We are feeling comfortable, after years of costly battling, that we now have the water. It is flowing. It is not a paper claim, but wet water. The tragedy is that we had to go to such lengths and spend so much time and money. The most frustrating aspect is that the people who were supposed to have been our legal trustees were the ones responsible for the dams and reclamation projects that diverted our water in the first place, and dried up our agricultural lands. For decades both the Department of Interior and the Salt River Project had the authority to make decisions to correct our situation. They never used it. We've had to force them.

The situation Makil refers to shocks even the experts who know a great deal about discrimination against Native Americans. The reservation, created on June 14, 1879, lies at the confluence of the Salt and Verde rivers, within the boundaries of the Salt River Project (SRP), one of the federal government's first large reclamation projects. The project includes most of Phoenix, Scottsdale and surrounding Salt River Valley communities. Yet the Salt River Pima-Maricopa Indian Community has never been included in the generous subsidies Salt River Project doled out for decades—with federal acquiescence—to non-Indian users, notably farmers, who surround the reservation. Makil asserts, "Every other agricultural district has been getting cheap Colorado River water except the 5,200 enrolled members of our community. This has meant that the per-acre cost of farming our 12,000 acres has been $130, compared to $40 for non-Indian farmers literally just across the street. Everybody around here has been getting subsidized power and water except us, yet it was our water for thousands of years before the non-Indians arrived."

Ivan Makil, father of seven children, sits in his busy office in the center of the reservation, gazing out the window to the east across the open desert at Four Peaks and Red Mountain, long a sacred place to his tribe, known historically as the "River People." In answer to a question about what happens next, Makil describes how Pima and Maricopa Indians farmed this region for tens of centuries, using the highly developed irrigation systems of their ancestors, the Hohokam. He explains that today agriculture employs only 6 percent of the reservation's people. Many work off the reservation, in nearby metropolitan Phoenix. Still, tribal unemployment is nearly 35 percent. Rich, green farmland takes up nearly a third of the reservation's 52,000 acres, and Makil's people are in the midst of deciding whether to expand agriculture, pursue light industry or enter new businesses. "We are in no hurry. We are taking our time. We have the water." But being able to put that water to use is another thing.

The tribe won't commit to investing in a new irrigation system, or doing something else, until a tribal consensus develops. "The priorities will come from the people. It will not come from the tribal leaders down to them. We have been asking the people how they see the next twenty to fifty years. We want as natural a development as possible."

Although squeezed for water in the past, the tribe has built a large shopping center and operates a major sand and gravel business; other economic ventures are in the wind. Yet they haven't lost the old ways. Some tribal members still weave baskets in the traditional way, and Makil listens to them as eagerly as he does to more development-minded members. "What we do will be reflective of the community and what it stands for, the cultural aspects. We believe it can be done to blend the new ways and the old.

"Whatever we do," he says, looking across the desert to Red Mountain, "you will be able to come back here many years from now, and you will always be able to have an unobstructed view of Red Mountain."

Judge Goodfarb's order comes none too soon. The tribe's water supply situation has been deteriorating for the last several years. Makil says, "We haven't been growing to our full potential because we haven't had sufficient water." Those days are over, but it took the Salt River Pima-Maricopa Indian Community eighty-three stormy, dry years to get its water. Their efforts started in 1908, when the U.S. Supreme Court ruled in *Winters vs. the U.S.* that Indian water rights were created when the government created a reservation, and that those rights are senior to the rights of most Anglo settlers. Crack non-Indian tribal lawyers for the Salt River Community have argued for the past decade—and tribal members have argued for much longer—that the U.S. government, the tribe's trustee, was refusing to enforce the Winters doctrine. Instead, the tribe's lawyers said, the U.S. government echoed the line of the Salt River Project, which had cut off most tribal waters in 1910.

In 1980, the tribe, despairing of ever getting help from its guardian, formally asked the Justice Department not to represent it in legal matters because of its conflict of interest. However, the Justice Department refused, leaving the Department of Interior locked into two opposing positions. One favored enforcing Winters and restoring the tribe's water rights. The other favored maintaining the status quo, and refused to recognize tribal water rights claims.

Until last fall, the tribe's efforts to regain control of its water had led to one frustrating development after another. The worst took place in the 1930s, during the Roosevelt administration, when Indian affairs were supposedly becoming more progressive under the leadership of John Collier. A group of Makil's forebears went to a sharp non-Indian lawyer in Phoenix. After study, the lawyer reportedly expressed amazement to the tribal elders that such a situation could exist in the United States, and he told them he would take their case. But, Makil recalls, first Collier, at the new Bureau of Indian Affairs in Washington, D.C., had to grant the attorney permission. Collier refused, saying in effect, Makil recounts, "Thank you very much but we are doing quite well with our wards in Arizona."

Wounded but not beaten, the tribal community kept its hopes alive. "We knew we weren't being unreasonable," Makil declares. "We weren't being greedy. We just wanted our fair share and we didn't want to have to battle it out of court." Late in the Carter administration, the tribe's hopes were again lifted when a high Interior Department official came to Arizona, met with all the parties, and was just as amazed at the discrimination as the first non-Indian lawyer had been forty years earlier. What caught the official's attention was a satellite map of central and southern Arizona, showing areas of water and vegetation in red. Indian reservations had little red, and the lines of demarcation between red and white were usually Indian reservation boundaries. "His eyes lit up," a participant at the meeting recalls. "He said, 'There is something really wrong here.' "

The upshot: Interior set a deadline for filing a suit against the Salt River Project. But the deadline passed, and the Salt River Project refused to engage in settlement talks. "Department of Interior Secretary Cecil Andrus could have ordered the Salt River Project to deliver water on his own authority, but he chickened out," a tribal lawyer recalls. In response, the tribe sued in the Washington, D.C., U.S. District Court, but under pressure from Salt River Project lawyers, the Department of Justice persuaded the judge to transfer the case back to Arizona. The tribal officials were furious, but they didn't stop fighting. "The tribe kept insisting," Makil recounts, "that no matter how many times we got beaten, that we had to keep going back until we wouldn't be able to get up anymore."

And keep on fighting they did, largely through tribal lawyers Philip Shea and Dick Wilks who, operating on a long leash from the tribal council, raised a legal racket with a flurry of lawsuits. "They are good, real good," says a senior Department of Interior attorney. "They really hung in there," adds Mike Jackson, senior staffer on the U.S. Select Committee on Indian Affairs and an aide to Arizona Senator John McCain.

Finally, about four years ago, after countless tumultuous meetings, a settlement was reached between the main players and forged into legislation. The result was Public Law 100-512, passed by the 100th Congress on October 20, 1988, and titled the Salt River Pima-Maricopa Indian Community Rights Settlement Act of 1988. In a sense, all parties won because passage of the act avoided further litigation, the tribe's water rights claims were quantified once and for all, and non-Indian water users could plan for the future more confidently. Judge Goodfarb's ruling last November put the icing on the cake. In it, he dismissed all objections from some non-Indian water users who had kept up their fight to the end.

The parties to the settlement were the tribe, on the one hand, and the state of Arizona, the Salt River Project Agricultural Improvement and Power District, the Salt River Valley Users' Association, the Roosevelt Water Conservation District, the Roosevelt Irrigation District, the Arizona cities of Chandler, Glendale, Mesa, Phoenix, Scottsdale, and Tempe, and the town of Gilbert. Essentially, the new law directed the secretary of Interior to come up with the water, through exchanges and purchases, and the cities to come up with funds to buy the water needed to meet the tribal claims. "All the water will come to the tribe from the Salt River Project," tribal attorney Philip Shea told *High Country News*. "The tribe, which has been getting 12,000 to 15,000 acre-feet, will now get more than 85,000, and that is water that is no longer available to those who once could use it."

There are various theories as to why the non-Indian water users surrendered these water rights, and why the state of Arizona, not normally celebrated for its progressive politics, is achieving the goals of *Winters vs. the United States* through settlement rather than through the costly litigation that is often the case in many other Western states.

First, Arizona's delegation has taken the view that Indian water rights questions should be nonpartisan. In addition, the personalities in Arizona differ from other states in the sense, says Mike Jackson, "that there have been many skilled players in key positions who want to put the issue to bed." Finally, the push to complete the Central Arizona Project also drove parties to settle Indian claims, to clear up the uncertainties over future control of water supplies. As a result, settlement has been the focus, rather than litigation, at Ak-Chin, Fort Yuma, and Tohono O'dam.

The Salt River Pima-Maricopa Community was also aided by a massive miscalculation by the Salt River Project. In an attempt to put the tribe's water claims to rest, the Salt River Project in the 1970s set the massive Gila River Adjudication into motion. The project knew it could lose some water, but was willing to endure the loss to gain certainty. And that was how it played out. "Our opposition had skeletons in its closet," says a knowledgeable adviser to the Salt River Pima-Maricopa Community. "SRP has manipulated the government for years, and has entered into all kinds of contracts that are in violation of reclamation laws. Under the settlement, SRP got its whole system ratified in exchange for surrendering some water." A seasoned legal source in Phoenix was just as blunt: "SRP feared that Judge Goodfarb would give away the store to the Indians. Settling was better policy than losing more in the courts." The Salt River Project may also have been encouraged to settle by Arizona's unique political climate. In Wyoming and New Mexico, for example, the water and political establishments fight Indian water claims even after they have been ratified by the courts.

But the Salt River Pima-Maricopa Indian Community got help from many non-Indians on its journey through the water rights maze, including Representative Morris "Mo" Udall; Senator John McCain; Representative Jay Rhodes; Jack Pfister, the one-time general manager of the Salt River Project; and former Arizona governor and presidential candidate Bruce Babbitt. It was Babbitt who first pushed hard for negotiations between Indians and non-Indians. "Back in the late 1970s," Babbitt recalled, "most of the major players walked around with surly looks and said they'd never negotiate—now they are falling like ten-pins. A great balancing of the ledger is at hand."

Judge Goodfarb's decree—contested case No. WI-200—will change the tribe's economic future substantially. For openers, it will lease back varying amounts of its newly gained water to non-Indian users for a good price—an estimated $16 million for a ninety-nine-year lease. This will help the tribe on its way to meaningful self-determination and economic self-sufficiency.

One reason the tribe seeks to grow is to handle the influx of non-Indian tourists to the tribal lands, especially to the tribe's retail establishments. And here, the tribe has been shorted, and Judge Goodfarb's order offers no balm. Neighboring cities, such as Mesa, Tempe, Phoenix, and Scottsdale, collect sales taxes from sales on the reservation, but return nothing to the tribe. This is because the tribe leases some of its operations, like markets, to non-Indians, and according to state law they can't get a share of the taxes. Makil says, "We have been forced to deal with a major influx of Anglos but don't get paid for their impacts. There is a net transfer of funds off the reservation. And we have our needs—social services, better housing, medical requirements and education."

At the moment, however, the tribe is in a state of happy shock and in no hurry to cut deals with non-Indian companies, formed overnight to tap into the tribe's new bounty, or to announce major developments. "The reaction of my people is not very visible," Makil observes. "They are not coming out and yelling and screaming in the streets. The fight has been going on for so long that now that we have victory, my people can't quite believe that it has happened." But it is no pipe dream. "The settlement is bomb-proof," says William Swan, a veteran attorney with the Department of Interior's solicitor's office in Phoenix. "Non-Indian parties are contractually committed to the terms of the settlement. If they break any part of it, the U.S. government will sue them."

Mike Jackson, arguably the most experienced Indian water rights expert on the U.S. Congress staff, agrees and sees a broader trend: "Across the West the players are pulling back from each others' throats and moving to settlement. Arizona has set the process in motion in a very big way." Jackson believes that "win-win" examples like the Salt River tribe are becoming the rule, rather than the exception. Citing the Gila Adjudication in Arizona, the Fort McDowell, and the San Carlos Apache cases, also in Arizona, the Jicarilla Apache case in New Mexico, the Ute settlement in Colorado, and Fort Hall in Idaho among others, Jackson says: "I'm bullish on the entire outlook. A lot of settlements are on the verge of resolution. In many places, the personalities are changing. The Salt River tribe's outcome provides a great example of the way enlightened tribes are going."

Interior Department lawyer Bill Swan agrees: "There have always been two ways to solve this problem: kick the feathers out of each other in litigation or to sit down and work out a settlement. Parties are sitting down but Arizona is on the cutting edge of the whole country."

Despite widespread skepticism that change is under way, Prior Appropriation, the sacred theory that won the West—"first in time is the first in right"—is under attack as never before. In Arizona in particular, its death rattle can now be heard above the wail of non-Indian water-users. "The bottom line," states Joe Sparks, lawyer for the San Carlos Apaches and others, "is that Arizona and the West have grown on water to which Indians have, at least in part, a superior right."

As for Ivan Makil, he's taking on the future one day at a time. "But one thing is for sure," he concludes. "Indians will no longer be invisible. We are an effective force and we have been more effective than non-Indians in many of these matters."

*June 15, 1992*

# The River Comes Last

## George Ochenski

**D**eep in the Wyoming wilderness and high above tree line, glacial cirques collect and funnel pure alpine waters from Cloud Peak's 13,000-foot summit down to the muddy torrent of the Bighorn River. Draining north into Montana, the river transects the Crow Indian reservation, where it is joined by the Little Bighorn, famous as the site of "Custer's Last Stand." Finally, the Bighorn merges with the Yellowstone just downstream from Pompey's Pillar, a rock formation that bears the carved initials from the 1805 Lewis and Clark expedition.

Much has changed since Lewis and Clark crossed the uncharted wilderness that was to become Montana. Crow Indians still speak the language of their ancestors, but the thundering buffalo herds that once formed the center of their "wheel of life" have vanished. And the "furious and formidable" plains grizzlies that terrified the Corps of Discovery are gone, their remnants driven into remote mountain ranges. Even the Bighorn itself has changed. Nearly half of the islands and gravel bars that once filled the river's braided channels are gone, their riparian habitat lost to Yellowtail Dam's regulated outflows. But in exchange, cold, clear water pouring from the depths of the 70-mile-long reservoir has created one of the finest wild trout fisheries in the world. Where buffalo calves once drank from a plains stream, drift boats packed with fly anglers now compete for trout that commonly exceed 4 pounds. With up to seven thousand catchable browns and rainbows per mile, it is no wonder this productive waterway hosts more than a hundred thousand angler days a year. This activity generates $18 million annually in an area where, as one local legislator put it, "the economy sucks." In a state ravaged by boom and bust industries and ranked at the bottom nationally in wages and per capita income, the fishery offers a welcome and much needed form of sustainable economic activity.

Given the world-class status of the fishery and the economic value to the state, it would seem an obvious public policy goal to protect this resource. So why did Montana's Legislature recently ratify a water compact with the Crow Nation that doesn't protect the Bighorn's fish? The answer, like the compact itself, is complex.

Montana, like most western states, wrestles with who owns what water and whether "paper rights" correlate with actual use and availability. This is important because those with water rights get to take a certain amount of water from the river, lake, or ground and use it for irrigating crops or for a wide variety of industrial and domestic purposes. Collectively, these activities are known as "consumptive use" and they sometimes suck rivers dry. The opposite of "consumptive use" is "instream flows," which means leaving water in the streams for the fish. While some consider this a waste of good water and a luxury arid lands cannot afford, it is increasingly common to view a healthy river and fishery as a value worth protecting. Under the Crow Compact, all valid, existing consumptive water rights are guaranteed, yet no instream flow rights protect the Bighorn's trout. The promise to honor all existing water rights was probably enough to garner the votes necessary to ratify the compact, and other agreements addressing long-standing disputes "sweetened the pot" for compact supporters.

One side deal settles a major Crow lawsuit against the state. For twenty years, the tribe has sought hundreds of millions of dollars in compensation for what it believes was illegal state taxation of Crow coal. In the out-of-court settlement, the state agrees to pay the tribe $15 million over fifteen years and promises not to tax Crow coal in the future. The tribe, besides dropping the lawsuit, agrees to use the payments for economic development and water and sewer infrastructure on the reservation. Another side agreement could settle a long-standing contention that the federal government did not enforce limits on how much reservation land could be owned by non-Indians. If everything goes as planned, the tribe will get a share of hydroelectric revenues from Yellowtail Dam that it will use to buy back non-Indian lands within reservation boundaries.

"I believe in miracles," said Clara Nomee, Madame Chairman of the Crow tribe, "and putting the compact together in eight months was a miracle. Negotiating solutions to any one of these issues usually takes years, not months." Some, however, think the short time frame had more to do with political term limits than miracles. The governor, attorney general, and most of Montana's legislative leaders have held office for much of the last decade and are now "termed out." In a state where the "Indian vote" can sway an election, having a role in a major negotiated tribal settlement can help candidates running for a new office. In addition, Nomee has been under federal investigation for possible misuse of tribal funds, and a popular settlement won't hurt her, either.

But Chris Tweeten, the state's lead negotiator, says politics didn't have much to do with it. "We did it for the good of the state. The stars may not line up like this again and we just had a limited window to get it done." The "limited window" caused real problems for instream flow advocates. "We never got to see a copy of the compact until it was finished and by then, no changes were allowed," says Bruce Farling, head of Montana Trout Unlimited. "We walked in the card game late, got dealt two deuces, and did our best to protect the fish." Those efforts resulted in a memorandum of understanding that the state, tribe, and federal government would develop a streamflow and lake level management plan within a year of the Legislature's ratification of the compact.

The short time frame also caused problems for the federal government's representatives. They refused to endorse either the compact or the memorandum and said the fast-track negotiations simply did not provide sufficient time to determine if enough water is available for all the guaranteed appropriations, let alone for instream flows. The federal government is an important player because the Bureau of Reclamation operates Yellowtail Dam, and it must agree to both the timing and amount of water releases. "We're worried about the feds," says Trout Unlimited's Farling, "because the Bureau of Reclamation is in the consumptive water business, not the instream flow business. Throughout the West, whenever the Bureau has a choice between fish and consumptive use, the fish lose."

Federal negotiators point out that, as trustee for the tribe, their primary duty is to make sure that it is the tribe that ultimately decides whether to use its share of the Bighorn's water for irrigation, municipal, and industrial needs or for instream flows to maintain the fishery. Being asked to trust the future of the Bighorn fishery to a shaky memorandum of understanding in the face of federal opposition was too risky for some. "It's not easy standing in front of a political steamroller, but other tribes have instream flows quantified in their compacts and it should have happened here" said Representative Bob Raney, D-Livingston, a conservationist and fifteen-year legislative veteran. "I usually vote with the Indians, but I couldn't support this. Everybody else gets their water first and the river comes last."

Representative Bill Eggers, D-Crow Agency, an attorney and Crow tribal member, called himself "a lone wolf, a voice in the dark" when he warned fellow state legislators that instream flows are only one of many issues left unresolved. "This agreement leaves way too much hanging in the air. We may be carrying lawyers on our back into the next century over this." Even Pat Graham, director of Montana's Department of Fish, Wildlife and Parks and part of the administration that negotiated the agreement, cautioned the legislature that the memorandum fails to "adequately protect this wild trout fishery."

Representative Hal Harper, D-Helena, wanted something better than just the memorandum of understanding—he wanted language in the compact itself. Although Republican leaders had told him no amendments would be accepted, Harper, a former speaker of the House and well-known fly angler, gave it a shot. With help from fellow Democrats and a few Republican sportsmen on the House Natural Resource Committee, Harper succeeded. His amendment says: "The Montana Legislature intends that the streamflow and lake level management plan should provide enforceable mechanisms that protect the long-term biological viability of the blue-ribbon, wild trout fishery on the Bighorn River." Like a lone remora on a great white shark, the amendment stuck to the bill as it knifed through the Legislature and across the governor's desk.

The next stop for the compact is the U.S. Congress, which could cast a more critical eye on the agreement. While Harper's amendment expresses legislative intent to protect the fishery, it doesn't specify what flows are actually required. Consensus is that 2,500 to 3,500 cubic feet per second would protect the fishery and Congress could write in those levels before approving the compact and sending it back to the state and tribe. But downstream Wyoming could object in the Congress, since lowering Bighorn Lake to protect the fishery could leave that state's water users dry.

Thanks to heavy snowfall in the mountains, letting water run down the river this year is no problem. But in dry years, there simply may not be enough water to meet all the demands. When that happens, there are no guarantees that sufficient quantities of cold, clean water will remain in the river to keep those fabulous fish healthy and their spawning beds covered. In this compact, irrigators and other consumptive users of water come first, and the river comes last.

*August 2, 1999*

# 7

# Watershed Restoration

# Bringing Back the Range

## Jim Stiak

I t is late August 1989 in central Oregon. A
sparkling brook runs along the bottom of
a canyon in the dry, juniper-dotted hills. Tiny
rainbow trout swim in the clear water. Sedges, grasses, and young
willows hug the stream banks, their bright green contrasting sharply
with the brown slopes rising above. In a Bureau of Land
Management cap, sunglasses, and an aw-shucks grin, Earl McKinney
is standing alongside Bear Creek explaining what sounds like a
minor miracle. With chainsaws, torches, and cattle, he's saying, this
stream has been transformed from one that used to trickle dry every
summer. Now it flows year-round.

"The BLM watershed program," says McKinney, "is to cut
junipers, wait three years and burn, (then) have a good cattle grazing
program lined up." McKinney is a range conservationist with the
BLM in Prineville, Oregon. In the early 1970s, his district began
cutting trees, burning fields, and allowing selective grazing to
rehabilite watersheds long overgrazed. Thinning the junipers,
McKinney explains, lets the grass trap more of the meager water that
falls in this country. Fires keep junipers from resprouting and
stimulate grass to grow, and the cattle, if grazed at the right time of
year, also help the grass along.

McKinney and a medley of people roam along the stream, poking
in the soil, snapping pictures, swapping stories. It's the quarterly get-
together and tour of the Oregon Watershed Improvement Coalition,
an ad hoc group of seventeen people from academia, the cattle and
timber industries, federal and state agencies, and wildlife and
environmental groups. The coalition was formed in early 1986 to
improve not only damaged lands, but also relations. "The
environmentalists said grazing on public lands should be
eliminated," recalls one member, but "the ranchers said the
environmental community should be eliminated." Bill Kreuger, a
professor of rangeland resources at Oregon State University, is
coalition chairman. He arranged the first meeting, seeing it as a test

of whether quarreling factions could stay in the same room for a
couple hours. They did, and the group has been meeting ever since.

Part of the friction among the different parties centered around
an obscure fish, the Lahontan cutthroat trout, that was rare and
getting rarer. The Lahontan, also known as the black spotted trout,
dates back to the day when the Great Basin was one big lake and the
fish was the largest trout in North American waters. In the 1930s, for
example, a 41-pounder was caught in Pyramid Lake, Nevada. But
with commercial overharvesting, irrigation dams, and interbreeding
with introduced species, the pure strain was decimated until it
survived in just a few small streams. Then came years of drought,
and on three streams in central Oregon, the Lahontan population
plunged. On Big White Horse Creek, its population dropped 87
percent in four years. Although the U.S. Fish and Wildlife Service
currently considers it only a "sensitive" species, pressure could
mount to list the trout as endangered. Like the spotted owl, the
spotted trout could be the center of a political mess. The coalition
hopes to avoid that by repairing both trout habitat and community
relations. In an effort to save the Lahontan, cattle have been fenced
out of Big White Horse Creek for the first time ever.

"Once the riparian habitat gets back in shape, we expect the
stream will deepen and the fish population increase," explains
coalition member Cal Cole. He is the executive director of Oregon
Trout, a group that he calls a voice for the fish rather than the
fishers. But preventing grazing on public lands is not the answer,
Cole adds. That will just put pressure on private lands, and much of
the best land—the bottom, riparian lands—are private. The answer,
Cole and other coalition members hope, is education about
enlightened ranching practices.

The coalition has only one on-the-ground project of its own, at
Bridge Creek, but members respond to calls for help or advice from
all around Oregon's rangelands. Every few months, the group takes a
tour to see the work being done, not only streamside, but also high
above in the upper watersheds. The 1989 tour is on Doc and Connie
Hatfield's "High Desert Ranch" outside Brothers, Oregon. Doc
Hatfield leads the group through a series of windswept fields, and at
the first stop, he tosses his grey Stetson onto a patch of earth
surrounded by scattered tufts of Idaho fescue. "Notice how much
bare ground there is here," he says. "This field hasn't been grazed for

twenty-five years." He reaches down and tugs on one of the clumps, which comes out easily. "Not much root vigor," he says.

He comes to a fence. On the left, where bushy grasses reach high, there's heavy animal use, he says. On the right, with few grasses, there's no animal use. He says grazing helps vegetation by recycling nutrients—held in the cowpies—and by stomping down dead vegetation and pushing seeds into the soil. "The big animal influence," adds McKinney, "is the critical driving force in the grassland ecosystem."

Doc Hatfield leads the group to a field where the juniper trees were burned off several years ago. When a storm came, he says, the water ran off quickly, but clean. The sediment was trapped by thick grasses that grew in place of the junipers. Bill Kreuger holds a quick class in erosion. He says there was a study that compared rates of erosion under different vegetation covers. The most erosion was under big juniper. Less occurred under sagebrush but the least— something like one hundred times less than under juniper—was under grass. Junipers also steal water. When the trees are cut in the hills the water table rises in the lower lands. Willow and Bear creeks, which used to be intermittent, are now year-round, Kreuger reports. Kreuger points to a 20-foot high juniper. "According to data," he says, "on a warm, saturated spring day, that tree'll pump up about 50 gallons of water a day. Like any evergreen," adds McKinney, "juniper transpires all year. So in the spring, the grass is already wilted from lack of water."

The tour heads up a pair of dirt tracks, past a hand-painted sign reading "Connie's Point" to a rocky knoll with a stand of twisted junipers and a 360 degree view. The country is gorgeous, the air scented with sage. This, says Doc, is the upper watershed of Camp Creek. He points to a nearby slope with fewer junipers than the other hills. We've cut the trees, Doc says, leaving enough shade for cows and cover for deer, but mostly grasses for our watershed. He turns to Dave Lumens of the Izaak Walton League for approval. Lumens slowly looks around and nods. "This looks good," he says. "Wildlife needs diversity, which this has."

Doc heads down the hill, pointing out the fluffy tufts of grass. The slope is grazed twice a year, but only for a short time, which Doc Hatfield says is timed to encourage its growth. "You can imagine water rolling off this when it's frozen ground," he says, "It'd have a heck of a time building up any speed with all these cracks and crevices and clumps."

"Now you gotta hurry up," he says, playing tour guide. "This is real exciting." He stops at a gully with a trickle of a creek and a large willow. "This willow is fifty years old," he says, "but this flow wasn't here except for a couple months in the spring—until we cut the junipers."

"We've come a long way in three years, after a hundred and twenty years of misuse," someone comments. Maybe the Oregon Watershed Improvement Coalition can change the world, says Doc Hatfield. "Like this, where ranchers and environmentalists are talking together, realizing there is common ground." There's work being done all over the state, says another coalition member. A rancher in southeast Oregon is working on improving 35 to 40 miles of Trout Creek. He wants to meet with people to talk about it, but not with environmentalists, another member points out. "It takes time," says Doc, "for these things to happen."

The tour winds back down the road toward Bear Creek. Earl McKinney takes over, and points to downed junipers lying along the stream banks. The BLM started cutting junipers in the early 1970s, he says. The trees dangle in the water, but not so thick that they block the sun from the riparian vegetation. The tree is pointed so the butt sits on the ground and doesn't easily shift in floods. Back eddies form behind the junipers, depositing silt. "The junipers are the symptoms of 125 years of man and his livestock," says McKinney. "The real damage to some of these creeks was in the first twenty years cattle and sheep grazed on them. They've never had a chance to recover."

Besides cutting junipers, the coalition has also protected riparian vegetation. "Any vegetation along the creekbank slows water," says McKinney. "Grass is great, willow is wonderful. Willow slows more water, makes for less erosion and more bank building. Beavers keep them thinned—many small trees are better at slowing water than a few big ones. This is just my viewpoint, that the beavers' function is to keep trees young. But they've been trapped out."

He stops at a wide, flat area where tall bunch grasses sway in the breeze. It is the floodplain of Bear Creek. "This area was grazed in the spring for a month," McKinney says. "It gets some heavy stomping. Where grazing is allowed, perennial grasses are establishing. Where grazing isn't allowed, it's annuals, and they were washed away by last year's flood. The water table is rising," he continues, gesturing over the field of grass. "Eventually this should be meadow. And the floods aren't as big as they used to be. That's the payoff for the upper watershed work."

He moves along the creek, to a spot where the floodplain narrows, and holds up a faded photo from 1976. The area in the photo is bare and rocky. He points over his shoulder to the same area now, lush with young willow. Tiny rainbow trout fry gather in the shade of the overhanging banks. Two coalition members swap fish stories about the 14-inch rainbow caught last year.

This time of year is when we kill our creeks around here, says McKinney. "The cattle graze the riparian zone, which is green and attractive, but not rich enough to put any weight on them. The creeks get ruined and the cattle don't thrive. Nobody wins. Down in the riparian zone," he continues, "the idea is to graze after the runoff, after the vegetation has grabbed the mud flowing down the creek. This area was grazed three times heavier than before, but is in much better condition. It's all a matter of timing."

"There aren't any two systems where you can use the same prescription," adds Oregon Trout's Cal Cole. "Some systems, such as narrow canyons, just can't be grazed." There are places where keeping the cattle off entirely works. On Willow Creek, one of the many Willow Creeks here, rainbow trout have returned to healthy levels. The fate of the Lahontan cutthroat trout is still in doubt, but, Cole insists, the coalition's work will make a difference. "Fish are at the end of the line," he says. "First you've got to have good water quality, which is a product of good land management. You've got to get the management together first." That management, says McKinney, is coming around. Every BLM district in Oregon is working on watersheds, as are private landowners throughout the state. "It's their working together that's making a difference. On nearby Salt Creek," he says, "the BLM began the watershed rehabilitation work there, but it wasn't until a private rancher also did some that the water began to flow year-round. After all," he says, "streams don't care if they're on public or private land."

*December 4, 1989*

# Incarcerated River May Be Paroled

## Angus M. Thuermer Jr.

I n the late 1950s, the Army Corps of Engineers began building dikes along the banks of the Snake River in Wyoming to keep water from flooding the town of Wilson and nearby ranches. In the early 1990s, the Corps and Teton County embarked on the nation's first program to let water through these barricades. Within two years, federal and local officials expect 1,800 acres of property beyond the dikes to once again gurgle with rushing streams.

Technically it's called a Section 1135 wetlands restoration demonstration project, says Dale Smelcer, study manager with the Army Corps in Walla Walla, Wash. In plain language, it's giving something back to mother nature. "The U.S. Fish and Wildlife Service says there are a hundred and sixty-four bird and nearly fifty mammal species—from shrews to moose—directly associated with wetlands in Jackson Hole," says Kim Springer, Snake River representative for the Greater Yellowstone Coalition conservation group based in Bozeman, Montana. Most are "negatively affected" by levees, Springer adds.

"Over the years the areas behind the levees have gotten quite dry," Smelcer explains. "It changes the vegetation from a wetland zone to a drier zone. You had cottonwoods as predominant vegetation in the past—now you get spruce coming in and some other types of vegetation that adapt to the drier conditions."

That change isn't good for spawning fish and other living things, says Springer. "Something like 80 percent of our breeding birds are associated with cottonwoods. It's prime habitat for all our wildlife. We're trying to restore some of the dynamic system that used to be there."

Whether it has been seven years of unusually dry weather or the dikes themselves which have caused the deterioration is still unknown. But the demonstration project—expected to cost the Corps $360,000 and the county $120,000—will show how such areas can be brought back to life. The proposal is relatively simple—breach the western dike a mile north of the Wilson bridge and install a headgate capable of controlling water flows. The meandering Snake is relatively constricted at this point, and the chance of it wandering away from the outlet is considered small.

The headgate would control the flow of water—up to 200 cubic feet per second but usually much less than that—into a series of ponds at the new Tucker Ranch development. Once a series of pits from which gravel was mined, the area is being converted into a residential subdivision. From the Tucker ponds, water will flow south, outside the dikes, in a series of abandoned river channels and ditches. Along the way it will recharge the water table, keep marshes wet, and preserve the riparian vegetation important to animals. Channels that are home to spawning Snake River cutthroat trout would benefit. Bald eagles, an endangered species that populates the Snake, would take advantage of revitalized creeks.

The water would flow south for approximately three and a half miles until it rejoins the Snake at its confluence with Fish Creek. The project boundaries extend approximately a half mile west of the dike, and the supplementary flows from the Snake would occur during the summer and fall. In addition to the property beyond the dikes, the project would also preserve a stand of cottonwoods on a river island by preventing erosion. Island erosion has increased since the river has been confined by the dikes.

Smelcer said the project is precedent-setting. "This will be one of the first ones," he says. "There are some others in the process in the United States to my knowledge, but this is the first one of this particular type." Altogether the rehabilitation project will cover 1,800 acres, 960 of which are classified as riparian. It will involve numerous landowners and requires their cooperation. "We will be working with all the property owners to direct the water so it doesn't do any damage," Smelcer says. "Some people might think they might get flooded out—that's not the case. I think most everybody realizes it's an asset to their property."

The county will have to obtain easements from landowners, but water rights might not be needed because the project proposes only "non-consumptive use." Obtaining the landowners' approval, however, may be difficult. Constructing canals on private property is an act some fear will lower their property values. Since the county is not willing to condemn land for the easements, landowner opposition could still kill the project.

But one of those who sees the value of water is developer Mike Potter. "We bend over backwards to recreate habitat and aesthetics," he says. "Here it's really turning something back to close to what it was originally, and the value is tremendous." Potter, who must keep a keen eye on the salability of lots that approach $500,000, sees water as an amenity. "Running water, the beauty of it, the sound of it, the waterfowl, the reflection of trees—it's all aesthetically very positive," he says. Potter said a key to developing sensitive property is restraint on the part of future owners. "There's no question purchasers of these types of properties are extremely sensitive to the need for wildlife habitat, the merit of it and the enjoyment of it."

The rehabilitation project was authorized in a 1986 law that turned over operation and maintenance responsibilities for the dikes to the Corps. As part of that responsibility, the Corps is assessing environmental impacts from the levees and could propose more projects like the one under way. Springer says the transformation of the Army Corps from a dam-building agency to one that restores the environment is beneficial. "We felt victorious that they were doing mitigation," she says.

*April 20, 1992*

# Raising a Ranch from the Dead

## Ed Marston

For years I have been biting down on Sid Goodloe's story as though it were a suspicious gold coin. I have also been telling bits and pieces of it to audiences, testing ideas I wasn't ready to put on paper. Putting it on paper meant confronting the audacity and complexity of Goodloe's story, and the fact that so many experts dispute his conclusions. Goodloe's story is about land. It is about a ranch in New Mexico that he has spent his working life transforming from a tree-covered, waterless scrub land into a savanna—an open grassland dotted by stands of trees, ponds and a flowing stream.

The land speaks for itself. The audacity comes in the conclusions that Goodloe draws from his work as a landscape gardener on a large scale. He says that the Southwest has been deprived of fire for a century, and that before it is too late, we must move against the piñon-juniper forests that have come to cover much of New Mexico and Arizona. He says we must also act against the upland thickets of ponderosa pine. Unless we move decisively, he warns, the region's watersheds and wildlife will be lost as surely as we have lost those of Los Angeles and Phoenix.

The West in these unhinged times is not short of radical thinkers. But Goodloe is different. His ideas, instead of flowing out of some fevered ideology, flow off his 6 square miles of land. Goodloe is anything but a New Ager—he's an Aggie, with two degrees from Texas A&M and a deep Texas twang to prove it. Nevertheless, he was led to his vision of the land by six hundred-year-old drawings Indians had incised into rocks on his land. Any doubts he had about the meaning of the petroglyphs were erased by a sign from the more recent past—notes from 1880 left by federal surveyors.

There is another audacious thing about Goodloe: he apparently developed a working grasp of ecosystem management long before he, or most of us, had heard the phrase.

We live our lives by the stories we tell. Goodloe's story is powerful because he promises us, and the land, redemption.

If you ask Goodloe why he bought a 3,500-acre, beat-to-death, unfenced ranch with fifty starving mother cows in south-central New Mexico exactly forty years ago this month, he gives a careful answer.

> *This ranch was badly abused, so I could afford it. But I also saw the potential. I knew I could make a living cutting firewood to buy food and clothes. I knew the soil was good. It was close to wildlife, so I could rent the land out to hunters in the fall. I knew if I integrated all the resources, I could make a living. I wasn't going to operate the way they taught us at Texas A&M. If I'd have been a purist cattleman, I'd have starved to death.*

When Goodloe says the ranch "was close to wildlife" he is being euphemistic. In plainer language, his ranch had so little grass that wildlife stayed away. And what had been Carrizo Creek when Anglo settlers came to the area in the 1880s was by 1956 a deep, eroding arroyo that ran only when the snow melted or rain fell. Goodloe could use windmills to make up for the lack of flowing water. But lack of grass was a much more serious problem. One of his first acts after taking ownership was to evict a team of archaeologists exploring an Indian village. Researcher Jane Kelley, recalling that event forty years later, says, "I worked on the ranch in 1955. In 1956, we went back. Goodloe had just bought the ranch. He said to us: 'I can't stand it. You're running over blades of grass.' So we left."

The archaeologists didn't go far. The region is thick with ruins, and they found research sites on neighboring ranches. Kelley, now professor emeritus at the University of Calgary in Canada, came back to the area year after year. She kept an eye on Goodloe's ranch, and says that it became clear that his land, bit by bit, was becoming healthier. "He let us back on the ranch in the 1980s. He had been incredibly successful in turning a raw arroyo into a stream with grass and sloping banks—it was hard empirical evidence of what he's done." Jane Kelley says she wondered why Goodloe was almost the only rancher in the area to transform his land. In the course of her research, she had become good friends with one of Goodloe's neighbors and she asked him why he didn't restore his ranch. He agreed that Goodloe had improved the valley and the hydraulic system, but Kelley says he had no interest himself in changing how he did things. It wasn't his way, the rancher told Kelley.

Goodloe sympathizes. He says he was able to turn his land into a productive ecosystem only because he was an outsider, and saw things freshly. Even so, "It wasn't an overnight deal. It took me fifteen years before I could see what to do. And if I had been an old-timer, it'd never have happened."

One of the first hints about the true nature of the land came from archaeologists who told him one thousand people had lived in a village on his land. "It didn't strike me for years—the meaning of all those people living on my land six hundred years ago. In the 1950s and 1960s, I was working for New Mexico State University or for the neighbors ten to twelve hours a day. I had five little kids and a little ranch. I left home at dawn and came home after dark. I didn't have time to meditate on things." Goodloe recalls that "it finally hit me some time in the mid-1960s, when I saw fish and beaver petroglyphs at the village." He realized that not only had the land supported hundreds of people, where he was having trouble supporting seven, but that there had also been live, year-round streams with fish and beaver.

Archaeologists say that just because the Indians were drawing fish and beaver doesn't mean fish and beaver were on the ranch. It could have been wishful thinking, like the Norman Rockwell paintings many Americans are still so fond of. But Goodloe takes the village and its art literally. His next insight into the land came when he decided to fence the ranch in the 1960s. To find the property lines, he got the notes the U.S. survey team had made on its trip through the region in 1880. With their help, he found the brass caps set in concrete that mark the section, or square-mile, corners. But he also needed the quarter-section corners. The surveyors' notes said they were marked by cut stones because there were no witness trees nearby. When Goodloe, starting at the section corners, used a compass and tape measure to find the quarter-section corners, they were in the middle of a piñon-juniper forest that looked as if it had been there forever. "The penny fell from my eyes right there. I said: 'There's something drastically wrong here.'"

It took ten years, Goodloe says, but he finally put it all together. His ranch had once been an open grassland with a stream and fish and a village housing several hundred people. Now he had to figure out how to bring back that lost landscape.

He had made one major attempt at improvement the year after he moved onto the ranch. With help from the U.S. Soil Conservation Service, he brought in a crew to drag a huge anchor chain, hung between two bulldozers, across half of his 3,500 acres, knocking down the piñon and juniper trees. The same thing was being done all across the Southwest. Ranchers and federal land managers were trying with varying degrees of urgency to turn back the "brush" that was invading the region's federal and private grasslands. All efforts depended on the same thing: generous help from the U.S. Treasury. The chaining worked for Goodloe. Grass grew and wildlife moved onto the ranch. He expanded his herd. And, he got another clue. After the chaining, the arroyo started to run. With the piñon and juniper trees no longer soaking up and transpiring all the rain and snowmelt, and with grass now on the land, the water table had risen and was emptying into the arroyo. The arroyo was still eroding and rockbound, but it was no longer dry.

Then, in the early 1960s, about five years after he had chained, Goodloe got a shock. He realized that the big trees the anchor chain had knocked down and left for dead were alive. "The chain had just pulled the trees over, but some roots were still in the ground." Even worse, the smaller piñon and juniper trees had been bent over by the chain, and then had snapped back up. With the big trees barely alive, the smaller trees were "released," as foresters say. They began to grow quickly. Goodloe realized that if he didn't do something, the land would soon be worse than before it was chained. Using all the time he could spare from working jobs off the ranch on the task, he bulldozed downed trees into windrows and burned them. When he wasn't bulldozing and burning the big trees, he was on his tractor, "popping the small trees out of the ground" before they grew too large to handle. It took him four years, from 1962 to 1966, to clean up the mess that the 1957 chaining had left. He hasn't chained since.

By 1966, Goodloe had some open meadows and a fair amount of grass. But he knew the ranch wasn't healthy. And economically, it still couldn't support him and his family. Looking back, he says, he just didn't have the knowledge to see what had to be done. "When I was in the university the first time, there were no words 'riparian' or 'ecosystem.' I had no background that would help me. I didn't know anything but to get rid of brush and rotate cattle." So in 1966, in search of cash and education, Goodloe leased his ranch—"with strict limits on how many cattle the tenant could graze"—and headed for Kenya with his family to manage a ranch.

There, he says, "I learned the true meaning of a savanna that functioned properly." On Kenya's wildlife preserves, he saw how periodic grass fires kept the land free of small trees, while allowing the large trees and grass to remain healthy. He also heard in Africa of a remarkable game warden in Rhodesia (now Zimbabwe), so he flew to that country and met Allan Savory. At that time, Savory's holistic resource-management approach to grazing was unknown in the U.S. Goodloe wrote the first American paper about Savory's methods.

In 1968, Goodloe and his family returned to the U.S. with $10,000 they had saved. Goodloe still didn't feel ready to tackle the ranch. He didn't know enough, he says, "so I decided to invest that money in me." He went back to Texas A&M for a master's degree in range science. This time there were courses on ecology and watersheds and hydrology.

In 1970, the Goodloes returned to the Carrizo Valley Ranch. "By then," he says, "I had things figured out." The phrase probably didn't exist at the time, but Goodloe was about to try ecosystem management.

What Goodloe had doped out was how cattle had altered the balance of the land, allowing trees to conquer grass, not just on his land but throughout much of the Southwest. He saw that it began with the fact that a thirty-year-old piñon or juniper stands only a few feet high. It has spent most of those years putting down roots. The trees grow so slowly, it takes much of a ranching generation for them to become noticeable. By the time the rancher sees what's happening, it's too late. Thousands, or tens of thousands, of trees will have taken over, the grass will have disappeared, and the rancher and his cattle might be starved off the land. By the time this happened, even the federal treasury would be of little help. As Goodloe had learned, sloppy chaining practices of the 1950s and 1960s were no match for the trees.

From the rancher's point of view, the worst thing was that he had done it to himself by grazing the land too heavily. In pre-Anglo times, Goodloe thinks, grass fires started by lightning swept away the seedlings, keeping the land open. Because the trees stay small for so many years, the fires wouldn't have to come too often, or burn too hot, to kill them. There had always been piñon-juniper trees in the area, trees that by luck, researchers say, had escaped fire. These had regularly seeded the grasslands, and then the seedlings, except for a few lucky survivors, had been burned off. But then came enormous herds of sheep and cattle to slick off the range, stop the wildfires, and allow trees to take over. Goodloe says that, once established, the trees are fierce competitors, sending roots out long distances just below the surface, crowding out grass. As a result, he says, the ground is bare in a mature piñon-juniper forest.

He has spent a lot of time on the land, digging fence holes, stretching barbed wire from post to post, searching for cows. Sometimes—not often enough, he complains—he has been caught in thunderstorms. "I've watched the water flow out from under the piñon-juniper. Trees are supposed to halt erosion. But this water comes out brown. It's heavy with soil." Soil-laden water flowing off of grassless land led Goodloe to see the trees, or at least too many trees, as his enemy.

Because of what he had seen in Africa, Goodloe no longer wanted to totally clear his land. He cored each tree before he decided to cut it. If a tree were older than a century or so—if it had been around when the first Anglo settlers arrived—he let it stand. "If I was a purist cattleman, I'd want to get rid of all of them. But I leave corridors for the wildlife. And I leave trees for me, for the aesthetics. A place that's completely cleared off is the pits. I want to look out on beauty."

Once Goodloe had created meadows by cutting down the post-settlement piñon-juniper, he went into the stands of old growth to cut out the younger trees. In the old days, he says, periodic lightning fires would have protected the large trees by burning out their youthful competitors. But even on Goodloe's ranch, fires are rare, and he plays the role fire once played; he cuts down the young trees before they can kill the older trees by taking their water and nutrients.

By the mid-1970s, Goodloe had much of the ranch under control: he had cleared out much of the brush and created open meadows. The ranch was looking more and more like the savannas he had seen in Africa. Speaking to groups, he likes to include an African landscape, complete with wildebeests, among slides of his ranch. It takes a moment or two for even a professional audience to realize that they are no longer looking at New Mexico.

But, though the macro-landscape was in good shape, down on the ground, the ranch was still in trouble, with only one kind of grass.

"Ninety percent of what I had was sod-bound blue grama grass."
Blue grama, he says, grows only in hot weather. Over the decades,
the cattle had wiped out all the grasses and legumes that grow in the
cool seasons. Goodloe's cattle and wildlife had enough to eat in the
summer, but were on thin rations in spring and fall.

Ranchers with irrigation water and a summer grazing allotment in
the mountains solve the lack of natural year-round feed by growing
grass or alfalfa hay on their irrigated valley land, and putting it up in
bales to feed cattle during the winter. Goodloe, however, has no
federal grazing permits and no irrigation water. Buying hay from
other ranchers would bankrupt him. To survive, he needed to
convince his land to produce grasses for all seasons.

It was a situation made for Allan Savory's short-duration grazing
method that Goodloe had brought back from Africa. In 1970, he
divided the ranch into twelve paddocks. The paddocks allowed him
to move the cattle around, protecting the cool-season grasses from
overgrazing. And all the time, he kept cutting trees, waiting a year or
two for the grass to grow and dry, and then burning the cut-over
land and seeding it with native grasses. Gradually, Goodloe says, he
created a diverse array of grasses. Now, unless he is hit by an
exceptionally heavy winter, he survives most years without having
to feed much hay. His cattle get through the winter because he keeps
them off two of his hot-season paddocks during the summer. These
grasses grow high, where high means about 10 inches, and then dry
out. When the snows come, he turns the cattle into these paddocks
to feed all winter. It's not totally free, he says. He still has to feed
them supplements. But it beats having to feed hay all winter.

Come spring, Goodloe turns the cattle onto the ranch's higher-
elevation paddocks (the ranch runs from 6500 to 7200 feet), which
are dominated by cool-season grasses. "I let them start eating that
about late April. Then they go to oak brush from about May 10 to
June 15." Goodloe loves the oak brush, which he burns each year.
New oak brush, he says, is very nutritious, and "every bite of oak
brush is one less bite of grass." By June 15, however, the cattle are
done with oak brush. "That's when I usually get in trouble. Our
monsoon rains don't start until July 10, and then we get our warm-
season grasses. But from June 15 to July 10, things are tight in this
country."

With the trees under control, and with a broad array of grasses on
the ground, Goodloe turned his attention to a riparian area—to the

eroding but now flowing gash in the ground known as Carrizo Creek. The arroyo was flowing because Goodloe—unlike almost all land managers—had started his restoration project by healing his watershed, rather than by protecting his stream. His theory, he says, is that it makes no sense to restore a riparian area if the watershed above it is sick. "The first big rainstorm will send enough water and mud down to simply rip out your new stream and its vegetation."

Goodloe says he began protecting Carrizo Creek in 1970 through cattle rotation. He fenced off the stream in the early 1980s, keeping the cattle out completely. Then grasses grew in the eroded streambed each spring and acted like the teeth of a comb, screening dirt out of the flowing water and gradually building the arroyo back into a stream, with a flat bed and grassed-in banks.

Goodloe says his downstream neighbor was not happy about his improving land. Before Goodloe brought his watershed back to life, the land had shed the spring snowmelt from the Lincoln National Forest the way concrete would, giving his neighbor a nice burst of irrigation water each spring. Now Goodloe's land sops up the spring flood, releasing it only gradually into Carrizo Creek.

When Goodloe fenced his riparian area, he planted willows. "Once the willows get bigger, I will bring some beaver in and they can dam the stream. It will be a complete reconstruction job." That will give Goodloe what he thinks the Indians on his land had six hundred years ago. In the meantime, Goodloe plays the role of beaver. He has dammed the stream next to his house, and created a pond that is home to ducks and fish.

For years, Goodloe says, he was grateful to the Forest Service for sending the soil that rebuilt Carrizo Creek. But now he no longer needs more dirt, and he has been campaigning for a land restoration project on the forest. He has even helped out, cutting firewood and vigas off the forest, hoping to repeat on federal land what he had done on his land. Originally, Goodloe recalls, it was a tough fight. The gods are ironic, and they gave him as a neighbor the Smokey Bear Ranger District—home place of the small, burned bear cub that became the Forest Service mascot. Goodloe's talk of thinning trees and reintroducing fire did not go over well. But over the past few years, the local Forest Service office has become a believer. "They're working on it," he says, "but they let this thing get so far ahead of them that they'll never catch up."

Would a major flood off the national forest wipe out Carrizo Creek? Goodloe says it won't. "I think my watershed is strong enough that I can be physically wounded but not destroyed." Goodloe was wounded in 1994. The forest's thickets of ponderosa pine above his ranch burned. Heavy rains then washed a river of mud onto his land. He used a bulldozer to divert the mud away from Carrizo Creek, but it filled seven of his thirty-five ponds with silt. He was disgusted. "A stream," he warns, "is no healthier over the long term than its watershed. It's like everything else in nature."

This, then, is how Sid Goodloe has spent the last forty years of his life: using energy and brute mechanical force to shove his ranch out of one ecological state and into another. While Goodloe is worse for wear—one hip is now artificial—the same can't be said for his land. "When I bought it, the ranch was overstocked with fifty cows. I now run about a hundred head and I could run more in average years. But I stock for drought years. In my first year on the ranch, my calves weighed about 375 pounds on average. Last year was a dry year, but the steer calves weighed 640 pounds. I won't tell you what the heifer calves weighed; no one would believe it." That means Goodloe is getting almost four times as much beef off the land as it was producing forty years ago.

He is also getting beams called vigas, firewood, Christmas trees, live trees for landscaping, wood for the small kiva ladders he makes when he can't work outside, increased numbers of wild turkeys and mule deer. It's a holistic system, he says. The deer do better because he cuts and peels young ponderosa pine trees for vigas in the winter. The mule deer eat the tree tops he throws away. That green browse, he estimates, has increased the fawn crop by 30 to 50 percent. It pays off for Goodloe in the fall, when hunters rent a cabin and the right to hunt his ranch.

Turkeys are also a game crop in New Mexico, but not on the Carrizo Valley Ranch. If you want to see Goodloe angry, ask about the turkey season. "This is where the game department is stupid. The season is too long and too late. They're interfering with reproduction." Why does he care about the native Merriam turkeys? "They absolutely keep my ranch free of grasshoppers. And they go through the (ponderosa pine) needles and scratch them up so they burn better. They're more important to me than anything else in the way of wildlife."

Goodloe's mantra is "not all trees are good and not all fires are bad." But he is no more a purist when it comes to fire than he is a "purist cattleman." He uses fire where he can—he religiously burns oak brush, and he'd love to see the ponderosa pine forests above him thinned enough to allow for cool fires. But when it is too wet or dry and windy to burn, Goodloe climbs on a four-wheeler and rolls from seedling to seedling, administering a drop of herbicide to each.

Goodloe estimates that his job at home is done; he has brought almost all of his land back to its pre-settlement condition. But he says the entire Southwest is at risk of losing its watersheds, and that if the watersheds go, the rivers and cities won't be far behind.

*April 15, 1996*

# A River Becomes a Raw Nerve

## Michelle Nijhuis

<p>

here are only a couple of customers at Moe's Place one afternoon in June 1999, so owner Moises Cordova has the time to sit down and talk. "This time of year, people don't usually come in until after dark, when they're done irrigating," he says.

Less than a mile from New Mexico, the town of Garcia hangs on to the south end of the wide, windblown San Luis Valley in south-central Colorado. Moe's Place—"where warm friends and cold beer meet," says the slogan on Cordova's baseball cap—is the town's only business, unless you count the backyard tire shop owned by Moises' brother Dave. Trailers are more common than houses among the sagebrush, and lawns are nonexistent. Except for the occasional kid on a bike, the two dusty roads through town are quiet.

A few hundred yards to the north, a row of tall cottonwoods outlines the riverbed of the Rio Costilla, a small tributary of the Rio Grande. In its upper reaches, high in the Sangre de Cristo Mountains in New Mexico, it's a fast-flowing stream. By the time it runs a gantlet of diversions above Garcia, it's so small and shallow that you can wade it in a moment. Nevertheless, this modest stream is the heart of Garcia. "We don't have as much water as we used to," says Cordova, whose family farms a few acres near town. "But there have always been fights over the water. Even when I was growing up, my dad would say, 'Yeah, I got into it with so-and-so about the ditches.' "

And this is going to be another contentious year, maybe even more so than others. Over the past few months, long-standing tensions over water rights to the Rio Costilla have risen to a very public boiling point. The small communities along the Rio Costilla—Garcia, Jaroso, Costilla, and Amalia—are again finding themselves at odds. But this year, there's something new on the scene. A New Mexico environmental group, Amigos Bravos, has set its sights on restoring the Rio Grande—not just the river, but also the small towns that depend on its water. The group is attempting to change the way local residents deal with the Rio Costilla, working with a handful of farmers, ranchers and urban refugees as it tries to mesh environmental goals with local needs.

As Amigos Bravos struggles to put its values into practice, one of the Southwest's heavy-hitting environmental groups, Forest Guardians, has joined the fray. Unlike Amigos Bravos, it's operating in the rarefied world of state and federal water law, serving notice that it intends to get water back in the river by challenging the aging compacts that govern the Colorado River and the Rio Grande. Its attention-getting case has thrown a spotlight on the Rio Grande watershed, including the Rio Costilla.

The scuffle in Garcia is testing the tactics of these two groups, and helping to decide the direction of the small towns along the Rio Costilla. The outcome may also foretell the fate of the Rio Grande and its human community. The Rio Grande is an immense river, stretching from southern Colorado to the Gulf of Mexico, and it's rarely dealt with as a whole. Instead, it's usually looked at piece by piece, through isolated battles over tributaries like the Rio Costilla. But these battles, drawn out over decades and muddied by local politics, may eventually jump their banks: they may add up to the future of the Rio Grande.

Garcia, like many of the largely Hispanic small towns in southern Colorado and northern New Mexico, is organized around an *acequia*, or irrigation ditch, system. *Acequias* and the associations that run them have been around longer than the U.S. government in this area: in Garcia, some of the ditches were established in the mid-1800s, and there are *acequias* in New Mexico that date back to the 1600s. New Mexico is one of the poorest states in the U.S., and rural Taos County, which includes most of the Rio Costilla's course, has an unemployment rate of nearly 20 percent—the third highest in the state. In a region without much cash flow, the *acequias* provide irrigation water to *parciantes*, or small landowners, who raise alfalfa and subsistence crops. An elected ditch rider, called a mayordomo, oversees the division of water.

In Colorado and New Mexico, the age of each *acequia*'s water right determines its place in the pecking order, with higher-priority ditches filling their decrees first. Once the water has been diverted from the stream into the *acequia*, it is allocated among users, usually according to the acres each person farms. It's a simple, flexible system, one that's met the needs of New Mexico's small farmers for centuries. But in the Southwest, water that remains in the river is considered wasted water—by both *acequia* associations and modern water engineers. Colorado now allows permit holders to keep river water flowing for the benefit of wildlife, and the New Mexico state engineer recently opened the door to the possibility of instream flow permits. Most river water, however, is still dedicated to agriculture and other human uses. "It really is true that the people who manage water here manage it as a commodity to get from point A to point B in the most efficient way possible, with no regard for what used to be a river," says Ernie Atencio, projects director for Amigos Bravos. "It turns into a network of canals and lateral ditches replacing what the river used to do."

Rio Costilla flows through two states—New Mexico and Colorado. As a result, the small creek and its 215-square mile watershed are governed by an interstate compact that was approved by local water users, two state legislatures, and the U.S. Congress in the midst of World War II. The Rio Costilla and the Pecos River in Texas are the only Rio Grande tributaries with their own interstate compact commissions, each including the state engineers and their advisers. The compact's few pages determine how much water each state gets from the 40-mile-long creek, which begins in New Mexico, curves northward through Colorado, and dips south into New Mexico again. Rio Costilla's confluence with the Rio Grande is 15 miles downstream of Garcia. But in four years out of five, Rio Costilla has been drained by the time it reaches the Rio Grande. Costilla, Spanish for rib, describes the arc of the river's course.

From the start, the compact has been a source of controversy. In 1944, immediately after its signing, the New Mexico state engineer said his former counterpart in Colorado "seemed to be a little perturbed" about the document. "He seemed to think it was too complicated to administer effectively," wrote the New Mexico engineer in a letter to a colleague. Many citizens of Garcia call that an understatement. They've complained to the commission for years that the neighboring towns of Jaroso, Colorado, and Costilla, N.M., with a combined population of about three hundred, were getting an unfairly large share of the water. By the time the river reaches the fewer than one hundred people in Garcia, they said, the trickle that remains isn't enough to farm with. "Filemon, my uncle, has probably been in the record (of commission meetings) longer than anyone," says Cordova. "He never gave up. He was a constant pain in the butt. The people here have been bitching and moaning for so many years, they can't be doing it just for practice."

Now, those who have been complaining for decades have new allies, recent arrivals who'd like to see more water stay in the river. Over the past twenty years, a few people have moved into the area, mostly Anglos escaping from coastal cities. Some bought property near the river in Costilla or Garcia, expecting to enjoy a backyard view of a lush riparian area. Instead, they were shocked to see the flow drop to nothing during the hot, dry late summer. Donna Crawford, who moved here from California with her sister Joanna to start a bed and breakfast, lives beside the river near Garcia. There was never much water in the river, she says, and during the unusually dry summer of 1996, "the water just stopped coming." Their bed and breakfast is now for sale. "Who wants to live by a dead river?" asks Helen Doroshow, a philanthropist and real estate developer who has lived in Costilla since the early 1980s. "I'm not going to sit here and watch my properties go down." Her properties, a few houses and another bed and breakfast in Costilla, are also now for sale.

These relative newcomers, along with some longtime Garcia residents, wanted more than a chance to complain to an unresponsive commission. In late 1996, the Crawfords and Doroshow enlisted the help of the Taos-based river conservation group, Amigos Bravos, with Doroshow's Levinson Foundation offering to fund some of the group's early research. Their invitation landed in the lap of Atencio, who had just joined Amigos Bravos as its projects director. Amigos Bravos' concerns are not solely ecological: its mission statement says "environmental justice and social justice go hand in hand," and its long-term goal is to restore the Rio Grande to drinkability. Because the group tries to find common ground with local water users, Atencio started looking for people to talk to.

Amigos Bravos joined forces with a fifteen-member local group, now called *Reviva el Rio Costilla* (Revive the Rio Costilla), and began to puzzle through the area's complex water-rights history. The coalition also set some goals: it especially wanted to see water flowing through Garcia, for the benefit of both the *acequias* and the upstream fisheries. "From our first meeting, it seemed like everyone had the same concerns," says Atencio, who was born in northern New Mexico and returned to the area after many years' absence (including a 1993 *HCN* internship) to work for Amigos Bravos. "We were looking at ecological issues, the Crawfords and Helen Doroshow were worried about aesthetic issues, and the *acequias* wanted water, but ultimately it all came down to keeping water in the river."

Longtime locals were initially suspicious. "We asked them, 'Hey, what's in it for you? " recalls Moises Cordova about Amigos Bravos. "But most of them seem pretty sincere about what they do. They're a plus, most definitely a plus."

"Amigos Bravos has been in the forefront of this," says Lonnie Roybal, a Costilla farmer and the leader of the local citizens' group. "They've got more experience, and they've got the time, no?"

Although Amigos Bravos tries to find a local consensus, it's not averse to using legal tools to achieve the communities' goals. The group obtained the help of an attorney, Peter White, a water-rights expert who spent twenty-seven years working for the New Mexico state engineer's office. He examined the 1944 Costilla Creek Compact, and then wrote a report that Amigos Bravos distributed to Costilla Creek water users and the state engineers. When the compact was negotiated, White says, the engineers assumed that each user would be limited to 2 acre-feet of water for each acre farmed. "The documentation of the negotiations clearly supports it," says White. On the ground, however, water users aren't limited to 2 acre-feet per acre. In Colorado and New Mexico, irrigators measure out their water by rate, in cubic feet per second. That means, White estimates, that some higher-priority ditches may use closer to 4 acre-feet per acre each year. At the same time, the lower-priority acequias in Garcia get less than half that amount in most years. "My focus is whether or not the compact commissioners are violating the compact," says White. "It's not an ironclad case, but I think the commission's just been kind of sloppy in carefully administering the water so it's fairly distributed."

The Costilla Creek Compact Commission rejected White's arguments. "There's nothing in the compact which forces that kind of restriction," says Steve Vandiver of the Colorado Department of Water Resources in Alamosa, Colorado. "In Colorado, at least, you're entitled to the flow rate of your decree as long as you use it beneficially." The response of the state engineers, Hal Simpson of Colorado and Tom Turney of New Mexico, was even more succinct: "The Compact Commissioners do not see a need at this time to change such practices," they said in a page-and-a-half letter to Atencio.

While Peter White pored over the compact, Amigos Bravos tried to figure out what was happening in the *acequias*. The group believed that water was being overdiverted within the system through poor oversight and unmetered ditches. But when they set out to find who was getting more than their share of the water, they found themselves in the middle of a water war.

"Here I am, this novice water-issues activist," says Atencio, "and Brian (Shields, the group's executive director) says 'Here, why don't you take this project on.' Right at the start, we went down there and, I confess, just started shooting in the dark. At the time, we didn't really know where to start."

Those shots roused people. The water that Amigos Bravos wants to see running through Garcia has to come from somewhere, and those who might lose water through the group's efforts haven't stood by quietly. Several local water users say they were, and still are, the targets of unfair accusations from the group and its supporters.

The first is Dean Swift, a 23-year resident of Jaroso, Colo., who owns a wildflower seed distribution company. He's the sole member of the Eastdale Ditch Company, which oversees the Eastdale Reservoir west of town. Each year, before the irrigation season begins, Swift draws 1,000 acre-feet of water from the main ditch feeding the town of Jaroso—the amount allotted to the reservoir by the Costilla Creek Compact—for his 700-acre operation. By May 15, the other parciantes on the canal, the members of the Jaroso Mutual Ditch Company, can open their headgates and begin irrigating.

Swift got some negative press last spring, when visiting reporters saw water flowing into the reservoir and thought he had access to the canal all summer long. "They were just dead wrong," he says.

Swift challenges Amigos Bravos' claim that its conservation work is community-based. "I think Amigos Bravos jumped into some politics of envy—it's such a small and unrepresentative group that they work with. The old conspiracy theory—their poor grandfathers getting swindled out of their rights—is very attractive, but I wish [Amigos Bravos] had looked into it before they got involved," he says. "They've antagonized almost everyone, and they could have [come in] in a nonconfrontational way. They've caused distrust among neighbors and friends, and that's very irresponsible."

Amigos Bravos and Reviva El Rio Costilla still believe that someone is overdiverting water, but their suspicions have now shifted to the Rio Costilla Cooperative Livestock Association. The organization was formed in 1942 and now numbers about 180 members, all of whom are blood relatives of the founders.

The livestock association owns 80,000 acres in the Sangre de Cristo Mountains near Amalia, N.M., where it grazes cattle and operates a recreational area for fishing and hunting. The association also manages the water in the 15,000 acre-foot Costilla Reservoir, which sits on mountain land owned by media mogul Ted Turner. Under Western water law, one person can control a reservoir or ditch that is on someone else's land.

Livestock association members use water from the Amalia ditches and Costilla's Cerro Canal, and the coalition thinks that association members are taking advantage of their management of the reservoir by using more than their share of water.

"It definitely started looking like they'd gained a lot of power in the community just through their control of water," says Atencio.

Vandiver does say that the distribution of the water isn't closely monitored. "There's some unanswered questions about the Amalia ditches," he says. "The watermaster can't be everywhere at once, and I think he relies upon what [livestock association] members tell him is being diverted up there."

Association president David Arguello denies that the association is overdiverting water. Amigos Bravos, he says, is "using some of the locals to say they want water back in the acequias, but (those locals) have minimal water rights. Naturally, some of that water's going to go down over the summer, but people don't want to face reality.

"I think the water's being administered according to the permit," Arguello adds, "and I don't see how it can be changed unless we amend the compact. They're threatening the livelihood of the farmers here, and those farmers are going to get angry. I'd hate to be the one to try and take the water away from them."

These tensions went public at the annual Costilla Creek Compact Commission meeting—held, like almost every other public meeting in the area, at Moe's Place—in early May. "It was a classic scene," says Atencio. "The citizens' group was on one side, and (livestock association) and Jaroso Mutual Ditch Association members were on the other. There were a lot of accusations thrown at us about being 'outsiders.' "

The livestock association also challenged Amigos Bravos' assertion that the water was not being distributed according to the compact. "After that compact meeting, they should have gotten their heads together and understood things," says Frank Ortiz, vice-president of the association.

And a new twist was added to the story that night. Forest Guardians, an environmental group based in Santa Fe, N.M., announced its intention to file a lawsuit. Lawsuits aren't unusual for this group, which fights most of its battles in the courtroom, but this one is particularly ambitious, designed to grab the attention of national policymakers.

Forest Guardians is challenging the long-standing interstate stream compacts on some of the Southwest's great rivers: the Rio Grande, the Colorado, and the Pecos, arguing that the implementation of the compacts doesn't comply with national environmental laws, like the National Environmental Policy Act. And because Rio Costilla is a tributary of the Rio Grande, the group has thrown the relatively small-time Costilla Creek Compact into the suit.

Forest Guardians isn't just pushing for a clarification of the Costilla Creek compact. If successful—and many say it's a long shot—its suit would fundamentally change all the compacts, requiring the engineers to consider endangered species and their habitats as they divvy up the waters of the Rio Grande and the Colorado.

"The Rio Costilla is a mess," says Forest Guardians' executive director John Talberth. "The situation there is having devastating consequences on the riparian area. It's a good test to see if we can get these compacts amended."

Although Talberth says the lawsuit is "one of our priorities," it's getting more notice than the group expected. A meeting of activists from around the region was well-attended, and a positive opinion piece from the Los Angeles Times has been reprinted in Southwestern newspapers. "We hit a raw nerve," says Talberth. Federal river managers were to have met with Forest Guardians Oct. 5 to discuss the case.

Amigos Bravos had hoped to build a consensus along the Rio Costilla through its local organizing, says Atencio. "That would be the ideal situation, but I'm starting to think that consensus isn't possible up there right now," he says.

The Garcia citizens' group represents a broad range of interests, he says, but so far they haven't been able to bring the bigger water users to the table. While Reviva el Rio Costilla has discussed a lawsuit of its own, based on Peter White's research, it has not yet taken any action. Atencio says it's possible that the national-level pressure from Forest Guardians' lawsuit will help Amigos Bravos' work at the local level.

So far, the two strategies seem to be compatible, or at least not conflicting. While Forest Guardians takes on "everybody and their grandmother," as Lonnie Roybal describes it, Amigos Bravos tries to make gradual progress outside the courtroom. Through its efforts, the New Mexico State Legislature has allocated $100,000 to install and improve water meters on the New Mexico side of the river, which Amigos Bravos hopes will resolve the question of upstream overdiversion. The commission has also agreed to produce an operations manual for the watermasters on both sides of the state line.

Steve Vandiver from the Colorado Division of Water Resources says the recent changes have been positive. "There's a heightened awareness in the community about the compact," he says. "People have made an effort to educate themselves, and they're more aware of what's going on and how it affects them." A report on flow levels in each of the ditches is now posted at the Conoco station between Garcia and Costilla, and Moises Cordova regularly checks the gauge at the Colorado state line to see if Garcia is getting its allotted flow out of New Mexico. If the flow isn't what it should be, he calls up Vandiver to report the problem.

"No one's asked these questions for 50 years, so these are big accomplishments, just in terms of shaking things loose," says Atencio. But, he adds, "it's been really exhausting and hard for us. We've scratched at a 50-year-old wound, and there's a lot of anger beneath it."

By wading into this untidy controversy, Amigos Bravos is causing itself and the local communities some headaches, and it touched off a firestorm with premature accusations. The group has also found that, for now, local efforts alone can't bring about all the changes it's looking for. But by altering the terms of a decades-long debate along the Rio Costilla—by bringing attention to complaints that have been repeated for years—it may also be setting a precedent for positive environmental and social change along the Rio Grande.

"I think people are expecting that this will be groundbreaking in the way it combines community and environmental concerns," says Atencio. "Costilla is a small example of much larger issues downstream."

In the end, the community may find it is fighting over a pie that's not big enough for everyone, at least not without major changes in land use. Alfalfa, a notoriously thirsty crop, is a common choice here. Flood irrigation is a habit.

"They probably need more water than we think they're limited to by the compact," admits Atencio. "Two acre-feet are allocated, but they might need closer to three to have a healthy crop."

"If you only had a little more of a drainage basin, it would be a Garden of Eden, as far as I'm concerned," says Vandiver. "But there's just not enough water up there."

"I'd like to see water running down the river," says Eric Galvez, a member of both the livestock association and the Jaroso Mutual Ditch Co. "I'd like to see my friends and neighbors in Garcia have water. But if it isn't there, it isn't there."

Some people are working on solutions. Lonnie Roybal is part of the ten-member Sangre de Cristo Growers' Cooperative, which grows organic wheat—a crop requiring far less water than alfalfa—for markets in Santa Fe and Taos. Now in its third year, the cooperative plans to start a milling operation and bakery here in town. And the livestock association has long since switched most of its efforts over to "hook-and-bullet" tourism, leading elk and deer hunting expeditions in Rio Costilla Park.

But the members of the coalition believe that the water, scarce or not, could still be distributed more equitably. Moises Cordova knows their efforts won't cure Garcia's problems. "Most people don't have enough water, or even enough acreage, to make a living farming," he says. He pauses, and adds, "But it does keep the traditions alive, it keeps hope alive, and it develops stronger family ties. Garcia could be green again. That's what this effort could do—make it green here. It could make it livable."

*October 12, 1998*

# 8

# Water Allocation and Management

# Water Marketing Is Becoming Respectable

## Steve Hinchman

*I*n the wake of the battle over Two Forks Dam, the mountain that is Colorado water law trembled. That trembling was most apparent at the thirteenth annual Colorado Water Workshop, held at the Western State College campus in Gunnison in July 1988. The workshop is the state's largest forum on water issues and that year it drew more than three hundred state and regional officials, water users, environmentalists, and concerned citizens. Colorado Attorney General Duane Woodard led off with the keynote address, saying that, with few exceptions, water conservation, re-use, transfers, banking, and marketing have replaced dam building as the state's primary method of water development. Woodard said non-traditional water supply methods, like sale of water rights—now a multi-million-dollar industry in Colorado—are preferable because they are more efficient uses of water and have less governmental interference. Water marketing is increasing, Woodard said, because of the rising cost of water and public resistance to dams. But he also cautioned that costs shouldn't be the only value controlling the market. When water is shifted from its historic use on farms to cities, both tourism and agriculture, the number one and three industries in the state, will suffer, he noted. Drying up farms in order to water cities will impact whole communities, from businesses to schools, Woodard added, and may also "foreclose a rural lifestyle for future generations."

Eric Kuhn, engineer for the Colorado River Water Conservation District, noted that the number of water transfers and other non-traditional projects is increasing in part because they are designed so the developer can skip the permit and environmental impact statement process and avoid public policy review, regulation and red tape.

However, Tom Griswold, manager of Aurora's utility department—one of the forty-two suburban entities supporting Two Forks Dam—said most of the agricultural water available to cities that can be cheaply put into existing pipelines has already been bought. New water transfers will require expensive delivery systems and likely will be subject to environmental studies for the first time, he noted. "The EISs will probably require a full assessment of the environmental and social impacts of drying up farm lands," Griswold said. "Replacement of the Two Forks yield with agricultural transfers would require drying up approximately 100,000 acres of crop production land. That seems like a significant impact to me and one that very well may not be in the overall best interest of Colorado."

Tom Havens, a consultant to California's Imperial Irrigation District, said the West was "on the edge of a virtual explosion in the price of water," and that the transfer of water from agricultural to urban areas would continue. Havens suggested Colorado consider a California law that allows farmers to sell or lease water they have conserved, as well as water banking and other ideas.

"Save water and sell it or lease it. I think that's the new standard, rather than use it or lose it," he said, adding that Colorado had a ready market for its water in California—an idea that was backed up by surprise speaker Dale Mason, head of the San Diego County Water Authority. Mason said San Diego was ready to lease Colorado's surplus water and pay the state a severance tax. He said the needed structures were already in place and a leasing arrangement would give Colorado cash for new water projects and local development, and water for instream flows without requiring new dams or diversions. By the time Colorado wanted the water for itself, Mason said, San Diego would have developed other sources. Mason admitted the legal obstacles are formidable, but added, "At least today people aren't saying, 'Hell no!' When we first proposed (water leasing) four years ago, we were branded as heretics throughout the West. Today we are holding seminars on it."

The workshop had an unprecedented number of calls for a state water plan, many from the state's leading water people, as well as a general acceptance of Governor Romer's demand for a Denver metro area water authority. Greg Hobbs, attorney for the Northern Colorado Water Conservancy District, said a water council composed of all the state's water conservancies and river districts should meet soon to plan statewide water development and formulate regulations. Their first task, he said, should be creation of a metro water authority for Denver. "To keep folks at the table we need some new institutions," Hobbs said. "We need an institution in Denver that we can deal with so those forty-two suburban water entities do not cut and run, and begin to dismantle our locally owned ditch companies."

Phillip Ray, an engineer and West Slope water consultant, said the state needs a broad policy, not regional conflict, or it would never be able to develop its share of water from the 1922 Colorado River Compact. Calls for water planning were joined by calls for other issues long taboo in Colorado water policy. Chris Meyers, attorney for the National Wildlife Federation, asked that conservationists be allowed to buy water rights and transfer them from consumptive use to instream flows for fish and recreation.

State Representative Scott McInnis, R-Glenwood Springs, and Bill Needham, Grand County commissioner and vice president of the Colorado River Water Conservation Board, both made pleas for caps on trans-basin water diversions. "Now, as communities on the West Slope grow, we need protection in the basin of origin," said Needham.

Bob Weaver, coordinator with the Colorado Environmental Coalition, asked for expansion of state water court jurisdiction to include review of public interest in maintaining rivers in instream flow and water transfer decisions.

*August 1, 1988*

# Irrigation Water Revives a Wildlife Refuge in Nevada

## Steve Hinchman

For the first time since the U.S. Bureau of Reclamation began its mission to harness the West's rivers for irrigated agriculture, water from a federal irrigation project is being purchased from farmers to be returned to dying wetlands. On June 2, 1990, before a crowd of seven hundred people, U.S. Senator Harry Reid, D-Nev., "turned" 25 acre-feet of water from northern Nevada's Newlands irrigation project into neighboring Stillwater National Wildlife Refuge. It is the first installment of 5,300 acre-feet of irrigation water that could be permanently transferred to the Stillwater marsh this year, pending final approval from the Nevada state engineer.

The water, however, is no gift from the Bureau of Reclamation. It is being purchased by The Nature Conservancy and the U.S. Fish and Wildlife Service. The two have teamed up in an unusual public-private campaign to save the embattled wetlands, enlisting the help of Nevada hunting and fishing clubs, local and national environmental groups, state wildlife officials and politicians like Senator Reid. The Nature Conservancy's market approach has found willing sellers among the irrigation project's farmers, potentially resolving one of the most bitter and long-running water wars in the West. As fresh water flows into the shrinking and polluted wetlands, Fish and Wildlife Service and Nature Conservancy officials hope the Stillwater rescue may serve as the model for environmental restoration for scores of similarly troubled wildlife refuges across the arid West.

The Newlands water reallocation breaks new ground in western water politics. "The purpose of federal reclamation projects has been to irrigate dry land, not save wildlife," says David Livermore, head of The Nature Conservancy's Great Basin office. "This is an exciting precedent." It may also be the first step in a more fundamental change: what David Yardas of the Environmental Defense Fund in San Francisco calls "a new regime for western water." Yardas and other proponents of reclamation reform—notably Senator Bill

Bradley, D-N.J., chairman of the Senate Energy and Natural Resources Subcommittee on Water and Power, and Representative George Miller, D-Calif., chairman of the House Interior and Insular Affairs Subcommittee on Water and Power Resources—want Congress to rethink the West's old irrigation projects, instituting modifications that reflect modern water needs.

The case in point is the Newlands project. The Bureau of Reclamation built Newlands in 1903 at a cost of $21 million. It supplies 214,000 acre-feet of water—the single largest source of developed water in the increasingly urbanized Truckee and Carson river basins. However, all of that water is owned by farmers. The project, with its dams, headgates, and canals, is run by the Truckee-Carson Irrigation District under a contract to the Bureau of Reclamation. To be on the TCID board, you must own at least 100 acres of irrigated lands within the Newlands project boundary. In effect, Newlands is a federally built project owned and operated by local farmers.

Watching with envy are the cities of Reno and Sparks, Nevada public utilities, two Indian tribes, and advocates for the Stillwater wetlands and for the endangered cui-ui fish in Pyramid Lake. All want a share of the overtaxed Truckee and Carson rivers and for years have lobbied in vain for access to Newlands water.

Their appeals have become more urgent, especially for the Stillwater National Wildlife Refuge. The Stillwater marsh once spread over 100,000 acres in the Carson sink, a glittering wet jewel in the northern Nevada desert and a critical fuel stop for millions of migratory waterfowl on the Pacific flyway. The marsh supported the densest population of wildlife in Nevada until the Bureau of Reclamation built Newlands. Although Congress designated Stillwater a national wildlife refuge in 1948, the wetlands slowly shrank to as little as 10,000 acres, while the irrigation project grew to almost 100,000 acres. In 1990, Stillwater depended entirely on meager agricultural return flows, which also cause toxicity and salinity problems. The past four years of drought cut the wetlands in half again, concentrating pollutants, killing millions of fish and triggering outbreaks of avian botulism that wiped out thousands of birds. "It's [now] 4,000 acres and we're still going into the driest part of the year, so it's going to be a lot less than that," reports Stillwater manager Ron Anglin. More than forty dead birds have already been discovered and Anglin worries about a repeat of the botulism epidemic, which he says is tied to low water quality. "We're trying to operate this refuge with water one, two, and three times as salty as sea water," Anglin says. Fish and Wildlife Service studies have found that such water is lethal to small aquatic organisms.

The only way to save the marsh, Anglin says, is to rebuild the ecosystem from the bottom up, starting with bulrushes, cattails, pond weed, invertebrates, and crustaceans. That will take fresh water, which means a lot of money. Fish and Wildlife Service biologists say that to keep the refuge healthy they need to maintain a minimum of 25,000 acres of wetlands: 14,000 acres at Stillwater marsh and 11,000 acres upstream at Carson Pasture. Anglin says that will require a total of 55,000 acre-feet of fresh water, which will cost $50 million or more. Anglin's passionate crusading has helped to create strong support in northern Nevada for the effort to revive the wetlands. Local groups like the Lahontan Valley Wetlands Coalition are raising funds to buy extra water for the marsh.

The only protest has come from some of the farmers, who have enjoyed almost a century of federal support favoring agriculture over all other water users. The Truckee-Carson Irrigation District says it will share water, but it wants water transfers limited to 20,000 acre-feet. TCID board president Ted deBraga says that would dry up 7,000 acres, or 10 percent of the project's 73,000 irrigated acres. "The land we targeted for going out of production is the marginal land," deBraga says. This would only cut the district's production by 2 to 4 percent. "I think there's room for both [wetlands and agriculture]," he adds, "but they probably won't be able to restore the marsh to what it was fifty years ago, so they will have to take somewhat less water." At $300 an acre-foot, however, there is no shortage of willing sellers among the farmers, many of whom are struggling with marginal operations. Ted deBraga recently sold Fish and Wildlife an option on 1,200 acre-feet of water, and he says many of his neighbors are considering similar sales.

So far the rescue effort has reached 10 percent of its goal. The Nature Conservancy has spent $1 million to buy 2,754 acre-feet that it will sell to the Fish and Wildlife Service at cost. Fish and Wildlife has bought options on another 2,562 acre-feet, utilizing $2.7 million appropriated by Congress in the last two years. Another $5 million may come from Nevada taxpayers if a Parks and Wildlife bond issue is approved this fall. Although relatively small, these purchases may have paved the way for bigger changes. A bill recently introduced by

Senator Reid would direct the Fish and Wildlife service to buy the water rights necessary to maintain 25,000 acres of wetlands at Stillwater. While this is only a quarter of the original marsh, most observers see it as a major victory for the environment. The measure also authorizes the Bureau of Reclamation to expand uses of the Newlands project to include flood control, recreation, wildlife, and municipal and industrial supplies.

The TCID farmers hate the bill. However, it represents thousands of hours of delicate negotiations and would settle California's and Nevada's claims to the Truckee and Carson rivers. These involve two Indian water claims, drought storage for Reno, writing off the irrigators' remaining debt on the project, and improved habitat for the cui-ui, in addition to partially restoring the Stillwater wildlife refuge.

Earlier this month, Senator Bradley took Reid's proposal one step further, inserting language that would dismantle the TCID and replace it with a new board representing all area water users. The new eight-member board would include representatives from Churchill and Lahontan counties, the towns of Fallon and Fernley, the Fallon-Paiute Indian tribe, a nonprofit wetlands advocacy group, and two irrigators. That revision has further outraged the TCID farmers, who now accuse the federal government of trying to steal Nevada's water by wresting control away from the local farmers. Senate staffers concede that the concept is probably too radical to pass this year. But Tom Jensen, counsel to the committee, said it was necessary to "throw some cold water around and wake people up."

"The Newlands project has grown up," Jensen says. "Newlands has crossed a divide from its original purpose of irrigation to being a fairly mature, urbanized region's water supply." He adds that there is a strong feeling in Congress that Bureau of Reclamation projects should now be run for the broadest possible public benefit.

*August 27, 1990*

# A Shrewd Farmer Drips His Way to Prosperity

## Tony Davis

For Howard Wuertz, "less is more" is not a cliché; it's a way of life. Wuertz, sixty-two, is a Coolidge farmer who has plowed $3 million into water-saving drip irrigation systems on his farms since the early 1980s. The drip system is a computer-driven network of underground steel pipe covering more than 5 miles on a single farm. It uses about half as much water as conventional irrigation, in which water rolls off an irrigation canal and floods the field. He says, however, that he grows twice as much cotton, melons, grains, and other crops as when he followed the traditional path. That, he says, is why his business thrives in an age of high-cost Central Arizona Project water, while other farms in the area fight extinction. Indeed, he says 1991, a disaster year for most farmers, was his best year ever economically.

Wuertz doesn't like to knock his fellow farmers. "They're my friends and drinking buddies, very good and dedicated people," he said. "But when they went to the crossroads and they had to make a decision (about how to irrigate), they went the wrong direction." Less water can be good for a crop because soil needs to be exposed to oxygen to break down elements such as nitrates, phosphates, and potassium so plants can use them and grow, he says. Too much water can smother the soil.

The brains of his system are computers no bigger than a standard lap-top-sized home computer. Five of these machines control networks of underground tubing underlying twelve to twenty-seven fields each. In each field, a tube lies 3 feet underneath every row of crops, and each tube is hooked to a sub-main line that ties to another line.

Wuertz traces his entrance into drip irrigation to what he calls "a propensity for survival." It started back in the late 1970s and early '80s, when he noticed his crop yields weren't rising as fast as they used to. He, like many other farmers, also had noticed that the water table underneath him had dropped ten to fifteen times since his family had moved to Arizona from North Dakota in 1929 to escape cold weather and the Dust Bowl. "I thought if we're going to have any chance at all to survive, we're going to have to figure out a better way," he says. "A blind person could see that if you had to use power to get to the water from 300 to 400 feet below ground, it's going to be more expensive."

He visited nurseries, strawberry growers, vineyards, orchards, and other specialty farms using drip irrigation all over the West. He observed that most or all of them had shown dramatically increased crop yields using a fraction of the water used in flood irrigation. He started investing slowly in drip, maybe a few hundred acres a year. He sold some real estate he owned in neighboring Casa Grande to raise money for the system starting in 1985. Until then, he relied solely on his yearly earnings to pay for his new way of growing, he says. Today, about half of his 4,000 acres are on drip irrigation.

Unlike his neighbors, who rely mostly on cotton, Wuertz puts 20 percent of his land in grains, 20 percent in specialty crops such as vegetables, and 60 percent in cotton. If farmers are to have any future, he says, it will only come if they don't put all their eggs in one basket.

Coolidge farmer Jamie Gellum, who went out of business last year after eleven years, calls Wuertz a risk-taker and an industry leader, but says some farmers are skeptical that he's doing as well as he says. "Farmers in general tend to be boastful," Gellum says. "You're not in competition with your neighbor, because what you make on a farm is not related to what your next-door neighbor makes. But you have a sense of pride; you like to make it look like things are going right."

Richard Lavis, executive vice president of the Arizona Cotton Growers Association, says that while drip irrigation worked for Wuertz, it isn't necessarily the right answer for other farmers. "You have different kinds of water conditions and different kinds of growing conditions in different places," Lavis says. "The financial realities are that Wuertz did what he had to do."

Other observers offer only praise. "Howard's planning horizon is a little longer than most farmers'," says Bob Moore, former director of the Agri-Business Council, an agricultural trade-lobbying group. "For most farmers, God bless 'em, it's season to season. For drip irrigation and the Central Arizona Project (CAP), you need a planning horizon that looks to the next generation, five to fifteen years out. Howard is one of the few farmers who knows that and understands it."

"Howard is a smart cookie," according to Bartley Cardon, retired dean of the University of Arizona School of Agriculture and a professor in Wuertz's animal and farm management classes in the early 1950s. "He was a poor boy when he was in my classes, but when he was making money, he plowed it into that drip irrigation."

Wuertz is no enemy of water projects or reclamation in general. He uses CAP water and spent nineteen years on the governing board of the Central Arizona Water Conservation District, which operates CAP. He's been president of the state's cotton growers and belongs to the state Farm Bureau and the Agri-Business Council. He says, however, that he always thought University of Arizona economics professor William Martin and his colleagues were "100 percent right" when they said most farmers couldn't afford to mortgage their futures to high-cost CAP water. "Any guy in his right mind would know that you can't take water out of Lake Havasu, take it into Pinal County with a 2,000-foot lift, and do it cheaply, even if someone gives you the power," Wuertz says. "The maintenance, the personnel, and the debt retirement alone would dictate it would cost $200 an acre-foot."

When the furor was boiling over Martin's work years ago, he says, he never went to a meeting of farmers when Martin and his colleagues' studies didn't come up in the conversation. "They didn't think about it. They got mad about it. They didn't deal with it rationally. Water has always been cheap and free in the West, and the attitude was that with reclamation projects this would go on forever. My attitude has always been that regardless of how we deal with water, it will become more expensive."

*August 10, 1992*

# Albuquerque Learns It Really Is a Desert Town

## Bruce Selcraig

For about as long as anyone can remember, the good citizens of Albuquerque have been living a fantasy when it comes to water. Despite receiving only 8 inches of rain a year, residents have grown up washing their cars in the street, playing golf on lush coastal grass, and using some 250 gallons of water per person per day—nearly twice as much as folks in Phoenix or Tucson. Yet, even in hindsight it's hard to blame them. Collectively, this high desert town of nearly five hundred thousand, which gets its entire water supply from an aquifer, was led to believe by public officials that it sat atop an underground Lake Superior.

The aquifer allowed Albuquerque to provide its citizens with some of the cheapest water in urban America—over 60 percent less than what Santa Feans pay. Better still, not only was the aquifer enormous, so the conventional wisdom went, but it was perpetually replenished underground by the Rio Grande River. "Albuquerque behaved as it understood the commodity," Mayor Martin Chavez says in defense of his town's water ethic. "If you think you have an infinite resource, using all you want is not wasteful."

Civic boosters in pursuit of boundless growth delighted in the Duke City's good fortune. Housing permits were handed out like balloons at a bank, and new business was lured with the promise that water would never be a problem. Sure, there were warnings as far back as the early 1950s that alternative sources of water must be found, but there were always experts willing to sound more optimistic, and, besides, the realists couldn't be heard for all the bulldozers. No less an expert than Steve Reynolds, the former (and now deceased) New Mexico state engineer for over thirty years, wrote in the *Albuquerque Tribune* in 1980 that the city could comfortably grow to a population of 1.5 million. "Albuquerque is probably better situated with respect to water," Reynolds said then, "than any large city in the Southwest." If Reynolds were around today some citizens might like to serve his misguided words to him fajita-style.

Albuquerque's long-overdue wake-up call came in August 1993 when the U.S. Geological Survey released a report showing that Albuquerque was pumping out its groundwater nearly three times faster than it could be replenished. Tests showed the underground water basin had dropped by as much as 40 feet between 1989 and 1992 and nearly 140 feet in some places over the past three decades. More important, the report shot down once and for all the notion that Albuquerque had a limitless source of water. The Rio Grande, according to the USGS report, was not replenishing (or recharging) the city's aquifer at anything approaching a steady state. In 1993 the Albuquerque area pumped about 160,000 acre-feet of water from the aquifer, while the aquifer is being replenished by rainfall and mountain snowmelt at close to 65,000 acre-feet a year.

The landmark USGS report set into motion a predictable but nonetheless fascinating political dance. The city's water experts said there was no immediate crisis, just a need for concern and more definitive studies; the city council approved higher water rates and a voluntary conservation program; business leaders promised cooperation, but told everyone how little water their businesses used compared to homeowners; community activists predicted that conservation measures would fall hardest upon those least able to afford them, and, from a distance, a few sages surveyed the tumult and said, "We told you so."

"Albuquerque has been told for twenty-plus years an approximate limit of its resource," says Tony Mayne, executive director of the Santa Fe Metropolitan Water Board. "And they have simply refused to believe it. They would have you believe the USGS told them one thing twenty years ago and a different thing last year. It ain't so. It just ain't so."

Suburbs spoke up for their water interests, as did everyone from Indian pueblo leaders to car wash owners. There was some civic introspection about the city-sanctioned urban sprawl of the '80s and some wonderment that a desert town could not have had a water conservation program in place, but a great deal of the public reaction to the water "wake-up call" of 1993 focused on one very large company and its enormous thirst.

On a mesa just northwest of Albuquerque sits a 200-acre complex of massive, square, beige and chocolate-colored buildings beneath a flock of gangly construction cranes. Grunting earth-movers and cement trucks plow up the mesa, as visitors churn through the temporary parking lot looking for office buildings named Jurassic Park and Godzilla. Surrounding this futuristic compound is an almost perfect demographic portrait of changing New Mexico: on one side an evangelical church, cookie-cutter suburban homes, fast food outlets, and shopping malls; on the other, beside the tranquil Rio Grande, a stylish bed-and-breakfast adobe mingles with horse stables, vineyards, and old Impalas on cinder blocks. New immigrants from Dallas and Chicago walk their dogs past the few remaining vacant lots of sage and cholla that defiantly remind everyone they're still in the desert.

This is Intel, New Mexico. When the world's largest independent maker of computer chips, the Intel Corporation of Santa Clara, California, came to this mesa in suburban Rio Rancho in 1980, the giant had but two dozen employees and gave hardly a clue that it would one day wield great influence in the Land of Enchantment. Intel now employs four thousand people in Rio Rancho, plans to hire at least another five hundred next year, and says it creates at least two spin-off jobs in the surrounding economy for every one inside the sprawling plant. Average plant salaries are $35,000—more than double the per capita income in New Mexico, the fifth poorest state. All of which made Rio Rancho the nation's fastest growing small city in 1993.

By far the state's largest private employer at one site—Wal-Mart ranks number one otherwise—Intel is a powerful constituency unto itself, rivaling most neighborhood groups or labor unions, and crossing all racial, religious, and political lines. New Mexico politicians would be certified fools to threaten those paychecks, and so, what Intel wants, Intel usually gets.

When Intel announced in 1993 that it wanted to build a new U.S. plant to make the new Pentium and next-generation P6 chips, New Mexico officials, longing to diversify from natural resource extraction and government jobs, unveiled the most lucrative come-hither campaign the state had ever seen. Their reward was Intel's $1.8 billion Fab 11, a project that would become the third largest industrial expansion in the world that year. Beating Texas, California, Oregon, Arizona, and Utah for Intel's affections, New Mexico laid out $57 million in property tax abatements, $36 million in waived new-equipment sales taxes, and $20 million in manufacturing tax credits. Taxpayers would foot a bill for $1 million for training Intel workers, air pollution permitting would be streamlined, and Sandoval County, in addition to floating a $2 billion bond issue for Intel, granted the chipmaker a lease on its mesa property: Intel may grant easements and build or raze improvements at will. It may sublease without the county's approval and it has the option to buy the Rio Rancho site for $1 at the end of the lease term.

An underlying assumption throughout this corporate courting process was that the Albuquerque area could provide all the water Intel would ever want. This was no small concern because Intel and all semiconductor companies freely admit they are, by the nature of their technology, world-class water hogs. The 6- and 8-inch-diameter silicon wafers Intel makes—they're later cut by diamond saws to yield the thumbnail-size chips that serve as the brains in personal computers—must be rinsed at least twenty times in hyper-clean water to remove impurities. Exactly how much water is used in these processes is something no company will divulge, but industry expert Graydon Larrabee, a former Texas Instruments fellow, says that among six companies he surveyed, an average of 2,840 gallons was used to produce one 6-inch wafer and perhaps twice that for an 8-inch wafer. If Intel's new chip factory makes about thirty thousand 8-inch wafers a month, which Larrabee says is standard, the amount of water used could reach 6 million gallons a day. (For comparison, the daily use of a really gluttonous golf course is about 1 million gallons. Intel says it returns 85 percent of this water to the Rio Grande through Albuquerque's treatment plants; however, that water never makes it back to the aquifer.)

In April 1993—five months before the alarming USGS report—Intel applied to the New Mexico state engineer, who decides water allocation issues, for a new water-use permit that would allow it to use 4,500 acre-feet of water a year, or about 4 million gallons a day. (An acre-foot is the amount of water it takes to cover one acre to a depth of one foot, or about 326,000 gallons.) In addition to Intel's pumped water allotment, it would continue to use about 3.5 million gallons a day from Rio Rancho Utilities, which also pumps from the aquifer. Intel's water request, arriving almost simultaneously with the aquifer alarm, quickly struck a nerve.

In the neighboring village of Corrales, just beneath the mesa on which Intel sits, residents had already complained of foul chemical emissions from Intel which they said caused skin rashes, nausea, and headaches. (Intel installed $11 million worth of oxidizers to remove the odor.) Now the Corrales citizens, fearing that Intel's request for three new deep-water wells might affect their own shallower wells and the stately cottonwoods along the Rio Grande, joined with the Sierra Club, the New Mexico Environmental Law Center, and others in formally opposing the Intel water request. "Just a few feet of draw-down would put a lot of people's wells out of business," said village board member Lawrence Vigil. Tim Kraft, once Jimmy Carter's appointments secretary and now a Corrales resident, said at a town meeting: "We've rolled out the red carpet, and now we're finding out our guest has bad breath and an unquenchable thirst." Intel hydrologists say a solid layer of underground rock separates its 2,000-foot wells from the 200-foot wells of many Corrales residents, and so should not affect their flow.

In June 1994, after a year of study and a four-week hearing, State Engineer Eluid Martinez granted Intel 72 percent of its water application, but required Intel to drill monitoring wells to ensure that its pumping would not affect wells in Corrales. The Intel request became a catalyst for what Albuquerque had avoided for decades—a serious discussion of water problems. "The Intel application raised a debate about what's good for the state," Martinez later told reporters. "It was a lot of water, but not more than would be used to irrigate 2,000 acres of farmland. Drying up a golf course or two would make that water available."

Doug Wolf, attorney for the New Mexico Environmental Law Center, is not nearly so sanguine about the Intel deal. "There's a real question," says Wolf, "about whether this is the right kind of industry for an arid state that's looking to the future." Says Wolf: "Intel argues that because it provides so many jobs they should get whatever they want. The logical extreme of that is that water should go to big business, tourism, golf courses, and exclusive, gated communities, which destroy what we care so much about in New Mexico and will homogenize us into Scottsdale or some kind of industrial center like Baton Rouge."

Wolf's colleague, water policy analyst Consuelo Bokum, points out that New Mexico water law requires the state engineer to consider "the public welfare" in allocating water—as does Alaska's and others—but that the standard is rarely applied and remains largely undefined by the courts. The state engineer "punted" on the issue of public welfare, Wolf says, by simply assuming that any use of water that wasn't a clear waste was beneficial. "If ever there was an argument for taking the public welfare into account," Bokum says, "it's in Albuquerque. The highest and best use of water has historically been defined as who has the most money, and anyone else be damned."

"Watch your head," shouts Intel's Richard Draper as he leads me under the scalp-high, finger-thick metal tubes that course for 44 miles through the windowless bowels of Intel. We're striding briskly past boilers and air scrubbers on a classic dog-and-pony plant tour where the company P.R. man could tell the clueless reporter everything is run by gerbils on treadmills and he would be none the wiser. Intel is a bit overwhelming for those who don't speak in gigabytes—a palace of science akin to the innards of a nuclear submarine, only much taller and wider and cleaner.

We peer through two narrow, vertical windows in the doors of a "clean" room, where workers in white, air-filtered, Gore-Tex "bunny" suits control the robots that imprint the wafers with millions of electronic circuits. How clean, you ask, is a "clean" room? Well, no particle in the air can be larger than one micron. The width of a human hair is roughly 75 microns. Intel likes to say the rooms are ten thousand times cleaner than a hospital emergency room. "I'm still pretty awed by what goes on in there," Draper says. "It's pretty 2001 stuff."

While Intel hardly needs anyone's sympathy—Rio Rancho did half of Intel's $8.7 billion gross in 1993, and Intel plans to build similar factories every year for the next six—it's not hard to see why the giant chipmeister feels unfairly picked upon by some in Albuquerque. Like 'em or not, Intel has never hidden the fact that it uses enormous amounts of water. Knowing that, New Mexico politicians tripped over themselves to offer Intel tax breaks and never expressed doubts about the water supply. Yet, through unfortunate timing with the USGS report, Intel—rather than dairy farmers and golf courses—became the convenient scapegoat. "The blame game kicks in early in the conservation debate," Draper tells me back in his gray-carpeted cubicle office. "You've got to put in perspective how much water we really use. Industries use only 3 percent of Albuquerque's water. Add Intel (which is not on Albuquerque's water system) and it's 6 percent. After our expansion it's 8 percent. Residential users make up 60 to 65 percent. We could

stop pumping tomorrow and it would be a blip on the screen."
Draper doesn't mention that Intel's presence has also created
thousands of new water users and new demands on sewers, roads,
schools, and such.

Draper says Intel has spent $260 million on environmental
safeguards at the Rio Rancho plant since the early 1980s and has
contracted with New Mexico's Sandia and Los Alamos Department
of Energy labs to improve its water conservation technology. Having
been an Albuquerque TV reporter before coming to Intel, Draper
wasn't surprised by some of the local anti-Intel attacks. "Our
expansion came at a time of debate about growth in New Mexico,"
he says. "We've had a rockier road in the last year than we would
like. I think New Mexico is more complex than (Intel's leaders)
thought. This isn't California or Arizona. There are different cultural
and economic issues here." That much is certain.

At a restaurant in Albuquerque's downtown neighborhood,
Jeanne Gauna, director of the SouthWest Organizing Project
(SWOP), heads for a back table and starts throwing punches at Intel
before the chips and salsa can arrive. "How could they have not
known about the water problems?" Gauna laughs. "All they know is
chips, right? Come on, they're exploiting a poor state. That's such
bullshit."

SWOP is a thirteen-year-old community group that has hounded
Intel on chemical emissions, hiring practices, and tax breaks, not to
mention water. SWOP released a sixty-page report on Intel's
activities that suggests New Mexico's incentive package might cost
taxpayers over $140 million more than expected, questions Intel's
commitment to hiring New Mexicans, and portrays the
semiconductor industry as one that fouls the environment, exposes
workers needlessly to dangerous chemicals, and breaks promises to
communities. Composed of veteran activists, SWOP also crashed an
Intel party at a local hotel by unfurling a 30-foot banner that read:
"*No grácias* Intel—Super Profits, Super Toxic Pollution—Real New
Mexicans Pay Taxes!"

One might think that however tempting a target Intel presents,
Gauna would tread lightly on the giant because it still holds out the
hope of doubling her constituents' income. But, based on recent
reports that suggest Intel has always planned to rely heavily on out-
of-state workers brought to Rio Rancho, Gauna has never let up.
"I'm absolutely certain," says the forty-eight-year-old grandmother

with the fiery Basque eyes, "that Intel will never be a good deal for Albuquerque. We're not anti-development or anti-growth, but Intel has yet to prove that we will benefit when almost half of the jobs are going to people from out of state. The taxpayers have underwritten their entire development, yet our communities aren't prospering."

But if not Intel, who? Ten different ways I ask Gauna if Intel is so bad, what kind of industry and which company of Intel's size would be better. She dodges, she weaves, she trots out the line about how New Mexico should grow chilies, not (computer) chips, but suggesting a real alternative proves difficult. "If they would pay their taxes and pay for all the infrastructure," Gauna says, "just about any industry could come in, but we should not have to pay for their profits. Intel is not sustainable growth. Their industry is famous for boom-and-bust cycles. There's no guarantee those jobs we paid so dearly for will even be there in ten or twenty years."

Fine points, but how should New Mexico grow out of its dependence upon government, the military, and exploiting the land? As long as states will grovel for any corporate prize it will be hard for New Mexico to turn down companies that promise thousands of jobs and at least the hope of environmental stewardship.

For the Lords of Sprawl, however, it is a laughable debate. For them, attracting and keeping Intel has been the state's greatest economic achievement in years, and they welcome all the new homes, roads, malls, and fast food emporia without a second thought. They see water conservation as a worthy topic for junior high school science posters, but never as a limit to growth and profits.

Albuquerque Mayor Martin Chavez can't afford to think that way. "If we don't act now about the water problem," Chavez told me, "we will have a crisis for which our grandchildren will condemn us." Chavez says he has already rejected the overtures of a California firm that wanted to relocate in Albuquerque but wanted a guarantee of 1 million gallons of water a day. "Three years ago Albuquerque would've been shining their shoes," Chavez says, "but their attitude wasn't one of conservation, so we basically just said, no thanks."

Chavez now heads into a city-wide water education and conservation program designed to cut water use by 30 percent in ten years. He's already pushed through an increase to monthly water bills and is preaching the new gospel to golf courses and gardeners alike. The city is also looking into injecting treated water back into the aquifer to replenish it, as some other cities do.

If Chavez is smart, say conservationists, he'll seize this historic opportunity to play the role of Head Water Miser to the hilt. Maybe he should walk the town handing out low-flow shower heads. People are willing to conserve if they see it as an equitable, community-wide effort; and Albuquerqueños, especially, know they must change their wasteful ways. But if they see water hogs being lured to the desert, they will know that politics and money still control their future—and Chavez will have squandered his chance.

*December 26, 1994*

# No More Ignoring the Obvious: Idaho Sucks Itself Dry

## Steve Stuebner

They stand like giant tombstones in a graveyard. Hundreds of black cottonwood trees—all dead or just barely hanging on— line the dry cobblestones of the Big Lost River. Charlie Traughber cusses state water authorities as he points out decaying groves of cottonwoods across the Big Lost River Valley. "Gawd, this is just terrible—it's total devastation," Traughber says, his voice rising with anger. "This used to be so green and pretty. Now it's all dead."

Traughber remembers a cool breeze in the 1970s rolling off the river, touching his face; he recalls wielding his fly rod in a box canyon, several miles south of Arco, the water's surface all abuzz with insects, and hooking 4-pound trout. It was a real river then, providing water for irrigation and aquatic life. But by 1995, the Big Lost had become a broken river.

Farmers with groundwater pumps have drained the Big Lost River and its aquifer to the point where the town of Arco, population 1,000, had to drill 640 feet recently to find water. Older wells at 120 feet have begun sucking air. Meantime, fish in the Big Lost River are also sucking air—there's no water left in the lower reach of the river—and that means farmers who irrigate from the river are left high and dry, too. "I say they're raping the groundwater," says Lew Rothwell, a longtime Arco farmer. "And it's not just happening in this valley." Traughber and Rothwell are angry at state water authorities who allowed farmers not only to drain the Big Lost dry 10 miles north of Arco, but also to pump down the aquifer to the point where it seems as though the river will be lost forever. Both men are disgusted for admittedly personal reasons: Traughber bought his home on the banks of the Big Lost twenty years ago so he could fly-fish from his backyard. He figured with prime river frontage it would appreciate in value. "Now," he laments, "it's not worth a thing."

Rothwell has been raising hay and grain crops on a 200-acre farm along the banks of the Big Lost for thirty-five years. But during Idaho's ongoing eight-year drought, he's been lucky to raise a single cutting of hay instead of the normal three cuttings. Last September, Rothwell's crop land looked like the Sahara Desert. His water right dates to the late 1800s, meaning he has a "senior" right that should give him a higher priority for water than those farmers who irrigate with groundwater pumps and whose water rights date only to the 1950s or later. But in the Big Lost, and in the Snake River Basin as a whole, the age-old water law of first in time, first in right, hasn't been strictly applied. Farmers who irrigate from the river grieve over brown fields, while groundwater pumpers have hundreds of acres of juicy spuds.

"They've ruined my place," says Rothwell, a soft-spoken man. Eight years ago, he refused a $610,000 offer to sell his farm. He held out for more, counting on the sale for his retirement. "Today, you couldn't give it away," he says. "I've kicked my butt ever since."

The fragility of the Big Lost shows clearly in the way the river peters out naturally to dust in the high desert after it leaves the mountains, even in healthy years.

Concerns about over-pumping in the Big Lost River Valley are mirrored across the Snake Basin. Unbridled groundwater pumping throughout southern Idaho has set up a heated clash between farmers who divert water from rivers for irrigation and those who lift water from underground. And even as they are being challenged by stream irrigators, pumpers are pointing fingers at each other for draining the Snake Plain Aquifer—one of the largest freshwater aquifers in the West—at the fastest rate in state history. In an attempt to foster the "full economic development" of the Snake River, state water authorities—and an Idaho Legislature dominated by ranchers and farmers—have pushed a policy that has led to legal chaos, rising tempers and environmental destruction. No quick fix is in sight.

But everyone, except for the pumpers, wants the state to enforce the doctrine of Prior Appropriation, honor senior water rights and stop "mining" the groundwater. Mining is defined as removing groundwater faster than it can be naturally recharged. "The department has handed out water rights and groundwater permits as if there's no tomorrow," says Gary Sledde, a water attorney with the powerful firm of Rosholt Robertson & Tucker in Twin Falls. The firm represents Idaho Power Co. and farmers with senior surface water rights. "The fish were there first, but they didn't fill out the (water rights) forms," adds Wendy Wilson, executive director of Idaho Rivers United. "Electricity has been so cheap (from hydroelectric dams) that farmers can afford to go deeper and deeper and deeper for water. Where's it going to stop?"

Longtime Idaho Water Resources Director Keith Higginson denies that either the Snake or the Big Lost is overtapped. "There's no such thing as an overappropriated stream in Idaho," he says. "There will be years when flood flows will fill all of the water rights in the basin." Higginson's philosophy of management is simple: if an irrigator's home stream dries up, drill a well. "The resource is so huge that the water being consumed is only a small part of what's there," he says of the Snake Plain Aquifer. "If we hadn't had a drought, it's my view that this issue would never have come up and no one would be complaining. But the drought has accentuated the problem and now everyone is complaining."

An even bigger water brawl is brewing for 1995. Federal authorities charged with saving endangered salmon and five species of snails are expected to take up to 1 million acre-feet of storage water from the Upper Snake—more than twice as much as they took in 1994. Due to the drought, farmers don't expect there to be enough water for them in 1995, much less for the salmon. When it comes to a choice, farmers seem to care more about their livelihoods than they do about endangered salmon. "I've fished for salmon and steelhead all of my life," says Hagerman farmer Dan McFadden. "But water is the most precious resource we've got. If we don't have water, we're out of business."

Tim Palmer, author of *The Snake River—Window to the West*, published in 1991, says the problems on the Snake Plain have been building. "For years, we knew that there wasn't enough water," Palmer says. "We knew there was too much water being pumped from the aquifer; we knew there wasn't enough water for salmon. Yet we failed to act on these problems—even in the face of alarming data—because the political leaders were so effective at protecting the status quo. Now, we're seeing so many of these problems coming down in an avalanche."

Rising in the southern end of Yellowstone National Park, the Snake collects runoff from the Tetons in Jackson Hole, Wyoming, and cuts across the crescent-shaped Snake River Plain before plunging through Hells Canyon, the deepest chasm in North America, along the Oregon-Idaho border.

In a new book, *Snake—The Plain and Its People*, editor Todd Shallat calls the Snake "the Nile of Idaho, the lifeline of the desert." Each spring, the Snake receives a fountainhead of water from mountain ranges that ring the plain. The river yields an average of 36 million acre-feet per year at Lewiston, Idaho. Its volume surpasses the Colorado River by two and one-half times. Because the Snake flows through the state of Idaho before it flows into Washington, Idaho farmers, food-processing plants, fish farms, and cities have enjoyed a magnanimous water supply. Today, Idahoans enjoy the dubious distinction of being the nation's second-largest guzzlers of water, just behind Californians. Idahoans use an average of 8.1 trillion gallons of water each year, with irrigated agriculture consuming 97 percent of the total.

Early settlers were Mormon farmers, who pioneered irrigation in the West. Eventually, thirteen dams were erected along the Snake in Wyoming and Idaho to hold back spring floodwaters and store billions of gallons of water for summertime use. Nowadays, Idaho farmers raise the nation's largest crop of spuds, the second-largest crop of sugar beets, and scores of other products, such as barley, wheat, mint, hops, and seed corn. The Snake's flows enabled pioneers to tame the plain and bring 3.6 million acres of dry desert soil into bloom. Today, agriculture nets $3 billion and enjoys clout as the state's largest industry. Water is the key to this economy, with pumpers holding 10,840 water rights and surface water irrigators holding 13,992 water rights.

From a political standpoint, it has always been state policy to fully consume the Snake to avoid water-grabs from Southern California and downstream interests in Washington and Oregon. "We are seeking—we always have been and we always will—the ways and means of developing every drop of water that tumbles from the snow packs of the Snake River watershed," former Republican Governor Robert Smylie told a U.S. Senate subcommittee in 1955. "And when we have used that water, whether to help grow a potato or turn a turbine, or both, then, and only then, will we willingly send it flowing into the canyons below Weiser to help develop still another empire further West." Current Republican Governor Philip Batt might well make the same speech today.

Since there seemed to be no need to conserve, until 1971 Idaho laws and policies did not even require farmers to apply for a permit to divert water from a surface water source. Permits for groundwater wells were first required in 1963, but the Idaho Legislature didn't give the Water Resources Department authority to shut down unauthorized wells until 1986. And until 1994, the Legislature did not require groundwater pumpers to measure their consumption. Full implementation of water measurement is expected to take at least five years. Many people argue that historical water policies in Idaho caused the Snake to be overappropriated and the Snake Plain Aquifer to be mined.

But laissez-faire policies are catching up with Idaho. Says farmer McFadden: "If they approve any more pumps out here, we'll have World War III."

Water Resources Director Higginson says although he knew in the 1960s that groundwater pumping affected surface water flows and spring flows in the Snake River Plain, he didn't force the issue. If he had, "We'd have been run out of town on a rail." State policy forbids mining aquifers, but does not address drought years: it banks on future wet years to replenish aquifers. But the Big Lost aquifer has apparently been pumped down so low during the drought that it will take a string of wet years for the aquifer to recover, if it ever does. Until 1994, Higginson relied on the "full economic development" clause in the law to approve new pumps, even if they affected senior surface water users.

What's unusual—compared to other western states—is that groundwater pumpers in Idaho have not been held to the Prior Appropriation Doctrine, which stream irrigators must obey. "There's two absurdities going on here," observes David Getches, a professor of water law at the University of Colorado. "Number one, a legal system that would treat groundwater and surface water as legally separate entities is absurd. Number two, you can have very efficient junior users who are pitted against very inefficient senior users." Getches adds, "The solution must be systematic. Idaho has to bring groundwater law into line with surface water law under the Prior Appropriation Doctrine. But senior farmers don't have the right to use as much water as they want."

State Senator Laird Noh, a Kimberly sheep rancher and chairman of the Senate Resources and Environment Committee, agrees that the state and Legislature should have been quicker to recognize that limits to development would emerge. But he says that Higginson could not have called for a moratorium in the 1960s, 1970s, or even the 1980s, when people saw the water supply as limitless. Former State Senator John Peavey, a sheep rancher, lost an election in the 1970s after calling for a moratorium on new Snake River development. He was later re-elected, but he singles out that loss as a prime indication that the people of Idaho were not willing to plan a progressive future. It wasn't until the 1994 legislative session that lawmakers approved a full moratorium on water development in the Snake River Plain. "We've put on the brakes," Higginson says.

Meanwhile, state authorities don't know how much water is being consumed by surface-water irrigators, spring-water users and groundwater pumpers. They can only guess. Only in 1987 did the state launch a legal process to get a full accounting of water rights and consumption—the Snake River Basin Adjudication. And it was only to ensure that the state could deliver a minimum flow to the Idaho Power Co.'s Swan Falls Dam on the Snake. More than seven years later, attorneys are getting rich, the program is $30 million over budget, and not a single water rights claim has been decreed. Some 150,000 claims await resolution. It's turned into a tangle of disputes between farmers who irrigate from a river or stream and those who pump groundwater. Legal disputes could put off the day when Idaho has a full accounting of water use until at least the next century, perhaps 2020. Observers call the program "The Idaho Water Lawyers Retirement Act."

As it stands now, the burden of proof falls on the senior farmer to pinpoint the injuring groundwater pumpers. The policy also indicates that farmers with senior water rights out of a stream may be required to drill a well instead of shutting off pumpers who are competing with them. "The law says that an irrigator is subject to a reasonable means of diversion," says Jeff Fereday, a Boise water law attorney who represents a variety of pumping interests. "Putting in a well might be a reasonable means of diversion." Fereday argues that pumping groundwater into a pivot sprinkler is a more efficient way to irrigate crops than sending water down a ditch. He also contends that it's not fair to shut off pumpers until their water rights have been adjudicated along with the rest. "The pumpers are entitled to due process under the law." Moreover, Fereday does not believe that the Snake Plain Aquifer is mined or overappropriated. "The Snake

Plain Aquifer is vast—there's more water in it today than there was when the wagon trains came through (in the 1860s)."

It's true that the outlet for the Snake Plain Aquifer at Thousand Springs—where spring waters issue from basalt cliffs and drop 150 feet into the Snake River—has a higher discharge today than it did in the early 1900s. But water experts say the higher flow is due to aquifer recharge from over one hundred years of irrigation—that is, water seeping into the ground as it travels down hundreds of miles of irrigation canals and ditches. Fereday argues that "we have this big nice 'gimme' that nature never provided naturally." The discharge at Thousand Springs, however, peaked in the 1950s, and it's been dropping ever since. An Idaho Department of Water Resources graph shows a bell-shaped curve. Chuck Brockway, one of the pre-eminent water experts in Idaho, notes that numerous monitoring wells throughout the Snake Plain show a sharp decline in aquifer levels since the 1950s. Since 1987, when the latest drought began, "the rate of decline is steeper than it ever has been," Brockway says, so that "when [groundwater pumpers] say they haven't had any impact, they're wrong."

*February 20, 1995*

# Afterword

## Ed Marston

*I*f it is a curse to live in interesting times, as the Chinese proverb holds, then when it comes to water, we in the West are much cursed. "Interesting times," of course, means changing times. And we are changing. Water, which had been a sacred bulwark of the traditional West of mining, logging, ranching, irrigated agriculture, and small towns, is no longer sacred and therefore no longer a bulwark.

The high priests of water—the water attorneys, the United States Bureau of Reclamation, the people who serve on water boards, the western congressmen who serve on the dam-authorizing and appropriations committees—no long rule water with the authority they once enjoyed. They no longer rule because the West's economies and values are in transition. On a thousand fronts, westerners are struggling against themselves and against the larger world to determine their future and their region's future. The struggle is fierce everywhere—in the forests, on the grasslands, and wherever bodies of ore are found. But it is fiercest with water.

Why is water so important? It is usually said that the interior West is arid, and therefore water limits how much land can be farmed; how many cattle can be raised; how much ore can be mined and milled; and how much electricity can be generated. If only there were enough water, westerners say, everything would be fine. Our problems would disappear, or at least recede until our expanded thirst ran up against the limits of the new supplies.

But to pin all of the region's limits on water is deceptive. The West was settled mostly by people from east of the 100th Meridian, and therefore they were most struck by the relative lack of water. But they came West because even though there was plenty of water in the East and the Midwest—water that fell from the sky—just staying even was hard, and advancement seemed impossible. The West, with its beaver and bison and gold and limitless land and grass and trees, seemed to promise liberation from the hardships of the East if they only had enough water—even though it should have been clear from the start that there is more to even an economy than water. Nevertheless, we westerners focused on water and devoted a century to finding it. And we did it in a single-minded way, heedless of the consequences. We drowned valleys under reservoirs, destroyed rivers and their fish and wildlife, dug tunnels under mountains so that we could take rivers from one watershed to another, and transformed the landscape.

The environmental movement has made much of the mess and confusion development of water caused in the region. But the West did something else that has been largely ignored. By concentrating on water development, we ignored other routes to the future. Western writer George Sibley raised that question when he asked: was the twentieth century the only possible path from the nineteenth century to the twenty-first century?

Sibley asks that question broadly. But we can narrow his question: were the Central Arizona Project and the Central Utah Project, the Glen Canyon Dam and the obstruction of the Columbia and the Snake and Platte rivers, the only way for the West to bridge the two centuries? And had we built a different bridge, would we be better or worse off? Would we be better fed and clothed; would our communities be more cohesive; would we be better educated; would we be more humane and less frightened? Or would we have less power and autonomy? Might we even be ill fed and shivering in the dark due to a lack of material advantages those dams bought us?

Such questions make practical people impatient. Why chew over what might have been? Deal with what is. That is usually good advice, but not when it comes to water in the opening years of the twentieth-first century, as what you have read in this book shows. The stories here are driven by the environmental movement's assault on traditional approaches to water. But there is another possible name for the movement: the nostalgia movement. At the heart of environmentalism is the conviction that rivers, and society, were better off before they were dammed, and valleys, and society, were better off before they were flooded or plowed and irrigated. Apparently, to paint the West with broad strokes, we were all better off when the Colorado River still flowed into the Gulf of Cortez, and when salmon spawned throughout the Columbia and Snake river basins.

The extraordinary fact about the environmental-nostalgia movement is the power and influence it has achieved. First, as you have read or already knew, the movement succeeded in halting progress by stopping the dams proposed for the Grand Canyon, and those proposed for Dinosaur National Monument, Two Forks Dam, the Animas-La Plata complex. Today, it is no longer possible to build large dams and reservoirs. But that has not been enough for this movement. It is now intent on restoration. It is intent on not just reintroducing wolves and blackfooted ferrets and lynxes on land, but on bringing back the creatures that depend on flowing rivers: the salmon, the whooping crane, the least tern, the humpback chub. The recovery of river species means the recovery of rivers, which means the removal or bypassing or reworking of dams. It also means the restoration of watersheds. If this book of articles is about anything, it is about returning the land and its waters to some semblance of what they were in the nineteenth century and, from that point, choosing a different path to a different future.

So in this particular case, the practical people may be the impractical ones, and the dreamers and visionaries are the ones who are reshaping the interior West.

You may say:

> That's not what I read in these articles. I didn't hear anyone say that they wanted to return to the past. They didn't even seem to be thinking that. They were just working away at particular problems, or involved in very local, on-the-ground issues.
>
> Plus, what you're talking about is impossible. It's not just the weeds and introduced species and several hundred thousand miles of paved roads and land that has been transformed by agriculture and mining and logging. We're also talking about an immense runup in population, and maybe even the transformation of the climate. We can't go back.

That is true. We can't go back as a time traveler would go back. But enough has happened over the past fifty years to show that we can stop building dams and clearcutting forests without falling into an economic depression. Far from it. The Grand Canyon State's economy is doing fine without those two dams in the canyon. Denver is being buried by growth without Two Forks water. The more the environmental movement has assaulted traditional natural resource development, the more the interior West seems to thrive economically. This development understandably encourages those who think the region would be better off without the dams now blocking the lower Snake River. It encourages those who want to use the water in Lake Powell to create beaches for wildlife and boaters in the Grand Canyon and to bring the Gulf of Cortez delta back to life rather than generate electricity. It encourages those who think that water now devoted to growing corn and soybeans in Nebraska could be partially diverted back into the Platte River to help the whooping crane and least tern.

We have also seen this cause-and-effect relation between economic prosperity and environmental restoration in the article on rancher Sid Goodloe, and his use of fire to restore a destroyed grassland and watershed. As the land came back to health—as it became capable of absorbing rain and melted snow and then measuring it out into streams over time—Goodloe became better and better able to make a living. The Goodloe article argues that we can have nature *and* material comfort. But there must be a catch. Tradition teaches us that we can have amber waves of grain *or* flowing rivers. We can have comfortable houses *or* old growth forests. We can have electricity *or* salmon.

There is evidence that the environmental vision is a chimera. Look at the New West that goes hand in hand with the environmental vision. In place of cattle and clearcuts we have subdivisions and shopping malls and subdivisions. Overgrazed grasslands may not be healthy watersheds, but paved over grasslands are even worse.

Environmentalists are often painfully ignorant of the reality of the interior West. This 1-million-square-mile region is not pristine and hasn't been for millennia. It has all been worked over, even where it looks beautiful and intact. When it comes to the land and its rivers and its wildlife, we have a tiger by the tail, and we cannot let it go. Goodloe didn't restore his land by "protecting" it and waiting for it to recover. He thought about it in detail, and he used not just fire, but bulldozers and poisons to kill off the invading trees. He attended endless meetings with the Forest Service and his neighbors, and worked as a consultant to wealthy landowners to raise the outside capital he needed to bring his land back to health. In other words, the biblical phrase about earning our livings by the sweat of our brows has not been repealed. It's just a different kind of sweat. A different guiding vision, a vision that should dominate our thinking in the coming years.

With the exception of the essay by Charles Wilkinson about the death of the Doctrine of Prior Appropriation, this is not a big picture book. Every story is about people in particular locations chipping away at their "issues"—at their stream, or their small watershed, or their salinity problem, or their dam. And usually, if not always, they are chipping in a vacuum. They are responding to their particular situation. They do not start with some global overview, and then apply it to a local situation. They do not say, "We can see now that dams are bad, and therefore I am going to fight this dam in my backyard." We operate on a much smaller scale. As former Congressional House Leader Tip O'Neill of Massachusetts once famously said: All politics is local.

We could as well say all development, and all anti-development, is local. But this book, by its collection of local efforts, allows you to see what they may add up to. It allows you to decide whether or not there is a pattern. I believe that there is such a pattern: a nostalgic quest for an earlier time when the interior West was more natural, and less developed. We are attempting to return some of the land and its rivers and streams to an earlier state, and those attempts are succeeding beyond what anyone would have dreamt even a few decades ago.

It is your job to analyze these articles and their interpretative focus through the lens of your experience and values and commonsense. It is your job to accept nothing on faith or authority until you have chewed on it, digested it, and made it your own. Go to it.

# Notes on Authors

**James Bishop, Jr.**, is a former *Newsweek* correspondent and federal official who is now teaching, writing, and organizing in Sedonia, Arizona.

**Dennis Brownridge** is a high school science teacher living in central Arizona.

**Debra Calling Thunder** of Lander, Wyoming, does freelance work and is a former newspaper reporter and editor.

**Peter Carrels** is a writer living in Aberdeen, South Dakota, whose book, *Uphill Against Water*, was published by the University of Nebraska Press in 1999.

**Jon Christensen** is a freelance writer and reporter in Carson City, Nevada, and editor of GreatBasinWeb.com.

**Katharine Collins** is a freelance writer living in Rock Springs, Wyoming.

**Tony Davis** is a reporter for the *Arizona Daily Star*.

**Pat Ford** is currently the executive director of Save Our Wild Salmon Coalition, an organization dedicated to restoring wild salmon in the Northwest.

**Steve Hinchman** is a former associate editor of *High Country News* and is currently director of the Western Slope Environmental Resource Council in Paonia, Colorado.

**Judith Jacobsen** is an adjunct professor at the University of Denver and speaks and writes on population and sustainability issues.

**Paul Koberstein** is editor of *Cascadia Times*, published in Portland, Oregon.

**Paul Larmer** is the senior editor of *High Country News*.

**Dan Luecke** is regional director for Environmental Defense.

**Ed Marston** is the publisher of *High Country News*.

**Dan McCool** is a professor of political science and the director of the American West Center at the University of Utah.

**Michelle Nijhuis** is associate editor of *High Country News*.

**George Ochenski** lobbies the state legislature on natural resource and Indian issues from his home in Helena, Montana, when he's not flyfishing or mountaineering (the truly important stuff).

**Marc Reisner** is the author of *Cadillac Desert* and other books and numerous articles.

**Hal Rothman** is professor of history at the University of Nevada, Las Vegas, and is the author of *Devil's Bargains: Tourism in the Twentieth Century American West* (University Press of Kansas, 1998), winner of the 1999 Spur Award for Best Contemporary Nonfiction from the Western Writers of America.

**Bruce Selcraig** (selcraig@ccsi.com) is a writer living in Austin, Texas.

**George Sibley** is a freelance writer and lecturer in regional studies and journalism at Western State College in Gunnison, Colorado.

**Steve Stuebner** is an Idaho freelance writer, the author of six books on natural resources and the outdoors.

**Angus M. Thuermer, Jr.**, is the editor of the *Jackson Hole News* in Wyoming and has covered environmental issues in Jackson for the past twenty years.

**Sandy Tolan** is a co-founder of Homelands Productions, an independent, public interest journalism organization. He is a frequent contributor to National Public Radio.

**Douglas C. Towne** is a widely published photographer of vintage neon signs and works as a hydrologist conducting regional groundwater studies for the Arizona Department of Environmental Quality.

**Susan Whaley** is a writer for the *Idaho Statesman* newspaper in Boise.

**Charles F. Wilkinson** is the Moses Lasky Professor of Law at the University of Colorado. His most recent book is *Fire on the Plateau: Conflict and Endurance in the American Southwest.*

**Florence Williams** is a freelance writer living along the Continental Divide in western Montana.

**T.J. Wolf** works as an ecologist for The Land Center in Taos, New Mexico. His new book, *Ice Crusaders: A Memoir of Cold War and Cold Sport*, has just been published by Roberts Rinehart.

**Dyan Zaslowsky** is a Colorado writer who has contributed to the *New York Times* and many other publications. She also co-authored *These American Lands* with T.H. Watkins.

# Index